The Expor
Services in Mauritius

The Export of Tradeable Services in Mauritius

A Commonwealth Case Study in Economic Transformation

Percy S Mistry and
Nikhil Treebhoohun

Commonwealth Secretariat

Commonwealth Secretariat
Marlborough House
Pall Mall
London SW1Y 5HX
United Kingdom

Published by the Commonwealth Secretariat
Edited by editors4change Limited
Designed by SJI Services
Cover design by Tattersall Hammarling & Silk
Printed by Hobbs the Printers Ltd, Totton, Hampshire

Copies of this publication may be obtained from

The Publications Section
Commonwealth Secretariat
Marlborough House
Pall Mall
London SW1Y 5HX
United Kingdom
Tel: +44 (0)20 7747 6534
Fax: +44 (0)20 7839 9081
Email: publications@commonwealth.int
Web: www.thecommonwealth.org/publications

A catalogue record for this publication is available from the British Library.

ISBN: 978-0-85092-892-1 (paperback)
ISBN: 978-1-84859-022-9 (downloadable e-book)

Contents

Acronyms

A&R	Accreditation & regulation
ABSO	Accounting and business support services outsourcing
ACP	African, Caribbean and Pacific (countries)
AfDB	African Development Bank
AIDS	Acquired immunodeficiency syndrome
AML	Anti-money laundering
ASEAN	Association of South East Asian Nations
ASO	Architectural services outsourcing
AU	African Union
BAC	British Accreditation Council
BFS	Banking & financial services
BoI	Board of Investment (Mauritius)
BoM	Bank of Mauritius (the central bank)
BPO	Business process outsourcing
CB-VTE	Vocational and tertiary education in central banking
CFT	Countering the financing of terrorism
CoE	Centre of Excellence
COMESA	Community of Eastern and Southern Africa
CRO	Contract research organisation
DEEL	Distance education & e-learning
DTT/DTA	Double taxation treaties or agreements
E/ASO	Engineering and architectural services outsourcing
ECB	European Central Bank
EDF	European Development Fund
EHL	*Ecole Hôtelière de Lausanne*
EPZ	Export processing zone
ESO	Engineering services outsourcing
EU	European Union
FATF	Financial Action Task Force
FDI	Foreign direct investment
FPI	Foreign portfolio investment

FSC	Financial Services Commission (of Mauritius)
FSF	Financial Stability Forum
FSS	Financial Services Symposium
GATS	General Agreement on Trade in Services
GATT	General Agreement on Tariffs and Trade
GBC	Global business company
GDP	Gross Domestic Product
GNI	Gross National Income
HIV	Human immunodeficiency virus
HLSS	Healthcare and life science services
HNWIs	High-net-worth investors
HR	Human resources
HRD	Human resource development
HRDS	HRD services
HRO	Human resource services outsourcing
HTT	Hospitality, tourism and travel
IBI	ICT-BPO-ITES industry
IBF	Islamic banking and finance
IBM	International Business Machines Corporation (of the US)
ICT	Information and communications technology
IFC	International financial centre
IFI	International financial institution e.g. IMF, World Bank etc.
IFS	International financial services
IMF	International Monetary Fund
IOR	Indian Ocean Rim
IOR-ARC	Indian Ocean Rim Association for Regional Cooperation
IPR	Intellectual property rights
IPR	International patent rights
IRS	Integrated Resort Scheme (a particular kind of development for foreign residents in Mauritius)
ITES	Information technology enabled services
JCI	Joint Commission International (for healthcare systems and facilities accreditation)
JSE	Johannesburg Stock Exchange
KPO	Knowledge process outsourcing
LDC	Least-developed country

LPO	Legal process outsourcing
LSE	London School of Economics
M&A	Mergers and acquisitions
MCAIR	Mauritius College of the Air
MEAO	Media, entertainment and animation services outsourcing
MEDIA	Mauritius Export Development and Investment Authority
MEF	Mauritius Employers Federation
MFED	Ministry of Finance and Economic Development (Mauritius)
MHQL	Ministry of Health and Quality of Life
MITT	Ministry for Information Technology and Telecommunications (Mauritius)
MOBAA	Mauritius Offshore Business Activities Authority
MQA	Mauritius Qualifications Authority
MTL	Mauritius Telecommunications Ltd.
NASSCOM	National Association of the ICT-BPO Services Industry (in India)
NCCT	Non-co-operative countries or territories
NGO	Non-governmental organisation
NICTSP	National ICT Strategic Plan (for Mauritius)
NPCC	National Productivity and Competitiveness Council (of Mauritius)
NSE	National Stock Exchange (of India)
ODL	Open distance learning
OECD	Organisation for Economic Co-operation & Development (Paris)
OFC	Offshore financial centre
OIA	Oxford International Associates Ltd. (Consultants to the Commonwealth Secretariat on the project)
PBWM	Private banking and wealth management
PCT	Pre-clinical trials
PPP	Public-private partnership
R&D	Research and development
RPO	Research process outsourcing
SADC	Southern African Development Community
SAP	Structural adjustment programme
SDR	Special drawing rights (of the IMF)
SEM	Stock Exchange of Mauritius
SMEs	Small and medium-sized enterprises
TCS	Tata Consultancy Services (a major Indian ICT-BPO company)

TEC	Tertiary Education Commission (of Mauritius)
TNC	Transnational Corporation
TPTM	Transfer pricing and tax management
UAE	United Arab Emirates
UK	United Kingdom of Great Britain and Northern Ireland
UNCTAD	United Nations Conference on Trade and Development
UNISA	University of South Africa
UoM	University of Mauritius
US or USA	United States (of America)
UTM	University of Technology, Mauritius
VTE	Vocational and Tertiary Education
WHO	World Health Organization
WTO	World Trade Organization

Preface

This book describes the growth pattern of a small island economy that has over the last four decades transformed itself from a poor, mono-crop sugar economy, to a diversified services economy and become a middle-income country, overcoming the constraints of economies of scale posed by an exiguous local market. The Mauritian experience reveals that size *per se* is not a handicap. Ultimately, economic transformation depends on: the will and the commitment of the political class to development, mobilisation and efficient management of resources, right market positioning, investment in human capital and policy flexibility to adjust to changing circumstances.

Dependent on sugar for 98 per cent of its exports earnings at independence in 1968, Mauritius successfully adopted an export-oriented industrial policy based on export processing zones (EPZs) and tourism. It harnessed the European Union's (EU) commodity protocols to maximise earnings from exports of sugar. Similarly, the country successfully built a world class textile and garment industry on the quota system that was established under the Multi-Fibre Agreement (MFA). However, new threats appeared with 'globalisation' in the 1990s pushing towards the liberalisation of international trade and highlighting the vulnerability of the economy to external shocks – in this case the erosion of preferences in the EU and the United States of America.

The new millennium called for a new economic trajectory. Thus, in 2004 a competitiveness foresight exercise, carried out by the National Productivity and Competitiveness Council (NPCC), concluded that Mauritius had to diversify into a wider range of services. Movement in this direction started with the Budget Speech of 2006, which engaged the country on bold economic reforms.[1] Once the political decision to open up the economy had been taken, the question that remained was how to transform intent into reality. The government of Mauritius approached the Trade Section of the Special Advisory Services Division of the Commonwealth Secretariat to assist in the elaboration of a roadmap for the exports of professional services from Mauritius.

The Commonwealth Secretariat team decided to follow up on the work done in the Competitiveness Foresight by adopting a similar approach, which relied on engaging key actors from Mauritius and abroad, including firms that had established a strong global presence in key markets for a variety of globally traded services. Hence, it was decided to: (i) involve the Mauritian government and business sector at policy levels as integral participants in the thinking and execution phases; (ii) focus on clear events – i.e. a series of symposia to enable full and frank dialogue by all participants – that would result in practical outcomes from which could be extruded what needs to be done by government (in terms of policy and administrative change) and business (by way of changes in strategic perspective, investment and employment); and (iii) enlist the participation of selected investors. The underlying assumption was that notions of what needs to be done, and probabilities of success, depend much more on the knowledge and expertise of investors who already have an established position in key global service export markets.

The vehicle used was the organisation of **sector-specific symposia** in January and April 2008. Given the emphasis on investment, the local counterpart agency was the Board of Investment, which had full responsibility for the organisational aspects of the symposia.

A priority list of four key sectors was drawn up after discussions with key stakeholders in Mauritius: (i) **financial services**; (ii) **information and communications technology services** (ICT/outsourcing sector); (iii) healthcare and wellbeing services; and (iv) export of **knowledge, education and training services** across a wide range of disciplines.

These discussions were expected to illuminate key policy issues affecting service exports in general as well as specific sectors; product, service, industry and institutional issues affecting export service capacity; resource constraints, especially in terms of human and financial capacity; and operational and behavioural barriers that prevented Mauritius from exporting services more effectively/extensively to a wider range of global markets.

The symposia would be deemed to have been successful if over the coming years there was: increased inward foreign as well as domestic investment by knowledgeable private players in key service export areas; development in a phased manner of all the resources needed to diversify and increase service exports in key areas – traditional and non-traditional; and progressive reduction of extant barriers that presently stand in the way of achieving such service export enhancement – i.e. policy, administrative, resource and supply-side constraints.

It is clear that a *sine qua non* of success is high-level commitment in political, policy-making and business circles to convert intent into reality. One of the fundamental factors explaining the relative success story of Mauritius is close collaboration between the public and private sectors. A commitment to social justice on the part of various governments since the country's independence in 1968 has also contributed to civil society's willingness to bear the costs of transition without any excessive opposition.

The findings of these symposia form the basis for an agenda for action (i.e. a roadmap) to be taken by the government and the private sector to enhance Mauritius's ability to become a significant exporter of global services in a number of key sectors. This book draws heavily from these discussions.

The primary objective of the book was to be a tool for the government of Mauritius to use in its investment promotion strategy and for potential investors to obtain a glimpse of the potential that Mauritius holds in the area of professional services. However, it was felt that the Mauritian experience contained valuable lessons to guide other small island developing states (SIDS),[2] which may be only at the initial stage of economic diversification.

Indeed, the Special Advisory Services Division of the Commonwealth Secretariat has received requests from several SIDS to assist them to either assess their potential for exporting services or to develop strategies for promoting the export of professional services. By August 2008, in addition to Mauritius, the following countries had received technical support: Malta, Cyprus, Sri Lanka, St Lucia, Barbados, Dominica, Trinidad & Tobago, Jamaica, Guyana, Malaysia, Kenya and Ghana.

A Pan-Commonwealth conference was held in Malaysia in February 2008 to provide a platform for the sharing of experiences among the countries and to listen to service providers as well as experts on the potential and prerequisites for the export of different types of services, whether business process outsourcing (BPO) or medical tourism, construction related or educational. The feedback from the participants coming from 35 countries revealed a consensus on the need for greater information dissemination and sharing of learning experience among commonwealth member states. It is hoped that this book will be the first in a series to bring to practitioners the issues that need to be tackled for effective diversification and transformation of their countries' economy.

Structure of the book

The first chapter introduces the concept of services and the opportunities they offer for enabling the process of economic transformation. Within the services sector, professional services trade has been growing the fastest. Although services have always been embedded in merchandise trade, it is only in recent years that the sector has received special attention in development literature. While developed countries have been benefiting from services trade and have been pushing for negotiations on services under the General Agreement on Trade in Services (GATS), developing countries are only now waking up to the potential of services for sustained economic development.

Chapter 2 describes the economic transformation of Mauritius from a single crop to a diversified economy within a 40-year span. The new challenges the island faces in the present World Trade Organization (WTO)-governed trade environment is also touched upon. To enable the reader to grasp fully how the process of change has been initiated from within, albeit with the assistance of an external facilitator, the *Competitiveness Foresight* document, the trigger for the adoption of a new paradigm that looks beyond preferences, can be accessed from the National Productivity and Competitiveness Council (NPCC).[3] This document should help to explain the context in which Mauritius finds itself today and the challenges it confronts, which are propelling it to adopt drastic reforms.

The four chapters that follow focus respectively on finance (chapter 3), ICT, BPO and information technology enabled services (ITES; chapter 4), health and life sciences (chapter 5) and human resources development (chapter 6). An attempt has been made to render each chapter as self-contained as possible. Each highlights the various components that make up the specific sub-sector, the current status of the sub-sector in Mauritius, its potential and the necessary conditions for its growth in Mauritius. The final chapter (chapter 7) brings together the main recommendations emerging from the symposia. While some of them are specific to Mauritius, most recommendations are relevant for any country wishing to engage on the road of professional services exports, especially in the four sectors addressed in the book, namely financial services, ICT, health and educational services. Moreover, the approach in developing the roadmap may hold useful pointers for other small states, though Gerschenkron's words in 'Continuity in History' still hold true: 'No past experience, however rich, and no historical research, however thorough, can save the living generation the creative task of finding their own answers and shaping their own future'.

Notes

1. Budget Speech 2006, Ministry of Finance, Mauritius.
2. At the sixth WTO ministerial conference held in Hong Kong, 15 Commonwealth Small States made a statement highlighting their specific characteristics which 'confer a high degree of vulnerability upon' them. These were detailed, inter alia, as: small domestic markets; exceptional high degree of openness to external economic developments with respect to trade, capital flows and technology; concentration of exports on a narrow range of commodities and markets; restricted range of resources; diseconomies of scale; dependence on foreign resource flows; limited capacity to manage the social and economic environment; vulnerability to natural disasters; geographical isolation; and susceptibility to external shocks.
3. NPCC (2005) *Competitiveness Foresight: what orientations for Mauritius?* See http://www.npccmauritius.com/ [accessed 5 January 2009]

1

Introduction

'...Global demand for knowledge-intensive services sectors (finance, business services, education and healthcare) is growing at breakneck speed; they face less competition than manufacturing from low-cost countries and suffer less than manufacturing from the rise in energy cost'. *Financial Times*, 17–18 September 2006.

Just a few decades ago a developing country was deemed to be successful when it reached the status of a NIC (newly industrialised country). The development model viewed economic progress as a transformation from exporting commodities to industrial goods. Services (the tertiary sector) were considered to provide support to the real economy. The prevalent belief about services was that they were not tradeable and could not be sent across borders like industrial products. The problem was compounded by the difficulty of obtaining proper statistics.

There are obviously some basic differences in trade in services and in goods. First, many services require proximity between the supplier and the consumer, and hence factor mobility is necessary for international transactions. Secondly, the limited scope for 'border' restrictions implies that domestic regulations have a much stronger influence on trade in services. A key difficulty is distinguishing between regulations that are necessary (and may even need to be strengthened) to achieve legitimate objectives – such as financial stability, competitive market conditions and universal service – and those that have a protectionist impact.[1]

While world exports of services totalled US$388 billion in 1980, by 2007 this figure had reached $3 trillion. The share of exports by developing countries was obviously much lower than that of developed countries, but had nonetheless been rising by leaps and bounds (see table 1.1). The figures, while they may not reflect the precise situation,[2] do however reveal an interesting trend. Only a few developing countries are leading the pack. For example in 2007, the African, Caribbean and Pacific (ACP) countries exported only US$67 billion out of a total of US$848 billion.

Table 1.1: Value of exports of services[3] US$ (billion)

	1980	1990	2000	2005	2007
World	388	830	1,527	2,538	3,337
Developing countries	71	150	348	622	848
ACP	12	18	31	52	65
Mauritius	C.1	0.5	1.1	1.6	2.2

Source: UNCTAD Handbook of Statistics, 2008

The OECD expects services to grow in the coming years as companies outsource more of their functions, with less need for face-to-face contact due to their intensive use of information technology. These functions include work by clerks and computer operators, data handlers and claims processors, as well as programmers and certain types of scientists and engineers, i.e. both high- and low-skilled white-collar jobs. OECD estimates place the total number of jobs that could potentially be affected by domestic or global outsourcing at close to 20 per cent of employment in certain countries. According to OECD reports, the direct benefits of international sourcing are currently accruing to a number of OECD countries (e.g. Ireland and the Czech Republic) and non-OECD countries (e.g. India), which have become highly competitive in business services. Sourcing business services from lower-wage countries could reduce the prices of services as diverse as finance, transportation and health. Research[4] carried out in 2005 by Walmsley and Winters found that if OECD countries were to allow temporary access to foreign service providers equal to just 3 per cent of their labour force, the global gains would be over $150 billion – more than the gains from the liberalisation of all trade in goods.

Worldwide services exports increased almost nine fold between 1980 and 2007, driven mainly by ICT and finance.

According to Synergist, the global ICT/BPO/ITES industry (onshore and offshore outsourcing) was expected to reach $850–900 billion in 2008, with BPO-ITES accounting for $550 billion. The largest 20 BPO-ITES providers will together account for less than 25 per cent of total market share. The 2006 Global Insight Report on Outsourcing concluded that, by 2008, IT offshoring would account for roughly US$125 billion in additional GDP for the USA annually, a US$9 billion jump in real US exports, and a net increase of 317,000 jobs in the US. Increases in the rest of the OECD (EU, Japan and Singapore, Hong Kong, Korea and Taiwan) would imply those numbers increasing by 2.5 times. According to Gartner, a market research firm, the size of the global BPO-ITES market (excluding ICT) in 2007 was a much lower US$173bn, of which US$25bn would be outsourced to offshore contractors. Of this, India would account for US$14bn in revenue. Both Gartner and Global Insight identified North America as the dominant market for ITES-BPO services, accounting for 60 per cent of the total market in 2006. The main BPO verticals for the US were telecommunications, financial services, healthcare and energy. Commonly outsourced processes include internal auditing, payroll, human resources, benefits management, contact centres/customer care/payments/claims processing, real estate management, and supply chain management.

The EU's ITES-BPO market accounted for 22 per cent of the global market in 2006, with the financial services sector consuming the largest amount of BPO-ITES services, followed by utilities and telecommunications. Human resources (HR), finance and accounting were the fastest growing service lines. The Asia Pacific ITES-BPO market accounted for 18 per cent of the global market in 2006. Given the relative infancy of this market, the region is expected to experience rapid growth over the next few years. Growth will primarily be driven by costs reduction and the need to focus on core competencies. HR, finance and accounting are expected to be the key growth areas in the Asia-Pacific region in the years ahead.

The global international financial services sector generated revenues of US$1.1 trillion in 2005, against world output of US$44 trillion, with forecast growth by 2020 to reach US$6.9 trillion against world output of US$122 trillion by the same time. Although the global financial crisis is expected to change these absolute figures, the trend is likely to be the same. In addition, the regulatory framework is likely to be strengthened and should provide better guarantees for future growth.

There has also been an increase in the number of financial centres worldwide. Financial centres may be global, regional, ordinary or offshore. Global financial centres, like New York, London, Singapore and Hong Kong, serve a global market with the widest possible array of financial services. Regional centres, like Shanghai and Dubai, serve their region rather than their domestic market. Ordinary financial centres, such as Paris, Frankfurt and Tokyo, are non-global and non-regional and cater mainly to the needs of their national economies. Offshore financial centres, such as Switzerland and other tax havens, specialise in wealth management and tax management, with limited provision of international financial services.

The development of financial services centres has not been so widespread, though the volume of transactions has been increasing, possibly because some basic factors are essential for their development. First and foremost, there must be a high level of human capital with appropriate skills. Second, the telecommunications infrastructure should be world class and should ensure round-the-clock connectivity. This also implies that the energy sector should be well developed to ensure that there are no power outages or significant fluctuations. Third, there must be state-of-the-art IT systems. Fourth, the financial system must be well developed with liquid markets. Fifth, the regulatory framework has to provide for 'best in class' financial regime governance. It is also an advantage for a financial services centre to have a hinterland that is growing, as well an extensive network.

From the above discussion, it is clear that there is a global market for services and countries need to gear themselves up to be able to exploit these new opportunities. However, a different approach is required, where services are considered to be exportable and not just for local consumption. More importantly, policy-makers must cease to view some services, like healthcare and education, only as 'public goods'.

Health services exports can take several forms: they can be traded across borders as a result of technological improvements in telecommunications, e.g. medical transcriptions; consumers can travel abroad to benefit from medical and health services, e.g. in 2005 India welcomed 500,000 patients from abroad for medical treatment; private clinics can be opened in a foreign country; and finally doctors and medical staff may offer their services on a temporary basis in a foreign country.

The exports of healthcare services are often classified as 'health and wellness tourism'. This market, estimated at US$40 billion worldwide, can be subdivided into four segments: i) medical tourism; ii) wellness and spas; iii) nursing and elderly care; and iv) research and diagnostic services. Medical tourism covers a comprehensive range of therapeutic services, including general surgery, orthopaedics, urology, gynaecology, ophthalmology, dialysis, cardiology and cardiac surgery. Other areas that have witnessed rapid growth in recent years are: cosmetic surgery, dentistry, and spas and wellness tourism (e.g. Ayurvedic medicine and acupuncture).

Moreover, a country can benefit from medical tourism if certain conditions are present. Apart from the obvious ones such as air access and appropriate infrastructure in terms of hotels, hospitals and spas, these include: portability of health insurance in target markets; respect for client privacy and confidentiality; institutions accredited by recognised bodies; ease of visa obtainment; recognition of professional standards; and a framework for malpractice insurance of out-of-jurisdiction personnel.

Similarly, the education industry is becoming increasingly global. Educational services can be exported via the internet (e.g. Indian teachers giving private tuitions in mathematics to American students); students can travel to a foreign country to obtain these services; universities can open branches abroad; and teaching staff can migrate on a temporary basis to provide services abroad. Exports in this sector have taken place from developed to developing countries over a long period of time. However, many developing countries, as well as small states like Malta and Cyprus, have also become exporters of educational services. At the same time, because of supply capacity constraints for some subjects like medicine and engineering in countries like the US and India, medical colleges have been set up in some Caribbean countries.

This growth in the exports of services has resulted from a combination of factors. First, technological improvements in telecommunications, in particular, and the advent of broadband technology have rendered possible the fragmentation of services. While the manufacturing process had been amenable to being broken up in specific operations, which could be performed in different places and then be brought together for assembly, this was not possible in the services sector because of the need for proximity between the consumer and supplier. However, great strides in ICT have led to more reliable telecommunications at a decreasing cost. Offshoring and outsourcing can be engaged in on a massive scale.

At the same time, business leaders have been searching for innovative ways to improve their competitiveness. Business schools have revisited 'small is beautiful', as the jargon in the 1980s pushed towards lean manufacturing, world-class manufacturing, focus on core business and business process outsourcing. Management philosophy at the enterprise level was ready to accept the avenues for rapid expansion that were being opened by the new technology, and the new international trading environment characterised by globalisation.

A third factor was the establishment of the World Trade Organization in 1995, which provided the institutional catalyst at the international level for placing trade liberalisation high on the agenda in a bid to build a 'level playing field'. Meanwhile, domestic regulatory reform in many OECD countries and some developing economies, as well as the emergence of a global labour market of highly skilled workers, provided the platform from which services could take off, especially as the basic framework was created with the General Agreement on Trade in Services (GATS).

What are services?[5]

A 'service' is better understood in contrast to 'merchandise', which refers to tangible goods while a service is intangible. However, services are embedded in many cases in merchandise trade, as they include activities such as distribution, marketing, design, communications, transport and insurance amongst others. It is interesting to note that the GATS does not provide a definition of 'services'. However, it defines the 'supply of a service' to include the production, distribution, marketing, sale and delivery of a service. The agreement covers all services sectors, except the core of air transport services (i.e. measures affecting air traffic rights and directly related services), and services provided in the exercise of governmental authority (i.e. services supplied neither on a commercial basis nor in competition with one or more service suppliers).

While defining trade in services in terms of four modes of supply, the GATS contains no definition of what actually constitutes a service. It is no different in this regard from its counterpart in merchandise trade, the General Agreement on Tariffs and Trade (GATT), which contains no definition of a good.

The 12 major categories in the list published by the World Trade Organization (WTO) in July 1991 and known as the 'W/120 list' are:

1. Business services
2. Communication services
3. Construction and related engineering services
4. Distribution services
5. Educational services
6. Environmental services
7. Financial services
8. Health-related and social services
9. Tourism and travel-related services
10. Recreational, cultural and sporting services

11. Transport services

12. Other services not included elsewhere

These 12 sectors are sub-divided further into 155 sub-sectors.[6] While all of these services could be included potentially in the schedules of commitments of WTO members, in reality binding commitments only apply in regard to those sectors or sub-sectors that are chosen specifically by the member.

The GATS defines four modes through which an international supply of a service can occur.

Mode 1: Cross-border supply

Cross-border supply takes place when a service is supplied 'from the territory of one member into the territory of any other member'. That is, the service is rendered by a resident in one economic territory to a resident of another economic territory and only the service 'crosses the border'. This is similar to trade in goods where the product is delivered across borders and the consumer and the supplier remain in their respective territories. Such supply of a service may be enabled by communication tools such as telephone, fax, Internet, courier or post. For example, a law firm delivering legal advice by phone to a consumer, a physician providing medical diagnosis to a patient via email, or a financial services supplier supplying portfolio management or brokerage services across the border. The boom in services exports originated for many low-cost countries with call centres. It has been roughly estimated that 35 per cent of world services trade are delivered via this mode.

Mode 2: Consumption abroad

Consumption abroad occurs when the service is supplied 'in the territory of one member to the service consumer of any other member'. That is, the consumer consumes the service outside his/her home territory: either the consumer or his/her property is abroad. Tourist activities such as visits to museums and theatres, or persons travelling abroad to receive medical treatment or to follow language courses are typical examples. Services such as ship repair abroad, where only the property of the consumer moves or is situated abroad, are also covered. It is estimated that between 10 and 15 per cent of world trade is found in this category.

Mode 3: Commercial presence

Commercial presence takes place through 'the supply of a service (...) by a service supplier of one member, through commercial presence in the territory of any other member'. GATS recognises that it is often necessary for services suppliers to establish a commercial presence abroad to ensure closer contact with the consumer at various stages of the production, distribution, marketing, sale and delivery, as well as after-sales, services. Commercial presence in a market abroad covers not only juridical persons in the strict legal sense, but also legal entities that share some of the same characteristics, such as representative offices and branches. Services supplied by a foreign-owned branch or subsidiary of a bank, medical services provided by a foreign-owned hospital and courses offered in its host country by a foreign-owned school are examples of supplies through commercial presence.

Commercial presence as defined in GATS means any type of business or professional establishment, including through the constitution, acquisition or maintenance of a juridical person, or the creation or maintenance of a branch or representative office, within the territory of a member for the purpose of supplying a service. In this case a juridical person has to be owned (i.e. the owner holds more than 50 per cent of the equity interest) or controlled (power to name a majority of its directors or otherwise to legally direct its actions). This is estimated to provide 50 per cent of world trade in services.

Mode 4: Presence of natural persons

Presence of natural persons occurs when an individual is temporarily present in the territory of an economy other than his/her own to provide a commercial service. GATS defines mode 4 as the supply of a service by 'a service supplier of one member, through presence of natural persons of a member in the territory of any other member'. Mode 4 is generally understood as covering contractual services suppliers, whether: (i) employees of a foreign service supplier; (ii) self-employed; (iii) intra-corporate transferees and foreign employees directly recruited by foreign established companies; or (iv) service sellers who enter the host country to establish contractual relationships for a service contract or persons responsible for setting up commercial presence. There is initially no actual service traded by category (iv). Mode 4 applies to service suppliers at all skill levels. The purpose of the stay in the territory of the member should be to supply a service. For example, mode 4 covers computer services delivered to the consumer either by an employee of a foreign computer company or by a self-employed computer consultant within the context of a services contract. Other examples include a computer programmer who is transferred temporarily to work abroad in the branch of his/her employer (intra-corporate transferee), a plumber present in a host country in order to work on a building site in the context of a services contract or a fruit picker going abroad to work temporarily in a farm in the context of a services contract between a foreign specialised employment agency (the employer of the fruit picker) and a host country farm (the client of the employment agency). This mode of supply contributes only between 1 to 2 per cent of world trade in services.

The different modes of supply are illustrated in the example below taken from the ICT sector (figure 1.1).

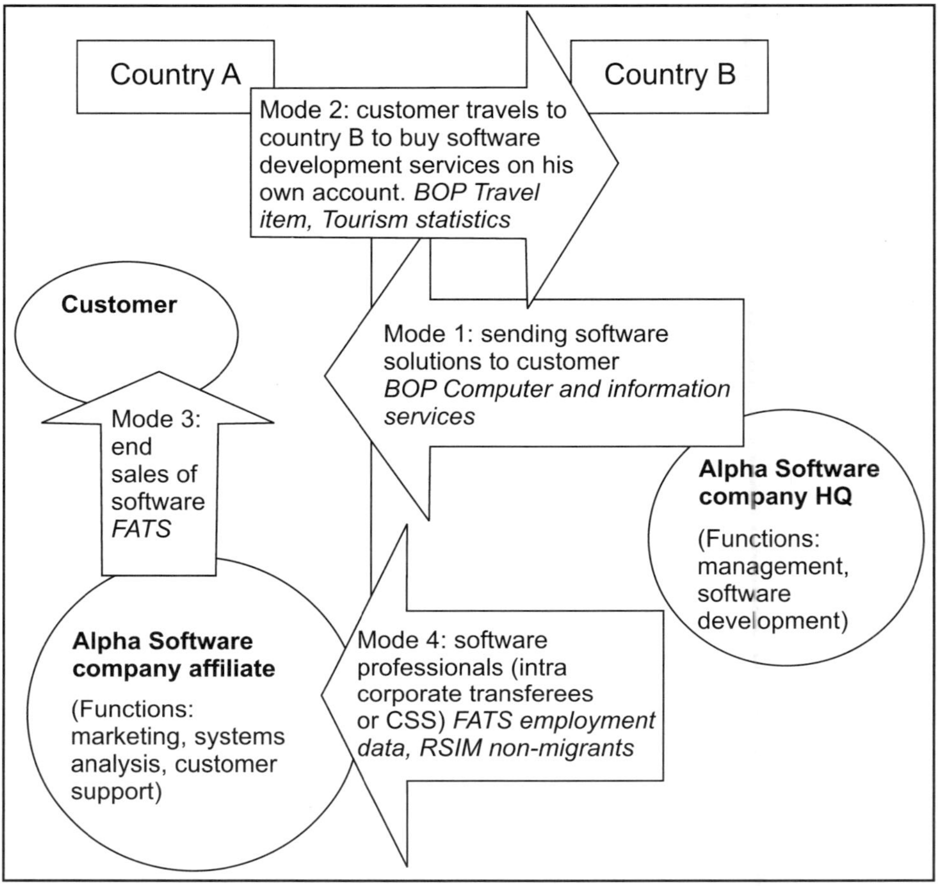

Figure 1.1: Global outsourcing of computer and software related services
Source: WTO website

Barriers to trade in services

Whilst there is definitely a market for services globally and these provide an opportunity for many developing countries, in particular SIDS (small island developing states), to diversify their economic base by securing some market niches, countries must be aware of the need for domestic reforms to overcome potential constraints and barriers.

Internally some of the challenges faced are:

- Scarcity of skilled human resources
- Poor infrastructure

- High telecommunications costs
- Inadequate knowledge of product and market
- Lack of capacity in the public sector to adapt to the fast-changing international environment (i.e. the persistence of a control, as opposed to a facilitation, mindset)
- Governance issues
- Lack of economies of scale
- Poor trade in services statistics
- Language proficiency
- Inadequate institutional support (trade promotion agencies as well as private-sector institutions still focus on traded goods)
- Lack of co-ordination among private-sector suppliers of services

Services trade barriers, on the other hand, may either take the form of discrimination against foreign suppliers or the protection of incumbent providers against all new suppliers. These barriers can take the form of:

- Non-recognition of qualifications by states
- High costs of accreditation as only a few bodies are recognised
- Nationality and residency requirements,
- Restrictive visas and work permits
- Government procurement laws
- Slow and inadequate legal processes
- Lack of transparency – e.g. publication of regulations
- Excessively high fees for obtaining services
- Inadequate protection of intellectual property – copyrights and trademarks

The General Agreement on Trade in Services

Many of these issues, particularly those concerning the GATS, continue to be discussed at the WTO. The following section, which explains the state of play in early 2008, draws on a speech delivered by Dr Harsha V Singh, Deputy Director-General of the WTO, at a pan-Commonwealth conference on trade in services.

Under the GATS, WTO members have made legally binding commitments on trade in services at the multilateral level. The structure of GATS comprises two different types of disciplines. One is a general framework of disciplines, which applies to all services activities. The other consists of the schedules of commitments, one for each WTO member, which specify the extent and nature of market opening.

The general disciplines include non-discriminatory treatment among members (the famous most-favoured-nation principle), basic transparency obligations, as well as a number of 'good-governance' provisions, including the availability of legal remedies for service suppliers that are adversely affected by administrative decisions. The regime also allows various flexibilities.

These general disciplines imply that even with the absence of specific commitments, there are obligations under the GATS. For example, the most-favoured-nation or MFN obligation is a powerful discipline as it prevents discrimination among service suppliers of different nationality. It also helps all WTO members, in particular the smaller among them, to benefit from the market-access opportunities that may be negotiated between or autonomously provided by the 'heavyweights' in the system.

The schedule of commitments identifies the service sectors in which market access and national treatment are specifically provided, and also the various conditions under which such access is granted. The GATS is a highly flexible regime. Market access and national treatment obligations apply only in sectors where members have undertaken 'specific commitments'. It is thus possible for each member to adjust its international trade obligations to the particular policy objectives and constraints of individual sectors. Limitations scheduled by members thus typically provide a legal basis for numerical quotas on the number of suppliers or their transactions, foreign equity ceilings or joint-venture requirements, or the exclusion of foreign-owned companies from domestic subsidy programmes.

An important feature of the GATS is that commitments can be phased in over time, enabling members to make preparatory policy changes and/or institutional (including regulatory) adjustments within a transition period. Nor do commitments have to cover an entire service sector. For example, GATS commitments on legal services often exclude the practice of domestic law, covering international and other countries' law only. Members are not constrained to open their public services to competition, and they retain broad scope to regulate for quality and other legitimate policy purposes, even in sectors where they grant full market access and national treatment (the principle of treating foreigners and locals equally).

While the absence of a WTO commitment in a given sector does not mean that access to that market is closed, without such commitments no guarantees of access are offered by a member state. If any country wants to have a predictable path for market opening and, ultimately, growth and development, such guarantees are most valuable. This explains why some countries have autonomously scheduled such access commitments, especially in telecommunications, outside of any negotiating context. Some countries that used to adopt a defensive stance vis-à-vis the GATS, have become a driving force in services negotiations in recent years.

Professional services

In terms of professional services, by far the greatest number of GATS commitments is found in engineering, accounting, architectural and legal services, while the lowest are recorded for veterinary services and the services of midwives, nurses and physiotherapists.

Regarding the special challenges faced by developing countries for professional services, not all modes of services supply are equally relevant. While the commercial presence mode (mode 3) offers valuable guarantees for investors in services, and the consumption abroad mode (mode 2) is of great significance in certain sectors, such as tourism, it appears that modes 1 and 4 are of special interest to many developing country members.

The Internet revolution has dramatically increased the tradability of services cross-border (mode 1). Developing countries are capturing a growing share of the world market for such cross-border services, ranging from remote call centres to sophisticated software development. In addition to software, medical facilities may have their records or patient interviews digitally transcribed overseas, while accounts and other data-related services may also be carried out cross-border. These developments are taking place not only in countries such as China and India. In Africa, countries like Ghana, South Africa and Kenya have also made inroads. In South Africa, for example, there are more than 400 call centres, employing 200 persons each on average. In Malaysia, third-party call and contact centres have been growing at triple-digit rates year-on-year since 2000. Similarly, countries in the Caribbean are major providers of back-office services such as data processing. Given improvements in telecommunications and the reduced cost of skilled labour, this is an area for potential future growth.

Mode 4 is a major focus for developing country exporters, as they have comparative advantage in labour-intensive services and much of their service exports take place through this mode of supply. In addition, they may be interested in transfers of managerial and organisational skills, together with semi-skilled workers.

With respect to this mode, it is worth noting that the GATS is concerned with trade in services – not with migration. Thus, mode 4 covers the temporary movement of persons across borders only to the extent that the purpose of their movement is the supply of a service. Mode 4 does not cover jobseekers and the GATS does not apply to measures related to citizenship, residence or employment on a permanent basis. As long as this does not impair their GATS commitments, governments remain free to regulate the entry and temporary stay of people in their territory.

Examples of mode 4 are many. In legal services, exports from developing countries often take place through the cross-border movement of persons, either as self-employed professionals or as employees of foreign-established law firms. More than one million Filipino workers were estimated to be abroad in 2006, many employed in professional services such as nursing, engineering, information technology and accounting. Similarly, in the last decade or so, Kenya has exported considerable quantities of professional services through the movement of its own professionals, especially to Southern African states, but also to developed countries. Likewise, Malaysian construction companies undertake projects such as roads, highways, housing, dams and power generation plants in countries as diverse as China, Vietnam, Chile, Argentina, Sudan and Namibia, while Malaysian architects design hotels, resorts, office buildings, factories and residential developments in countries like Vietnam, the Philippines, Australia and South Africa.

Of course, WTO members focus negotiations on market access through all the four modes. Consumption abroad and commercial presence (modes 2 and 3) are also seen as important, including by some Commonwealth member countries. Moreover, one particular track in services negotiations is dedicated to the development of disciplines with a view to improving the resilience, stability and predictability of domestic regulatory regimes.

WTO negotiations on services

To participate effectively in the WTO services negotiations, member states have to keep in mind the broader context, in particular:

- Stronger internal co-ordination and co-operation is needed than for other negotiations, given the diversity of interests and ministries involved;
- The process of negotiations is based on request and offer, which is time consuming;
- Several participants have emphasised parallelism with other key negotiating areas such as agriculture and industrial tariffs; and
- The recent proliferation of regional agreements risks diverting negotiating resources and attention.

These factors have led to the services negotiations moving at a slower pace than is desired by many. Nevertheless, the negotiations have moved beyond important milestones towards their final phase. First and foremost among these milestones is the Hong Kong Ministerial Meeting, in particular Annex C of the ensuing Declaration. It specifies common negotiating objectives and ambitions at an unprecedented level of detail for all four modes of supply. It also emphasises the need for full and effective implementation of the modalities for least-developed countries (LDCs), and to pursue work not only on market-access issues, but in rule-making areas as well. The Hong Kong Ministerial Declaration also clarifies that LDCs are not expected to undertake new commitments in the services negotiations. Further, for the market-access negotiations, Annex C opened a hitherto unused avenue to complement the time- and resource-consuming bilateral process, with plurilateral request-offer negotiations.

Though intense meetings have taken place periodically, the request-offer process still has some way to go. By the end of 2007, a total number of 71 offers had been received, covering 95 WTO members. Of these, 30 are revised offers. There are almost 20 developing country members (including a few Commonwealth countries) that still have to submit an initial offer.

Moreover, there is sense of disappointment concerning the 'quality' of offers, both in terms of new sector inclusions and improvements of existing commitments. The overall focus is on the sectors and modes that already dominate existing schedules, with relatively few significant changes in the pattern of bindings: sectors that had attracted a limited number of commitments in the past are not drawing many offers either – for example, education, health, distribution, postal-courier and road transport. While some progress has been made with respect to computer services, the level of new commitments and improvements for other professional services has so far been minimal.

In contrast, the plurilateral process had a promising start. Over 20 groups were organised to deal with collective requests in virtually all major service sectors and some cross-cutting issues such as cross-border trade (mode 1), commercial presence (mode 3), presence of natural persons (mode 4) and the legacy of MFN exemptions. For mode 4, there are two plurilateral requests, one from a broadly composed plurilateral group and another from LDCs only.

In these plurilateral negotiations, one group of WTO members requests the 'target' group to make new commitment or to further liberalise in a particular sector. Thus, membership of these groups may vary widely from sector to sector, depending on economic interest.

For Commonwealth countries, too, participation in plurilaterals is limited mostly to the main economic players in terms of market share. In other words, the developed country members are far more frequently involved than developing economies, both among requestors and respondents. Among the developing countries, Singapore is an exception. It is part of eight plurilateral requesting groups, and is the target of nine plurilateral requests. Otherwise, developing Commonwealth countries in the top rung of services exporters and importers generally have been associated with making few plurilateral requests, but are the target of a comparatively larger number of such requests. Thus, for instance, in the case of India, Malaysia, South Africa and Nigeria, they are respectively associated with requests by four, two, zero and zero plurilateral groups making requests, but are the targets of 14, 16, 14 and 7 plurilateral requests. Some smaller Commonwealth countries have also been the subject of requests, with Brunei Darussalam getting eight requests, Sri Lanka getting three, and Mauritius, Fiji and Namibia getting one request each.

This may indicate partly that the markets of these developing Commonwealth countries are seen to be attractive by others, but that these countries themselves do not take the initiative to seek market access from others in more sectors. This is even the case in sectors that may provide such countries with opportunities to improve their market share. Thus, among the 20 plurilateral requests on various sectors or modes of supply, Commonwealth developing countries (with the exception of Singapore) have been part of the requesting group only in computer and related services (India, Malaysia and Pakistan only), education (Malaysia only), tourism (Mauritius only), cross-border or mode 1 (India only) and mode 4 (India and Pakistan only). Hence, the intensity of participation is low in general and tends to be more defensive than focused on seeking opportunities. This is even given the situation where considerable actual liberalisation has already occurred in domestic policies.

With specific reference to professional services, plurilateral negotiations have taken place for architecture, engineering and integrated-engineering services; computer and related services; construction and related engineering services; and legal services. Professional services are also part of the plurilateral negotiations on cross-border supply and mode 4. In these and other areas of services for which there are plurilateral requests, it is possible for various countries to seek better conditions from others for their own service suppliers, as well as for services supplied through a consortium of suppliers involving various countries.

One expressed reason for the lack of greater interest in services negotiations is the belief that they will not lead to a substantive result. It may however be that this judgement is partial and premature, since a large number of those making requests in the plurilateral process have done so with the understanding that they themselves would be in a position to offer that same request. Thus, since these requests are quite substantive, the potential results would also be substantive and available to all members (given the most-favoured-nation treatment mentioned above). Of course, this result could potentially be even more substantive with the active participation of more countries.

One reason for a number of developing countries to hesitate opening up their services sectors is the view that they first need adequate regulatory capacity. The argument is thus not against greater interlinkages with the rest of the world, but preparing for such interlinkages with strengthening their regulatory capacity. GATS offers a number of ways to enable governments to properly sequence reforms and to take precautionary measures. Member countries also retain broad latitude to regulate as required under domestic policy considerations. These aspects provide members with enough leeway to prepare and fine-tune their commitments and to phase them in over a transition period, including having time to strengthen their regulatory capacity. This flexibility should encourage further commitments.

Improved regulatory capacity is also important because good domestic regulation is often critical to realising the benefits of services liberalisation.[7] While establishing or improving regulatory institutions may be costly and difficult, because regulation requires sophisticated skills in a world of rapidly changing technologies, adequate capacity in this area extends the scope of the market and the ability of domestic entrepreneurs to compete in the world. Better regulatory regimes also provide confidence to domestic and international investors. Creating regulatory infrastructure for services may be as important as building roads and ports (physical infrastructure) for merchandise trade.

There is major scope for considering innovative methods for upgrading regulatory capacity, both by linking up with other regulators and institutions that can facilitate the process, and by devising a technical assistance programme to supplement these efforts. The 'Aid for Trade' initiative being emphasised at the WTO is important in this context. Aid for Trade presents a key opportunity for developing countries to address wide-ranging technical assistance issues, including those relevant for regulatory and other technical upgrading challenges of market opening in services, as well as for utilising available market opportunities domestically and abroad.

An important part of the GATS negotiations is member countries' focus on disciplines for domestic regulation. The current work of the negotiations is to develop such 'disciplines' being applicable to licensing and qualification requirements and procedures, and to technical standards. The objective is to ensure that domestic regulations do not impede the benefits of market opening. Essentially, WTO disciplines on domestic regulation do not replace national regulations or limit governments' scope for setting regulatory objectives, but are instead agreed rules regarding the creation and implementation of government-required regulations. Most WTO members expect the disciplines to be applied in sectors where GATS commitments have been made, and to apply to regulations that are not trade restrictions as defined in the GATS (i.e. restrictions to market access or national treatment limitations). After consolidating the various proposals for disciplines made by member states, the Working Party on Domestic Regulation was at the time of writing in the process of revising and editing the draft text of the disciplines in order to reach agreement among WTO members.

Another important possibility for accessing markets is through mutual recognition agreements (MRAs). Of course, MRAs may be difficult, time consuming and expensive to negotiate. This is another area where technical assistance would be useful. In the meantime, the existing GATS provision in Article VI:6 applies, which requires that 'In sectors where specific commitments regarding professional services are undertaken, each Member shall provide for adequate procedures to verify the competence of professionals of any other Member'. Of course, the negotiations of domestic regulations disciplines may help define what 'adequate procedures' actually means.

An important concern that is often expressed is the likelihood of imbalances when small developing countries negotiate bilateral agreements with much larger developed country trading partners. In this regard, an important feature of the WTO negotiations is that they take place within a framework of carefully established rules, designed to encompass flexibility and fairness to all participants. In addition, individual developing countries have the opportunity to form negotiating coalitions around particular issues of interest, thereby magnifying their negotiating leverage significantly, as demonstrated by plurilateral requests on issues such as mode 4.

Notes

1. World Bank (2006) Trade Research Papers.
2. Please note that an Inter-Agency Task Force on Statistics of International Trade in Services has been set up to improve data collection in the sector and to produce an updated manual on services trade. The task force comprises representatives of the United Nations, the International Monetary Fund (IMF), the UN Conference on Trade and Development (UNCTAD), the Organisation for Economic Co-operation and Development (OECD), the European Commission (EC) and the World Trade Organization (WTO).
3. UNCTAD defines ...'total services to include 11 main service categories, according to the definition of the IMF Balance of Payments Manual (BPM5, 1993). The categories included are transport, travel, communications, construction, computer and information services, financial services, insurance, other business services, royalties and licence fees, personal, cultural and recreational services and government services n.i.e. [not included elsewhere]'.
4. Quoted in: *A Handbook of International Trade in Services* by Aaditya Mattoo, Robert M Stern and Gianni Zanini (eds). This book is recommended to readers who wish to have a comprehensive introduction to the subject of trade in services.
5. This section draws in part from a Commonwealth Secretariat publication for Barbados: *Frequently Asked Questions on Trade in Services* (2007).
6. See http://www.wto.org/english/tratop_e/serv_e/mtn_gns_w_120_e.doc for a full list [accessed 10 November 2008].
7. See *Regulation In Services: OECD Patterns And Economic Implications* by Giuseppe Nicoletti.

2

Mauritius: from Plantation to Knowledge-based Economy

The setting

Mauritius is an island of 1,865 km^2 situated in the South West Indian Ocean, far from its major markets and suppliers. Inhabited only since the 18th century, the island was a French colony for almost a century until conquest by the British in 1810 because of its strategic importance on the route to India. The British converted it into a monocrop economy, with sugar cane as the mainstay. Since the French era, slaves had been imported to the island from neighbouring Madagascar, Mozambique and Senegal. With the abolition of slavery, indentured labourers were brought from India and a small minority even from China. Thus, by the end of the 19th century, Mauritius was already a multi-racial society. It is today a veritable melting pot of European, African and Asian cultures, with a population that stands at 1.2 million. Of these, 51 per cent is Hindu, 32 per cent Christian, 16 per cent Muslim and less than one per cent is of Buddhist faith.

Since independence in 1968, the nation's diversity of races and cultures has not been a source of major strife as the political system, based on the Westminster type of parliamentary democracy, has maintained a precarious social balance by including the concept of 'best loser', whereby each ethnic group is guaranteed representation in the national parliament. Elections to the 70-member National Assembly are held regularly, normally every five years. Mauritius enjoys a robust democracy, where changes of government have not affected political and social stability inordinately as the major political parties have all been in a coalition government at one point or another since 1982.[1] Even though there have been regular changes of government since then, there have been no fundamental shifts in economic strategy, which has remained firmly export oriented.

Spared any major natural calamities, Mauritius nonetheless is visited by cyclones in the summer, usually between December and April, which determine to a large extent fluctuations in the country's growth. For example, agriculture and especially sugar cane suffer both when cyclones pass over the island and also when they do not, because of the drought conditions that then prevail. Consequently, so long as 'king sugar' reigned, the Mauritian economy was highly vulnerable to the vagaries of the weather.

The island underwent a significant structural transformation from independence to the late-1990s, when new challenges started to appear which demanded a rethink of the country's economic trajectory (see tables 2.1 and 2.2). This chapter provides an overview of the conditions and policies that led to a transformation of the economy.

Economic situation up until independence

At independence Mauritius was a textbook example of a monocrop (monoculture) economy. It had no mineral resources, no entrepôt trade and, except for sugar refining and its immediate by-products, few manufacturing enterprises. However, since the 1820s the economy of the island was open to international trade and was producing the crop for which it had the best comparative advantage – sugar, which is cyclone resistant and best suited to the volcanic soil of the island. Sugar exports were sufficient to pay for imports to maintain the population, so long as the price was high and the population did not increase faster than sugar production. This situation prevailed to the end of the 1940s, when malaria was eradicated from the island. Thereafter the rate of population increase grew, reaching 3 per cent per annum in the 1950s. Mauritius seemed destined to become a dismal Malthusian case scenario of population outstripping the food supply/productive output needed to survive.

Table 2.1: Mauritian structural transformation 1970–98 (US$bn and %)

Economic parameters	Amounts/proportions				Growth rates (%)		
	1970	1982	1998		1970–82	1983–98	1970–98
Nominal GDP and GDP growth per annum ($bn)	0.42	0.95	4.45		1.52	19.1	17.2
Real GDP (1970$) ($bn)	0.42	0.78	2.25	GDP growth	3.2	5.9	5.1
				GNP growth	*–4.8*	*6.4*	*2.1*
Population (mn)	0.73	0.92	1.10		2.2	1.1	1.4
GNP/capita (nominal)($000)	0.57	1.03	4.05	real growth	-6.3	5.4	2.0
Agriculture as % of GDP	26.1	15.7	8.8	real growth	-1.3	-0.6	-0.7
Manufacturing as % of GDP	12.0	20.1	25.2	real growth	4.5	7.4	6.0
Other industry as % of GDP	8.1	9.0	9.9	real growth	1.1	1.2	1.5
Services as % of GDP	53.8	55.2	57.9		4.5	6.6	5.8

Source: Annual Reports 1975, 1984, 1999 (Bank of Mauritius); *Country Economic Reports* (World Bank); *Global Development Finance Reports* (World Bank) 1998, 1999; and *World Development Indicators* (World Bank) 1998 and 1999.

Table 2.2: Mauritian economic performance and change 1970–98 (US$bn and %)

Economic parameters	1970	1982	1998e	Period – averages for 1970–82	1983–98	1970–98
Investment as a % of GDP	22.4%	24.0%	28.5%	21.1%	28.5	24.0%
Savings as a % of GDP	24.1%	21.5%	24.0%	19.3%	23.6%	21.0%
Inflation (CPI)	4.2%	14.5%	7.1%	11.0%	7.2%	9.0%
Overall budget deficit	-2.5%	-8.1%	-1.0%	-2.5%	-3.5%	-2.9%
Exports as % of GDP	54.2%	53.5%	59.6%	53.8%	57.6%	55.2%
Imports as % of GDP	55.6%	57.3%	65.4%	56.1%	61.8%	58.7%
Current account balance/GDP	2.0%	-5.8%	-2.6%	-3.1%	-3.4%	-3.2%
External debt	5.0%	69.1%	55.5%	30.3%	58.3%	46.5%
Average annual real growth rates						
Exports ($bn)	0.32	0.49	2.65	3.9%	7.7%	5.3%
Imports ($bn)	0.37	0.54	2.91	-2.1%	8.5%	6.1%
Government consumption				3.4%	6.6%	5.0%
Investment				-5.2%	8.0%	4.0%

Source: As for Table 2.1.

A turning point in the economic history of Mauritius was precipitated by an exogenous factor. In 1960, cyclone Carol devastated the island. This prompted the colonial authorities to set up a commission headed by Professor Meade[2] to report on the economic and social structure of Mauritius. The Meade report was to influence the island's economic and social policies during the 1970s. Meade stressed the need to control demographic expansion, which posed the greatest threat to economic development. Among the key recommendations was the need to diversify the economy away from sugar and to industrialise as fast as possible. However, he also noted the following potential impediments to industrial development:

- The 'sugar mentality', which obstructed capitalist development
- Shortage of capital
- Absence of financial institutions and intermediaries
- Racial division, which prevented commercial and financial co-operation between entrepreneurs of different ethnic groups
- Lack of knowledge in manufacturing outside the sugar industry

Therefore, the initial obstacles to transformation Mauritius faced were not only economic, but also psychological and sociological. The most urgent tasks in the early-1960s were to: attract capital, diversify the economy away from sugar to other employment generating sectors and to dampen demographic growth. To address the last problem, family planning and emigration (to Brazil and British Guyana!) were recommended by Professor Meade. In order to relieve unemployment, a policy of wage restraint was advocated to reflect the abundance of labour and to attract foreign investors (in common with most least-developed countries in the initial stages of development, Mauritius had no local class of dynamic entrepreneurs except for those already involved in sugar). Moreover, there was a large pool of semi-literate labour, as primary education had been free and universal since 1915. In 1965, the number enrolled in primary school as a percentage of the age group (5–11) was 101 per cent and 26 per cent for secondary school

A choice had to be made on the strategy to follow to bring about economic diversification. Either market forces alone could be left to create the right conditions for capital from sugar to move to other sectors, or the government could intervene to hasten the pace of diversification, as well as to ensure a more equitable distribution of income. The Mauritian government decided to intervene both for political and economic reasons. Politically, the country was moving towards independence and the government felt that it had to assist the development of a new class of entrepreneurs with no connection to the sugar sector. Racial heterogeneity and more than a century of specialisation in one crop would limit and delay the diversification of the economy if market forces alone were left to dictate the pace of change. On economic grounds, too, intervention seemed justified since returns in other sectors were not as high as in sugar. In fact, this and the imminence of independence resulted in capital outflows of over 15 million Mauritian rupees (MRs) in 1963 and MRs12m in 1964. Moreover, the market economy, such as it was, was entirely dominated by the smallest but richest ethnic group of sugar-baron landowners.

The first phase of import substitution thus started as early as 1962. This does not mean that a closed-door policy was pursued. In fact, foreign investors were encouraged to invest in Mauritius. The encouragement to import substitution was embodied in development certificates, which were awarded from 1964 and provided holders with the guarantee of quantitative restrictions on imports of competing goods, such that they effectively enjoyed a monopoly situation under high-tariff protection. The development certificates were granted on a firm-by-firm basis. Among the main import-substituting industries set up before independence were edible oil refinery, margarine, soap, fertiliser, matches, cosmetics and paper stationery. However, the limits of import substitution were reached quickly on an island of 800,000 people with a labour force of just 200,000.

Post-independence economic development

An overview of the economy

The remarkable performance of the Mauritian economy in the 1980s was due mainly to a set of policies that restructured the economy and provided the necessary stimulus to investment and savings. Growth was not smooth. Mistakes were made, corrective action was taken and policies that went against economic orthodoxy were adopted under certain circumstances, which fortunately did not create major insurmountable distortions in the short run. Indeed, moving from an alarming situation at independence in 1968 (when there was a nominal per capita income of about US$260, an unemployment rate of around 17 per cent and total dependence on sugar exports), Mauritius underwent major structural transformations over four decades to attain a nominal per capita income in 2008 of $5,250. As early as 1975, the island graduated from the International Development Association (IDA), which provides soft loans to the world's poorest countries.

Up till the late 1980s, the Mauritian growth rate always fluctuated with sugar production, which was itself dependent on the vagaries of the weather. During the 1950s, real growth averaged 2.5 per cent annually, but dropped significantly to 1.3 per cent in the 1960s. In the 1970s, the average annual growth rate was a respectable 5.6 per cent; it remained at around 6 per cent in the 1980s, before falling to around 5 per cent in the 1990s.

Population growth was brought under control through a vigorous programme of family planning, as well as through emigration. Whereas the population was increasing on average of around 3 per cent per year in the 1950s, it grew at a rate of 2.4 per cent in the 1960s and 1.4 per cent in the 1970s. During the 1980s, the rate further decreased to 0.79. Hence while Mauritius did come to grips with its demographic problem, a shortage of labour developed as a result. Meanwhile, the issue of an ageing population is looming.

Employment volatility has been a major problem for the island. The rate of unemployment stood at 17 per cent in 1968. After receding to around 6 per cent in the mid-1970s, it shot up again in the wake of the 1979 oil shock, reaching 17 per cent in 1981 and peaking at 22 per cent in 1982. While progress was made, with unemployment falling to less than 3 per cent in 1990, the rate went up again to 10.2 per cent in 2003 as income increased and other low-cost garment producers emerged on the international scene as protectionist barriers were being gradually dismantled.

The island's export performance has been quite remarkable. In 1968, sugar and its by-products made up more than 90 per cent of total exports of goods. Between 1970 and 1976, total export earnings, starting from a low base, grew by 31 per cent on average per year. The rate for the period 1976–82 was 16 per cent per year, averaging 22 per cent per year between 1983 and 1990. Merchandise exports totalled only MRs361.7 million in 1971 when the first export processing zone (EPZ) firms started operating. In 1990 they reached MRs18,246 million, nearly a fifty-fold increase in 20 years. Sugar accounted for only 32 per cent of the total. In fact, manufacturing brought in more foreign earnings than sugar in gross terms for the first time in 1985. The composition of exports underwent a major change as manufactured exports, especially textiles, gained in importance.

From independence to 1972, the situation for Mauritius both politically and financially was not a good one. However, then the price of sugar started rising, from 40

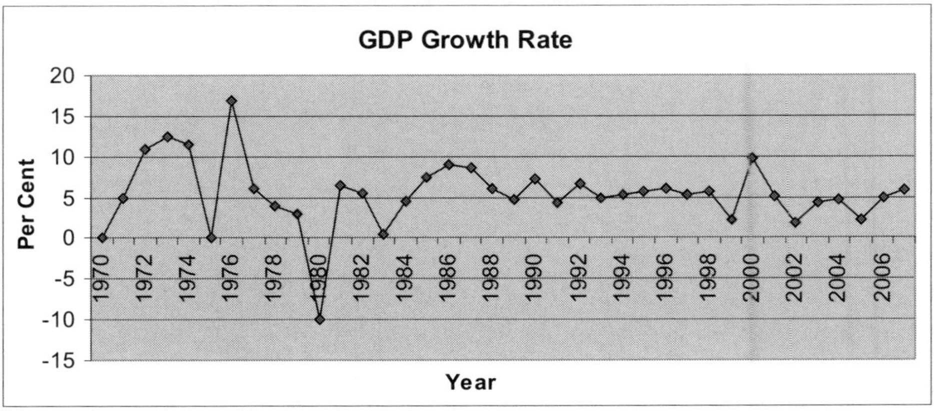

Figure 2.1: GDP growth rate

pounds sterling (£) to £330 per tonne. At the same time, the Mauritian quota under the European Economic Community (EEC) Sugar Protocol increased from 380,000 tonnes to 505,000 at a guaranteed price of £260 per tonne compared to the previous price of £57. The value of sugar exports reached MRs1584.2 million in 1974 from MRs321.6 million in 1971. The sugar boom cushioned the first oil shock and fuelled the illusion that the economy was on the path to sustained prosperity. Substantial wage increases, as well as end-of-year bonuses ranging from 1 month to 22 months in certain sectors were granted to compensate the workers for the austerity endured since 1968. Meade's warning that high wages plus social security plus cost of living allowances would spell inevitable ruin was forgotten. Both food subsidies and social expenditure were increased as the government pursued a policy of income redistribution and consolidation of the welfare state. Government budgetary expenditure as a percentage of GDP went up from 22 per cent in 1975 to 29 per cent in 1976 (an election year) to 32 per cent in 1978.

A sense of economic euphoria clouded the recession, which had already hit the rest of the world. The Mauritian government launched an ambitious investment programme in infrastructure – for example, a bulk sugar terminal, harbour development, roads and a hydro-electric plant – estimated at MRs7.2 billion for the plan period 1975–80. Moreover, since official development assistance was not forthcoming because of the international economic decline, the Mauritian authorities borrowed on the Euro market at commercial rates in the belief that the recession would be short-lived. This expansionist policy betrayed a disregard for macroeconomic management, with dire consequences for the economy. The heavy injection of money resulted in double-digit inflation – 14 per cent in 1973, 29 per cent in 1974 and 15 per cent in 1975. The balance of trade deficit widened and the government budget deficit expanded. Workers were laid off (567 in 1976, 3,581 in 1978 and 4,234 in 1980) and the unemployment rate soared.

Thus, even before the second oil shock in 1979, economic conditions in Mauritius had regressed to their 1968 level. In response, the government contracted more Eurodollar loans, controlled imports and regulated prices, but allowed the real interest rate to remain negative. Taxes were increased: the top income tax rate was 70 per cent, while the company tax rate was 65 per cent. Meanwhile the country's tariff structure did not give the right signals to firms whose products were not intended for direct export. The overvaluation of the rupee, which had been linked to the IMF special drawing right (SDR) since 1975, did not help to improve the situation. The economic deterioration, partly due to mismanagement under political pressure, was compounded by external factors – the rise in oil prices, cyclones, strikes and interest-rate hikes on the international financial markets, leading to a heavy debt-service burden. As a result, by the end of the 1970s the catastrophic economic situation brought home once again the need for the country to break away from the tyranny of sugar and engage forcefully in industrialisation and economic diversification.

Stabilisation and adjustment: getting prices right

Owing to the worsening external situation, Mauritius negotiated its first Stand-by Agreement with the IMF in 1979 with the immediate objective of stabilising the economy. Emphasis was laid on demand management schemes to reduce the budget and the balance of payments deficits and curtail consumption and imports. The Mauritian rupee was devalued in October 1979 by about 23 per cent vis-à-vis the SDR and in 1981 by another 20 per cent. In 1980 the country embarked on a structural adjustment programme (SAP) with the help of the World Bank. The aim was to lay the foundations for renewed growth by promoting export-oriented industries, by encouraging tourism and by diversifying agriculture

A series of measures were taken to curtail consumption and encourage investment a sales tax of 5 per cent was introduced, interest rates were liberalised and subsidies on rice and flour were reduced. Most important of all was the decision to de-link the local currency from the SDR and to attach it to a trade-weighted basket of currencies reflecting the trade patterns of Mauritius. This was intended to restore the competitiveness of domestic products, which had been partially eroded by the wage increases of the second half of the 1970s. Since March 1983, the rupee has been on a crawling peg, floating downward to maintain the real exchange rate at a competitive level. Further, a policy of wage restraint has been vigorously followed whereby negotiated wage increases have been lower than the inflation rate – except that every five years the salary structure of public servants is reviewed by the Pay Research Bureau, leading to a massive monetary injection.

The island's tax structure was reformed and the highest marginal rates were brought down to 35 per cent. Company tax was also reduced to 35 per cent, while new companies holding export certificates were charged 15 per cent for their whole lifetime. To encourage local companies to export, a graduated tax structure was set up whereby a 2 per cent rebate was given for every 10 per cent of output exported.

Hence, a firm exporting 100 per cent of its products would pay only 15 per cent taxes. Tariffs were rationalised to be more in line with export-oriented industrialisation, quotas were removed and price controls were eliminated on all except eight basic products.

In addition to monetary and fiscal policies, some institutional reforms were carried out under the SAP and these played a significant role in the economic recovery of the country. A basic weakness in the industrial strategy was identified in marketing and investment promotion. A parastatal organisation, the Mauritius Export Development and Investment Authority (MEDIA), comprising for the first time more members of the private sector than government representatives on its board of directors, was set up in 1984 to search for new markets to attract investors.

Government, unions and the private sector

The Mauritian government played a key role in institution building, infrastructure development and in creating an environment within which economic agents could function effectively to promote growth. Although this does not imply that all the policies followed were necessarily the correct ones, the government has been an active agent in fostering the economic growth of the island. It secured guaranteed prices and markets for sugar, it adhered to international conventions, which gave Mauritian goods access to the EEC and it negotiated quotas for its textile exports with the US government. The government also provided free primary and secondary education, creating a literate and adaptable labour force, and has invested heavily in physical infrastructure without neglecting social overheads.

During the 1960s and 1970s and inspired by Fabian socialism, the country's Labour government built a welfare state which provided free healthcare and education, cheap housing as well as subsidies on imported staple food (namely rice and flour). In fact, the priority objective of satisfying the basic needs of the population laid the necessary social foundations, which allowed the people to respond to changing external conditions relatively fast. However, it also laid a shaky economic foundation, which would have collapsed without the structural adjustment programme (SAP) of 1980.

The government also intervened positively in the early stages of development to mobilise domestic and foreign capital for infrastructure development. Domestic resources can be mobilised by the private sector if income distribution is such that savings may be made. However, the major constraint facing a new state is obtaining enough foreign exchange. This can be overcome by either exporting more or by obtaining grants/loans from other countries/institutions. Because Mauritius did not have any strategic or ideological importance at independence, it had to ensure that the flow of foreign exchange from sugar exports would be stable over time so as not to handicap investment efforts. The Commonwealth Sugar Agreement guaranteed a favourable price, but was due to expire when the United Kingdom joined the EEC in 1973. So the government had to negotiate stable prices and preferential treatment by the EEC, which could be achieved by enlisting the support of EEC member countries.

As a result, Mauritian foreign policy took on a dimension of its own. The country adhered to the Non-aligned Movement, to the Organisation of African Unity, as well as to the Organisation Commune Africaine et Malgache (the French equivalent of the Commonwealth), which was to disintegrate in the late-1970s. In June 1973, Mauritius signed the Yaoundé Convention, which gave preferential tariffs to EEC goods and duty-free and quota-free access to EEC markets. This treaty also enabled the island to benefit from financial aid from the European Development Fund and the European Investment Bank. The Lomé Convention not only provided Mauritius with sufficient market openings for its growing textile industry, but also guaranteed a market for 505,000 tonnes of sugar per year under the EEC-ACP Sugar Protocol at a price usually higher than the world price. During the sugar boom of 1974, the guaranteed price was lower than the world price, but Mauritius respected the clauses of the convention in violation of the profit-maximising motive.

A more debatable area of government intervention was in the labour market. The comparative advantage of small, labour-rich countries lies in keeping down labour costs – the only costs that can be effectively controlled domestically – which can be done by outlawing militant trade unions or recognising only pro-government unions, as was done in some countries of the Far East. In Mauritius this course of action was not possible because of the country's strong trade union tradition and because of its democratic system. Instead, a quite repressive law (the Industrial Relations Act [IRA]) was passed in 1973, which effectively made all strikes illegal.

At the same time, different institutions were set up to prevent industrial relations from becoming explosive. Tripartite salary negotiations, involving the government, the private sector and trade union federations, have been held regularly since 1977 prior to the budget being presented. After these discussions, compensation for the increase in the cost of living is arrived at and this is applied to both the private and public sectors. A special body, the National Remuneration Board (NRB) set up under the IRA, is responsible for fixing minimum wages and conditions of service in the private sector. If employers and workers cannot reach an agreement, they take their case to the Industrial Relations Commission, which has the power to settle conflicts. The Ministry of Labour also performs a conciliatory role in disputes.

These mechanisms for wage-dispute settlements and collective bargaining have contributed to social stability. There has not been a major strike in Mauritius since 1979. However, government intervention did introduce rigidities in the labour market, especially in the agricultural sector. Similarly, fixing a lower minimum wage for women than for men in manufacturing had negative repercussions, until corrected under the SAP in the early 1980s. More flexible labour regulations were established in the export processing zones, which were then seen as enclaves. Nonetheless, from an economic viewpoint, the system did not satisfy either efficiency or equity considerations. It was neither dynamic nor flexible enough to reward productivity and scarce skills. Although the system was meant to compensate employees for cost-of-living increases, it was guided by the principle of tapering compensation, with the lowest paid receiving the full increase. This led to a reduction in wage differentials, especially in the public sector, which became more 'bottom weighted'. To redress the situation, the salary structure was reviewed every five years, resulting in sudden massive increases in the salary bill and in the money supply, with its concomitant pressure on the government budget and on inflation.

Nonetheless, the tripartite committee with all its imperfections served the useful purpose of consensus building, which has been the cornerstone of the Mauritian success. It provided a critical forum for the major social and economic players to air their views. Of even greater importance was the effectiveness of collaboration between the government and the private sector. It was this collaboration (at times very informal) which led to certain key initiatives being taken, like the EPZs being set up in 1970, the first hotels being built, successful negotiations on the Sugar Protocol, the creation of a national airline, the establishment of a stock exchange and a freeport, investment in Mozambique and the implementation of a value-added tax. The public-private partnership in Mauritius overall had a positive influence. How did it happen?

Partnership between the public and private sectors

The private sector in Mauritius has always been well organised. Institutions like the Chamber of Commerce and Industry, and the Chamber of Agriculture were set up in the 19th century to defend the interests of their members. The private sector was then made up mostly of franco-Mauritians, who had to deal with the British colonial authorities. Their racial homogeneity surely played an important part in the strength of these institutions. They maintained their relevance after independence by opening up gradually, and here the advantages of smallness stand out.

The government, and especially the Prime Minister, had to trust the private sector and vice versa. At independence, the private sector therefore created the post of joint co-ordinator, and appointed someone who had been a minister before independence to provide an interface between the private sector and government. This facilitated high-level talks with the government, as the private sector could speak through (and with) one voice. Confidence building and consensus seeking could be carried out in a structured, constructive way to ensure that frictions did not develop into conflicts.

While there was still a good deal of mistrust between the private sector and the civil service in the 1970s, the relationship improved in the 1980s as private-sector representatives were appointed as members and chairs of various boards of administration of parastatal bodies. These much-maligned institutions helped to bridge the communications gap between civil servants and business. Nonetheless, this change in attitude occurred in the 1980s in the wake of the structural adjustment programme, which compelled policy-makers to think more in terms of efficiency than control. This approach was further encouraged by the 'business-friendly' attitude of the government in 1983. The single most important measure to kick-start the economy in 1984 was the drastic reduction in the top marginal rates of income and corporation tax from 65/70 per cent to 35 per cent. This was a powerful signal on the part of government; the private sector responded positively with economic results that led to Mauritius being touted as another East Asian economic miracle.

Indeed, the World Bank in a momentary lapse of inspiration entitled a book *The East Asian Miracle* (the expression 'Mauritian miracle' has also been used in the international press). Miracles in popular belief are attributed to supernatural forces, to completely exogenous factors, and the economic evolution of Mauritius has certainly benefited from a fair dose of externalities (as described above). The interesting question is why Mauritius is one of the rare ACP countries to have succeeded, when all were exposed to the same exogenous factors viz. oil price hikes, world recession in the early 1970s and 1980s, the Sugar Protocol, the Lomé Convention and absence of quotas on the US market. There is no doubt that Mauritius enjoyed a fair amount of luck – the sugar boom, which blurred the impact of the first oil crisis, and the EPZ, which started at a time when there was little competition yet a great deal of protectionism. No major cyclone hit Mauritius in the 1980s when the economy was booming. Nonetheless, Mauritius was also unlucky when unfavourable weather conditions in 1979 and 1980 hit and threatened to derail the first structural adjustment programme. Luck also comes to those who are prepared, to the practitioner who acts on 'gut feelings' ('animal spirits' in Keynesian terminology), to those who can identify and seize opportunities.

In Mauritius, exogenous shocks have been a major catalyst for change, as with cyclone Carol in 1960, the fall in sugar prices at independence, the oil shocks and the dismantling of protectionist barriers. Yet Mauritius was able to respond to these challenges by taking new directions: setting up the EPZ in 1970, adopting painful structural adjustment programmes between 1979 and 1983, going for industrial modernisation, capital markets and skills development and export of services. Implementation, though not always in the most efficient and effective manner, was facilitated by the creation of support institutions in key sectors.

Thus, the National Computer Board (NCB) was established in 1989 as ICT came to be seen as a key sector for the future. Since skills shortages were anticipated to be a major constraint, the Industrial and Vocational Training Board was also set up in the same year. As the end of the Multi-Fiber Arrangement (MFA, also known as the Multi-Fiber Agreement) was heralded at the beginning of the 1990s, the Export Processing Zones Development Authority (EPZDA) was set up in 1992 to assist competitiveness of exports enterprises by improving productivity and quality. While offshore banks had been encouraged since the mid-1980s, there was no institutional support until the Mauritius Offshore Business Activities Authority (MOBAA) was established in 1992 together with the Mauritius Freeport Authority (MFA), whose mission was to develop Mauritius as a transhipment centre in that part of the Indian Ocean. As the international trading environment changed under the aegis of the World Trade Organization (WTO), these institutional initiatives were streamlined. Thus, the investment portfolio of the MEDIA and the MFA were transferred to the Board of Investment housed in the Ministry of Finance, and the MEDIA and the EPZDA were merged to form Enterprise Mauritius in 2005.

Furthermore, since the development of the ICT sector depended on telecommunications, a Telecommunications Advisory Council was set up in 1994 to work on a telecommunications bill, which would make the sector more competitive, bringing down connection costs. The bill eventually became an Act in 1998. Mauritius set itself the target of becoming a 'cyber island', and the regulatory body, the ICT Authority, was set up in 2001.

Economy in the new Millennium

During different periods, the engines of growth of the Mauritian economy had been: sugar, textiles, to a lesser extent tourism and offshore financial services. However, by 2000 they were showing signs of running out of steam. While sugar's contribution to the national economy in terms of both job creation and value added had been declining since the 1980s, garment manufacturing also went through a downturn. The key challenge confronting Mauritius at the end of the last decade was the same one it confronted at independence and in 1980: namely, how to reduce the level of unemployment, which had been increasing steadily and stood at 10.2 per cent in 2003.

Macroeconomic indicators

An analysis of table 2.3 reveals: (i) that Mauritius enjoyed a growth rate averaging 4–5 per cent per annum; (ii) the inflation rate was under control, but steadily rising after 2004; and (iii) per capita income and (iv) total exports had been steadily increasing. On the downside, the budget deficit as percentage of GDP (around 6 per cent) was quite high and this, if not corrected, could lead to a dire financial situation, compounded by the high and growing level of public debt.

The success of the Mauritian economy, as described above, was largely dependent on preferential treatment in the main export markets for sugar and textiles. Mauritius was beneficiary of several trade preference schemes from its key trading partners, namely the EU (the Cotonou Agreement, formerly the Lomé Convention) and the United States (the African Growth and Opportunity Act [AGOA] – Wearing and Apparel Provision).[3]

According to the IMF, Mauritius was one of the economies most vulnerable to a fall in export revenues following the phasing out of preferential trade arrangements. The IMF study calculated the percentage fall in export revenues for Mauritius under three

Table 2.3: Selected economic indicators 1990, 2000–2007

Economy	Period	Unit	1990	2000	2001	2002	2003	2004	2005	2006	2007
Yearly											
GDP (market prices)	Year	MRs bn	39.4	120.3	132.1	142.5	157.4	175.6	185.3	206.3	235.5
	US$ bn	2.6	4.6	4.5	4.8	5.5	6.3	6.3	6.6	7.5	
GDP deflator (basic prices)	Year	%	+6.9	+2.1	+6.2	+4.8	+5.0	+5.7	+4.0	+6.8	+7.9
GNI per capita (market prices)	Year	MRs 000	36.9	100.7	110.4	118.0	128.0	142.0	148.9	166.0	192.8
	US$ 000	2.48	3.83	3.80	3.94	4.51	5.12	5.10	5.31	6.15	
Growth of household consumption	Year	%	+5.0	+3.7	+3.2	+3.3	+5.1	+7.8	+7.3	+5.9	+4.5
Savings rate	Year	%	25.3	26.3	28.4	27.4	25.1	22.6	17.4	17.1	21.3
Net international reserves	As at end of June	MRs bn	10.8	25.2	31.8	40.6	50.2	54.7	65.8	64.7	83.5
Net international reserves (weeks of import coverage)	As at end of June	No.	25.5	23.8	29.6	37.3	40.3	37.4	36.7	31.0	36.7
Investment rate	Year	%	30.6	22.9	22.7	21.8	22.6	21.6	21.4	24.3	25.1
Growth of investment (GDFCF)	Year	%	+23.3	-8.3	+4.7	-0.1	+10.3	+2.2	-1.9	+19.0	+8.6
Private investment as a % of total investment	Year	%	62.7	72.0	68.9	68.5	61.0	69.3	70.4	68.3	78.2
Foreign direct investment (FDI)	Year	MRs mn	609	7,265	936	979	1,966	1,796	2,807	7,222	11,514
Direct investment abroad	Year	MRs mn	8	333	83	278	1,156	970	1,942	1,134	1,826
Trade											
Growth of merchandise exports	Year	%	n.a	+2.7	+13.2	-11.5	-5.9	-3.5	+8.9	+10.1	-10.6

Growth of merchandise imports	Year	%	n.a	-5.6	+0.6	-2.9	-4.3	+3.9	+5.5	+11.1	-1.1
Terms of trade	Year	%	+98.0	+96.0	+90.0	+94.0	+97.0	+97.0	+88.0	+83.2	+82.7
Total exports of merchandise goods (f.o.b)	Year	MRs bn	17.9	45.7	54.8	54.0	53.0	54.9	63.2	74.0	69.7
Total imports of merchandise goods (f.o.b)	Year	MRs bn	21.8	54.4	59.0	60.2	61.4	70.9	86.7	108.6	113.7
Openness of the economy	Year	%	1.1	0.8	0.8	0.8	0.8	0.7	0.8	0.9	0.8
Growth of service exports (f.o.b)	Year	%	n.a	+6.3	+19.4	-13.0	-0.7	+4.3	+13.0	+4.6	+23.0
Growth of service imports	Year	%	n.a	+8.8	+9.4	-4.2	-0.1	+0.1	+8.4	+5.1	+8.7
Merchandise exports as a % of total exports	Year	%	70.7	55.4	52.5	61.2	59.7	57.9	57.0	58.2	50.4
Merchandise imports as a % of total imports	Year	%	76.6	73.0	71.4	71.7	70.8	71.6	71.0	72.2	70.2
Current account balance	Year	MRs bn	-1.8	-0.9	8.0	7.5	2.7	-3.2	-9.6	-19.6	-12.5
Current account balance as a % of GDP	Year	%	-4.5	-0.7	6.1	5.2	1.7	-1.8	-5.2	-9.5	-5.3
Overall balance of payments	Fiscal year	MRs bn	3.0	2.1	5.1	5.9	9.1	3.2	-3.1	-3.0	+6.6
Tourism											
Growth of 'hotels and restaurants' sector	Year	%	+11.0	+12.2	+1.2	+3.1	+3.0	+2.4	+5.6	+3.5	+14.0
Tourist arrivals increase over previous year		%	+10.9	+13.6	+0.6	+3.2	+3.0	+2.4	+5.9	+3.6	+15.1
Gross earnings per tourist	Year	MRs	12,451	21,683	27,511	26,888	27,656	32,618	33,774	40,521	44,860
Room occupancy rate (total)	Year	%	62	70	66	67	63	63	63	66	76

Agro-industry											
Growth of 'sugar' sector	Year	%	+11.9	+64.5	+9.9	-25.0	+3.7	+10.6	-9.2	-2.9	-13.6
Production of main commodities											
Sugar	Year	Metric tonnes	624,302	569,289	645,597	520,887	537,155	572,316	519,816	504,857	435,972
Sugar cane	Year	Metric tonnes	5,548,291	5,109,521	5,792,325	4,873,897	5,199,384	5,280,370	4,984,058	4,748,973	4,235,849
Tea	Year	Metric tonnes	29,868	6,110	7,440	6,870	6,973	7,229	6,798	7,649	8,027
Tobacco	Crop year ending March	Metric tonnes	799	563	556	477	426	357	296	298	327
Foodcrops	Year	Metric tonnes	65,840	114,484	129,119	103,876	103,455	111,633	96,782	106,902	99,130
Fish	Year	Metric tonnes	13,222	7,842	8,794	9,314	9,449	9,430	8,982	8,885	5,987
Export-oriented enterprises (EOE)											
Growth of EPZ/EOE	Year	%	+7.0	+6.0	+4.4	-6.0	-6.0	-6.8	-12.3	+4.6	+8.0
No. of enterprises	end of year	No.	568	518	522	506	506	501	506	434	404
Employment	end of year	No.	89,906	90,682	87,607	87,204	77,623	68,022	66,931	64,962	67,314
Investment	Year	Rs Mn	690	1,702	1,758	1,468	1,418	2,508	2,376	2,245	4,301
EPZ/EOE exports	Year	Rs bn	11.5	31.0	33.7	32.7	31.4	32.0	29.0	33.6	37.8
EPZ/EOE exports as a % of total exports of merchandise goods	Year	%	63.4	75.7	70.9	60.5	59.3	58.4	45.8	45.4	54.3

Source: CSO, Mauritius

different assumptions for export supply elasticities (e). These are summarised in table 2.4, below.

Table 2.4: Percentage loss in total export revenues

Elasticity	e=0	e=1.0	e=1.5
Mauritius	-11.5%	-19.6%	-23.7%
Mean for middle-income developing countries	-1.6%	-2.9%	-3.6%

e = elasticity of export supply

Source: IMF (2004) The Impact of Preference Erosion on Middle-Income Developing Countries. Working Paper, September 2004.

By the beginning of this millennium it became clear that Mauritius could not continue on its old trajectory, which had relied on preferential access to markets for just a few products. Diversification of the economy, which had been touted since Meade's days, had to be pursued vigorously if Mauritius was to maintain living standards.

Key lessons

As Mauritius engages on a new phase of structural transformation, key elements that facilitated its first transformation are just as relevant today.

Pursuit of an outward-looking strategy

Since it became independent, Mauritius's success depended on its adoption of an outward-looking strategy. The Export Processing Zones Act was passed in 1970, two years after independence. Unlike EPZs in other countries, the Mauritius EPZ did not refer to a specific geographical area. It was instead a legal entity that provided the holder of an export enterprise certificate with generous incentives: tax holidays, duty-free import of raw materials and equipment, free repatriation of capital and flexible labour regulations.

The essential element, however, is not the legislation, but rather the attitude of welcome. Foreign direct investment (FDI) was actively encouraged and sought out, and there was a consensus among the population as a whole that FDI was in the interests of the country. For instance, Mauritian nationality was offered to Hong Kong investors when the fate of the colony was still being discussed by the British and the Chinese in preparation for the handing over in 1997. The resulting surge of investment from Hong Kong formed the basis of the remarkable growth of the textile and clothing sector in the 1980s.

Moreover, if there is no consensus on the need to promote export-oriented policies, if there is no involvement by local entrepreneurs,[4] any outward-looking strategy is doomed to failure. An important feature during the early phases of industrialisation is the presence of local entrepreneurs. Foreign firms brought in new technology and an element of competition necessary to induce efficient production and enhance quality. However, if the EPZ had been grafted onto an economy not yet ready to receive it because of lack of infrastructure or preparation of the labour force, then it would probably have been rejected by the system.

Emphasis on good governance

The state played different roles in different phases of Mauritius's transformation as initiator, promoter, protector and arbiter. Yet it was a developmental state, a state committed to development of the country and not to sectarian interests. The rule of law prevails in Mauritius. Political leaders generally respect the country's key institutions and ensure social stability. For example, political vision was demonstrated when Mauritius joined the Organisation Commune Africaine et Malgache (OCAM), which opened the door to the Yaoundé Convention, and when it stuck to the Sugar Protocol although market prices were higher than the guaranteed price.

The country's civil service has also played an important role in implementing the various economic and social programmes. Without a proper public administration, without competent cadres in the economic ministries and the Central Bank, it is doubtful whether the adjustment programmes could have been as successful.

The island's close public-private sector collaboration also forms part of good governance as it shows willingness on the part of political leaders to engage in dialogue and a sense of responsibility on the part of captains of industry to participate constructively in the process of policy-making. However, a precondition for such effective dialogue is the existence of a structured private sector. One of the advantages of a small economy is in the area of communications: policies changes can be explained quickly and turnarounds are short.

Importance attached to social stability

An unquantifiable outcome of public-private collaboration has been the social stability that ensued as the fruits of economic growth trickled down to the population. Social stability has been and still is a major factor for attracting FDI and tourism to Mauritius. Although this was arguably achieved at the expense of optimal economic policies, the premium on social peace is high in a multiethnic society. However, care has to be taken to prevent temporary concessions from becoming permanent distortions. For, without economic progress, without perceptible continuous improvement in the standard of living, the social fabric can be easily torn. In the final analysis, moreover, only productive employment creation can guarantee long-term social peace.

Maintenance of political stability

An important factor in the sustained growth of the Mauritian economy has been political stability. Although the political landscape has experienced episodic turbulence, such stability has manifested in the broadly shared beliefs of the political class and consensual adherence to an economic strategy of outward orientation, market-driven development and the rejection of nationalisation and inward-looking policies. That is, there has been continuity in broad objectives.

Thus, although a Labour government had started implementing policies underlying the structural adjustment loan (SAL) in 1980, the accession of a strong, unopposed coalition to power in 1982 ensured that the proper psychological shock was created to sell the idea of austerity to the people. The fact that the Mauritian Militant Movement (MMM) had been closely associated with the labour movement made it easier for government to influence trade unions and impress upon the latter the urgency to take strict steps to redress the economy. Finally, the MMM, which for years had been clamouring for nationalisation of some sugar estates and for self-reliant development, began to espouse the existing development strategy and reassured political opponents that its objective was no longer social revolution, but economic growth, readjustment and tight financial management of the country's affairs.

This change in ideology explains to a large extent the fact that Mauritius was one of the rare countries where a SAP did not give rise to street demonstrations and riots. Even though the ruling coalition split and fresh elections were held in 1983, the same steady, rigorous economic management continued. Successive governments have helped in creating a business environment that is stable and in managing public opinion with respect to the need for economic discipline.

Emphasis on macroeconomic stability

An appropriate meso-micro incentive structure, consistent with macroeconomic objectives of stability, prudence and balance, is also crucial. In spite of the above elements, the Mauritian economy did not really take off before the mid-1980s. The main reason was the failure to get prices right, i.e. the exchange rate, interest rates, tariffs and tax policies have to be geared towards a clear-cut goal – development through the adoption of an outward-looking strategy.

Before the structural adjustment programmes of 1980 and 1982, fiscal policy was characterised by high government expenditure, financed by high taxes and external borrowing (short-term Eurodollar loans to finance long-term infrastructure development projects). The fiscal and exchange rate reforms undertaken in the context of the SAPs ensured more efficient fiscal governance (the overall budget deficit as a percentage of GDP remained at around 3 per cent between 1985 and 1995), removed the distortions of a dual exchange rate policy and ensured that the rupee was not overvalued.

Emphasis on human resource development

The design and implementation of a given economic strategy requires competent cadres and a productive labour force. Another precondition then is to have a literate and adaptable work force, as well as an efficient administrative system that is development oriented and not bent on enlarging its bureaucratic precinct.

Since its human resources are Mauritius's only real natural asset, human capital development was considered crucial to sustainable growth, as well as to equitable distribution of income. Although the private sector contributed significantly to education, standards varied across secondary schools. Primary education was free and almost entirely public even before independence. However, free secondary schooling was granted from 1976 only, this as a result of the Labour government's commitment to education as an instrument of social progress. The College of Agriculture, which was set up in 1925, became part of the University of Mauritius at the latter's inception in 1967 and World Bank assistance was sought to develop the education sector further, especially the secondary and vocational sectors. Heavy investment in human capital formation provided the semi-literate labour force that was necessary for the initial phase of industrialisation.

Adequate infrastructure

Without investment in physical infrastructure (roads, the harbour, electricity, telecommunications and so on), transformation would not have been possible. Although mistakes were made in the late-1970s with respect to the mobilisation of expensive commercial funds for long-term infrastructure development, there is no doubt that the investments facilitated economic success in the 1980s. Thus, a potential economic disaster was averted, because borrowed funds were used for development projects and were not siphoned off. This is another good point for governance – the objectives were the right ones, even though the economic means were not appropriate. It may also be argued that the government did not have much choice, as official development assistance flows had dried up and investment was needed for future growth. In this respect, there may be a case for revisiting the policies of official development assistance to small economies when they are in a transitory phase.

Labour market

Labour markets should function properly, such that conflict is minimised and wages are allowed to rise in line with productivity. The labour situation will vary from country to country, depending on the political and social structure. Government intervention in the form of arbitration may smooth relations between employers and employees and promote a productive work environment. The imperfections in the labour market in Mauritius did not prevent growth from taking place, because there was a consensus on the broad economic strategy and nobody wanted to return to a situation of high unemployment. If that tacit social contract had not been in place, market imperfections could have been a major obstacle.

Collaboration with donors

Compared to many other countries, Mauritius utilised foreign aid assistance from donor countries and multilateral institutions relatively well, thanks to the combination of factors mentioned above. Still, it is important to highlight the importance of technical assistance provided by UN agencies, the Commonwealth Secretariat and the European Union, amongst others. Many of these programmes were implemented successfully because there were consultations with local stakeholders in the conception and design stages. Without such technical assistance (often provided on a grant basis) it is doubtful whether Mauritius, with its limited human resource base, could have progressed so quickly. The flexible attitude of foreign institutions also helped, described by an outside observer as 'the willingness of international interlocutors like the World Bank to backstop with financial assistance a transition involving policy reform, structural adjustment and economic transformation without requiring Mauritius to suffer excessive social and political dislocation'.[5] Mauritius was perhaps lucky to be faced with interlocutors who believed in local ownership of development programmes and not in universal blueprints!

New challenges

The modern economic history of Mauritius reveals that small states reach turning points very quickly as international conditions change. Success usually translates in higher standards of living, but with accompanying increases in production costs. Thus, by the year 2000, Mauritius found itself again at a crossroads with the challenge of finding the right development path to attain the same objectives as in the 1970s, namely to attract FDI, and to diversify its economic base. However, the context had changed. Internally, the shortage of labour as well as of skills led to an increase in labour costs. Therefore, the major comparative advantage of Mauritius, upon which its early industrialisation had been based, no longer acted as a pull for foreign direct investment. In fact, it was not so much the costs as the unavailability of labour itself that served as a brake.

Mauritius had to re-think its industrial strategy, and the products it wished to sell to the world. Externally, the international scene, with the advent of new low-cost labour-rich garment producers, the World Trade Organization and globalisation, and the dispersion of foreign assistance with the opening up of Eastern Europe, created a situation of heightened uncertainty.

The response of the Mauritian government in the early 1990s was to push for a CMD strategy: consolidation, modernisation (of the textile and agricultural sectors) and diversification (into financial services with the setting up of a freeport and offshore business activities). The garment sector was still going through a phase of restructuring, but it consolidated itself through modernisation and increased productivity and quality. These measures were still not sufficient to prevent the closure of many garment enterprises in the period 2000–2005. The industrial structure still lacked depth, essentially because the approach to industry had been concentrated on building pillars instead of searching for clusters and for linkages between sectors. Within the garments sector, four products dominated the industry, namely pullovers, T-shirts, shirts and pants. Similarly, tourism was Eurocentric, as the bulk of tourists to the island mainly came from France and Britain.

However, Mauritius's attempts at diversification were not totally successful, mainly because of a lack of skills, a mismatch between the output of the education system and the needs of the country, an absence of critical mass, and a reluctance to break with the old paradigm, which had brought relative success to the island in the past.

A necessary condition for continued growth is a new mindset at the decision-making level (both in the public and private sectors), a mindset that is more geared towards taking risks than to preserving past gains. Decisions that face Mauritius in this new phase of transformation relate to the reform of the education and training system, public sector reform, competitiveness and productivity enhancement, an integrated economic system, a flexible labour market, the development of an export-oriented service sector (not only financial services), and a strategy of regional integration (expansion through strategic alliances) as opposed to simple de-localisation.

More specifically, at the beginning of the new millennium it was clear that the priority areas of focus had to be: the role of government; human capital; macroeconomic reform; and regional co-operation.

The role of government

With the new millennium the Mauritian government's role was evolving more towards that of a regulator, an arbitrator and a facilitator. Given the lack of critical mass, it might still have to be a catalyst in some sectors. Nonetheless, the public sector would have to put in place the proper legal and regulatory framework for the private sector to operate. The emphasis would have to be less on control, more on creating a business-friendly environment, less bureaucracy and more efficient delivery of services. The civil service would have to be streamlined and overhauled to acquire this new mindset as facilitator. It is a politically difficult and sensitive issue, but one that is fundamental to future growth. It is extremely important that the public service attracts and retains the best brains to identify potential bottlenecks fast and take remedial action.

At the same time, there should be a move towards decentralisation. A re-engineering of the parastatal sector is required, such that efficiency criteria prevail over political expediency. In practice, this could amount to a Herculean task in such a small and interconnected country. This is a challenge to the ingenuity of Mauritian politicians and policy-makers, as the social implications of inaction are far reaching.

Human capital

At the time of writing, the reform of the education and training system was under way, following almost a decade's delay. The outcome of this reform will be felt only after another decade or so. In the meantime, there is a need to obtain skilled staff, so a policy for the import of highly skilled human resources will have to be elaborated upon.

Microeconomic reform

While macroeconomic stability is necessary to create the conditions and environment for growth, microeconomic reform has to be addressed once the fundamentals are in place. Production is carried out at the level of the firm, and measures must be taken to increase productivity and efficiency. Structural adjustment helped put the Mauritian economy back on course, at the expense of optimal economic policies in some cases. Now, the time has come to correct certain distortions which, if left unchecked, could jeopardise the country's competitiveness. Key points on the agenda should be:

- **Anti-monopoly regulations.** A major handicap to being small is the absence of critical mass and the concentration of wealth. This creates a situation where monopolies and cartels develop rapidly, where invisible barriers to entry are erected by the links that exist among players in manufacturing and finance. A thorough reform of the financial sector is needed. The best prescription to fight monopolistic behaviour is to open up to global service providers; this will also enable faster transfer of technologies and will upgrade local skills.
- **Labour market reforms.** The mechanisms for wage fixing, cost-of-living compensation and salary restructuring must be reviewed to make the labour market more flexible and open, to encourage mobility of labour to efficient sectors. These reforms, which could not be carried out in 1982–83 when there was an unemployment rate verging on 17–20 per cent, should be set in motion.
- **Social services and ability to pay.** Food and housing subsidies used to be justified as circulating capital at a time when the majority of the population lived in poverty. With increases in the standard of living, pockets of poverty can be identified more easily. It makes more sense in terms of both equity and efficiency to provide social services on the basis of 'ability to pay', with subsidies provided on the basis of need. This would reduce government expenditure, keep down tax rates and ensure better social justice.

Regional co-operation

Regional co-operation is one of the avenues open to small countries if they are to progress economically. The Lomé Convention is a vivid example. If Mauritius did not have access to a guaranteed market, it would probably not have fared so well, despite implementing the right policies. Small countries that find themselves in direct competition with labour-rich countries may find it difficult to sustain growth if they cannot depend on secure markets. Such markets may be geographically regional. However, if a country finds itself in a crawling growth region (although this is not the case in the Association of South East Asian Nations [ASEAN]) then the limits to its own growth will be reached rapidly. Regional co-operation by itself will not help small countries, but it is a sure way of expanding markets – provided there is regional integration. In the case of Mauritius, there is need for a planned delocalisation (outward investment).

As at end 2004, when the *Competitiveness Foresight* was completed, Mauritius was signatory of four regional groupings, namely the Common Market for Eastern and Southern Africa (COMESA), the Southern African Development Community (SADC), the Indian Ocean Commission (IOC) and the Indian Ocean Rim Association for Regional Cooperation (IOR-ARC).

The main objective of engaging in these groups is to enhance co-operation among member states on the economic front and on trade relationships. Members also try to make maximum use of the natural resources of other member countries by investing in the opportunities for extraction and downstream processing (value-addition) offered by them.

Under the COMESA, Mauritius enjoys tariff-free trade with eight other African countries and reduced-tariff trade with 11 others. The COMESA comprises 20 member states of Eastern and Southern Africa, with a total population of about 385 million. The member states are: Angola, Burundi, Comoros, Democratic Republic of Congo, Djibouti, Egypt, Eritrea, Ethiopia, Kenya, Libya, Madagascar, Malawi, Mauritius, Namibia, Rwanda, Seychelles, Sudan, Swaziland, Uganda, Zambia and Zimbabwe.

Mauritius adheres to seven SADC protocols, including a trade protocol. The latter has been operational since 1 September 2000 and paves the way for a phasing out of a minimum of 85 per cent of tariffs within eight years, and all tariffs by 2012. It is expected that a free-trade area will be created by 2012. SADC was established in August 1995 with a view to enhancing the standard and the quality of life for people and to making the maximum use of natural resources of its member countries. SADC has 14 member states, namely Angola, Botswana, Democratic Republic of Congo, Lesotho, Malawi, Mauritius, Mozambique, Namibia, Seychelles, South Africa, Swaziland, Tanzania, Zambia and Zimbabwe.

The Indian Ocean Commission comprises Madagascar, Seychelles, Comoros, Reunion and Mauritius. The objective of the IOC is to enhance co-operation among member states, mainly in the diplomatic, economic, cultural and scientific fields. Among other achievements, customs duties have been removed reciprocally in Madagascar and Mauritius on originating goods.

Mauritius also forms part of the Indian Ocean Rim Association for Regional Cooperation. Established in 1997, this association's objective is to establish a regional framework for improving trade relationships among member countries. There are 18 members, with a total population of over 1,595 million: Australia, Bangladesh, India, Indonesia, Iran, Kenya, Madagascar, Malaysia, Mauritius, Mozambique, Oman, Singapore, South Africa, Sri Lanka, Tanzania, Thailand, United Arab Emirates and Yemen, with Egypt, Japan, China, the UK and France as dialogue partners and the Indian Ocean Tourism Organization as observer.

A new way forward?

By 2000, the Mauritian economy was showing signs of approaching distress: growth was slowing, unemployment was growing, there was a widening fiscal deficit, increasing internal and external public indebtedness, growing bureaucratic inefficiencies, relatively uncompetitive domestic private enterprises and an increasing welfare cost burden. All these factors pointed to the clear unsustainability of the strategic trajectory that was dependent on the four pillars of sugar, the garment industry, tourism and financial services.

Exacerbating the domestic situation was the fast evolving international context, with new rules and new players coming onto the scene: the end of quotas and preferences, a trading regime increasingly ruled by WTO and intense competition in traditional sectors from other low-cost economies (i.e. large ones like China and India, with their own massive domestic markets to sustain their industries, as well as smaller but competitive ones, like Bangladesh, Sri Lanka and Vietnam). External factors also included the failure of regionalism to provide Mauritius with growth options (although it may provide options for Mauritian firms to invest elsewhere regionally), increasing globalisation of the world economy, especially of world finance and world trade, and the growth of business process outsourcing (BPO) made possible by rapid changes in information and communication technology (ICT) as a new phenomenon in the global reorganisation and redistribution of economic activity.

Given the above, the questions that arose were:

- Has the response of Mauritius to globalisation been inadequate, as it tried to adhere to its strategy of relying on protected markets (sugar and garment production) to grow?
- How does Mauritius cope with the new situation? What options does it have? Does it really have an alternative to complete openness? and
- Is the future in services, rather than in manufacturing or agro-industry?

It was clear that some new directions had to be worked out if national living standards were to continue to be improved.

These were the questions that the Mauritian stakeholders debated at the 'Competitiveness Foresight' exercise organised by the National Productivity and Competitiveness Council in September 2004,[6] the main issues of which are summarised here.

The format consisted of round-table discussions bringing together a small group of key practitioners in their respective fields (industry, agriculture, the public sector, services, the trade unions, civil society and politics) to participate and contribute to disciplined, sharply focused brainstorming and deliberation with the assistance of an independent facilitator with a thorough knowledge of Mauritius (Mr P Mistry). It was felt that this was the best approach to ensure ownership of the ideas and improve the chances of successful implementation. There was only one question:

> **With Mauritius's future as a sugar producer looking bleak, powerful competitive pressures being placed on textiles and garments exports, the OECD placing limits on financial sector competition and finite limits on high-value tourism, what should the island's strategy for growth and development be for the next 10 years and beyond?**

The stark choice facing Mauritius was either to continue with the economic agenda that had been put in place under the structural adjustment programme, or to choose a new economic trajectory that would lead to an average growth rate of 7 to 8 per cent per annum.

To achieve continued increases in income and standards of living commensurate with Mauritius's achievements since 1982, and in order to assure the future political and social sustainability of the island's unique heritage of inter-racial harmony and its model of social justice, the consensus was that Mauritius needs to be a competitive, market-based economy that should aim for at least 7–8 per cent growth per annum. Without such a level of growth, Mauritius will find it increasingly difficult to deliver on its commitment to social justice and equity. Growth without equity is politically and socially unsustainable, if the benefits of growth are captured only by the business elite. Equally, Mauritius cannot have equity and social justice without a high level of growth, for the simple reason that the budgetary costs of delivering equity and social justice become unaffordable. The kind of welfare state that the broad majority of Mauritians want is sustainable only with a real growth of 7–8 per cent or more per annum. Table 2.5 sums up the number of years Mauritians need to wait under different growth scenarios.

If it continues to grow at an average of 4 to 5 per cent per year, the GDP per head would take 16 years to double. The country cannot adopt the approaches of previous decades. These, as described above, consisted broadly of the following. In the years 1968–80, autarchic development based on notions of self-sufficiency within a closed economy was the major orientation. This clearly did not work, because it led to virtual economic collapse and to the intervention of the IMF and World Bank to

Table 2.5: GDP per capita under different scenarios of economic growth

Average annual growth rate (%)	3	4	5	6	7	8
Year where 2003 GDP per capita doubles (given population growth of 1% per annum)	2039	2027	2021	2018	2015	2014

help Mauritius achieve fundamental structural change. Then in 1981–1996, the country was quite successful (more so than Africa and South Asia, but less so than East Asia) with an approach of partial openness practiced on an asymmetric, non-reciprocal, selective basis (i.e. open on the export side for goods and services, but closed on the import side for factors). However, during those years Mauritius remained 'effectively closed' to foreign investment (except on its own terms) and to foreign investors and entrepreneurs, as well as to most foreign transnational corporations. Now, the island's partially open, asymmetric regime is also running out of steam. So what is left? To go back to being closed, to stick to a partial openness paradigm or to go for more complete openness as a strategy to become and remain competitive in a globalising world?

The Competitiveness Foresight exercise decided that Mauritius must change its direction in order to grow. Its 'competitiveness' in textiles/garments and sugar has been bolstered by quotas that provided preferential access to key export markets. Sugar also benefited from a remunerative price, which came under serious pressure, and the sector's scope for further development was viewed as being quite limited. Nonetheless, the Competitiveness Foresight considered that the island had built up capacity and core competencies in sugar and garments that it might profit from if its firms invested in more competitive locations in the region or even further away. Such action may provide the country with dividend and remittance income from overseas investments.

It does not, however, solve the more fundamental problem that Mauritius, now a relatively high-cost producer, confronts in these sectors: that of sustaining a reasonable growth rate in an increasingly competitive environment and, for sugar in particular, limited scope for further expansion. It cannot hope to remain competitive by making marginal improvements in productivity alone.

Given this scenario, are there other areas of manufacturing or agribusiness (e.g. high-value horticulture) where Mauritius might be more competitive? Possibly. But has the island enough domestic firms with core competencies in these areas? To make risks manageable, it will need to open itself to global firms with the necessary technologies and market connections. Yet Mauritius itself provides too small a market for attracting inward investment in manufacturing or agribusiness. For inward investment to come to the country, it must be globally competitive in those areas of investment for at least the length of the life cycle of the large lumpy investments that need to be made in manufacturing and agribusiness to supply the global market.

With its limited human resource base (where sophistication and expectations tend to outstrip income generating capability), the main option for Mauritius (in a globalising economy that brooks no preferential treatment) seemed to the Competitiveness Foresight to be in services where investment capital needs are lower and 'factors' (people, capital, ideas, networks) are more mobile. Indeed, the island already relies on two pillars of services: offshore finance and tourism. It needs to expand those pillars and to develop new ones. However, if Mauritius's economic interests lie in newer areas that involve providing the wide range of outsourcing services that globalisation has created a need for, then which of these should it focus on? Where do its comparative and competitive advantages lie? What are the implications for human capital requirements that provision of such services necessitates? How should Mauritius address these?

It was agreed during the Competitiveness Foresight exercise that the main options for increasing and diversifying sources of export income lie in areas where ICT/BPO is making rapid inroads, as well as in transport services and in potentially new areas of outsourcing such as the provision of global health, education, global media and entertainment services. Mauritius also needs to develop much larger and more sophisticated domestic construction capability to respond to the needs of its own real estate development as the country transforms to accommodate globalisation and also to compete for construction contracts abroad (especially in Africa).

Activity diversification should be accompanied by market diversification. With its historical and cultural Franco-Anglo connections, Mauritius has been too reliant on preferential access to the EU through quotas, taking a market concentration risk that has now materialised. It needs to retain its presence in established EU and US markets through improved competitiveness and productivity. However, it also needs to make efforts to enter the markets of the present and future, i.e. India, China, East Asia, the Middle East and Central Asia. So strategically Mauritius needs to focus its attention on both activity and market diversification, looking to anticipate and accommodate the future rather than succumb to its vicissitudes.

At the same time, it was generally agreed that there is no single big idea (other than the idea of openness) or new sector that will save Mauritius. The world is changing and it is changing in entirely different ways. ICT/BPO is changing the work scene and creating job location shifts and opportunities that Mauritius can either capture or miss out on. The main constraint is neither resources nor financial capital. It is, rather, attitude, along with human, social and institutional capital. Relieving such constraints requires greater openness to human capital, trade and finance.

Another option that was much discussed during the Competitiveness Foresight exercise was that of transforming Mauritius into a 'city state'. The questions that were asked were:

- Is there a niche for another international city state/entrepôt in the Indian Ocean to play a role similar to that of Hong Kong, Singapore and Dubai? These city states are different in many respects, but similar in strategic outlook and the functional services they provide (freedom of movement of people, capital, knowledge and firms, along with low taxation and light-touch regulation of economic activity) to the international community.
- Can Mauritius play a similar role?
- What does it need to do?

- What are the obstacles and transitional problems it will face?

Table 2.6, below, reproduces some comparative indicators for Hong Kong, Singapore, Dubai and Mauritius to show that each state has been able to forge its own development path. However, the other three states have outperformed Mauritius. Why? Should Mauritius therefore aim to be an international city state?

An international city state is defined as 'a highly urbanised environment with exceptional infrastructure for transport and communications, an entrepôt for trade, finance, ideas, people and networks, acting as a regional node that connects its region to the world credibly. It is a corporate state with minimal barriers to entry of human, financial or physical capital. In a word, an international city state is characterised by openness'.

Mauritius has the potential to become a city state. There are, however, constraints linked to the political system and culture. The prevailing mindset is to control, to

Table 2.6 Some comparative indicators for city/island states

Characteristics	Dubai	Hong Kong	Singapore	Mauritius
Land area (sq. km)	3,900	950	620	2,000
Population (million)	1.01	6.82	4.21	1.22
GNI (2002/03, US$ billion)	32.41	168.03	88.10	4.68
GNI per capita (US$)	32,380	27,690	22,190	3,860
GNI growth rate (1990–2003)	10.5%	2.5%	3.2%	5.4%
Price deflator/inflation (1990–2003 av.)	1.1%	1.0%	0.7%	6.2%
Value-added in: agriculture	0.2%	0.0%	0.0%	8.1%
(as % of GDP) industry	39.2%	13.0%	36.0%	31.2%
(2002–03) services	60.8%	87.0%	64.0%	60.7%
Exports of goods & services as % of GDP	74	151	140	61
Imports of goods & services as % of GDP	72	142	138	57
Trade as % of GDP	146	293	278	128
Gross capital formation (% GDP)	45.3	23.1	24.7	22.1
Government revenues (% GDP)	3.5	5.2	26.4	20.3
Budget balance	+1.1	-1.1	+3.5	-5.1
FDI: inwards (US$ billion)	0.11	13.20	6.11	0.31
outwards (US$ billion)	3.23	4.51	4.14	n/a
External debt (US$ billion)	0.00	0.00	0.00	1.80
Phone connections (F+C) per 1000	1,146	1,507	1,258	559
Personal computers per 1000	153	422	622	117
Registered Internet users per 1000	401	435	504	100
Paved roads as % of total roads	99.2%	100.0%	100.0%	96.4%
Aircraft departures (in thousands p.a.)	42	91	72	14
Planned construction investment	35	5	4	n/a

protect, to be inward looking and to be closed to global human capital. Geography also does not favour Mauritius, as it is a 'micro-dot in the Indian Ocean'.

If Mauritius wants to become a successful international city state, it has to become more open by removing all barriers to trade, finance and people. The whole island must become an EPZ – indeed, there should not be barriers internally between firms or industries. Its foreign policy would then have to be geared towards connecting Mauritius much more closely to its geographic neighbours (i.e. South Africa, India and Australia) and to placing emphasis on new markets for its goods and services (i.e. China, East Asia, the Middle East and Central Asia) rather than remaining focused almost exclusively on maintaining its erstwhile colonial ties. Its health, educational and recreational facilities should be world class for two reasons: first, in order to attract human capital of a calibre capable of adding value to its own indigenous human capital base; and second to be competitive in taking advantage of the global BPO opportunities that are already emerging in these two key service sectors.

Engines of future growth

Changing economic trajectory is not an easy task. Consensus has to be developed at the national level on the new destination before all energies can be mobilised to advance in that direction. Re-engineering the national economy entails some pain before the gains can be enjoyed. What are the main obstacles that can prevent consensus building and the required paradigm shift?

The possible constraints on future growth identified by the participants were: (i) the political model of open democracy that is confrontational and divisive, rather than operating in a way that encourages unity and a rapid consensus for resolving and moving forward on key issues of national interest; (ii) the IT, transport and telecommunications infrastructure, which is inadequate for the demands of a broadband society capable of making its living in a global world; (iii) the budgetary deficit that limits room for manoeuvre and constitutes a constraint that will become even more binding unless growth momentum is revived with a change in strategy and direction; (iv) cultural inhibitions on the part of every segment of Mauritian society, which may obstruct greater openness; and finally (v) the absence of a vehicle for implementation.

Instead of the single new idea, there would be several engines of future growth. It was recognised that these engines would be able to produce output only if precise goals are set and a time frame for action agreed upon. There was a need for a roadmap, for a competitiveness strategy. The most important thing was to create a climate in which successful people, as well as flexible enterprises and competitive industries (that do not require a large commitment of up-front capital) from all over the world are attracted to Mauritius. This attraction should rest on 'natural' elements, i.e. the stability and suitability of macroeconomic policies and the overall business and socio-political climate Mauritius has to offer, rather than rely on 'artificial' measures such as selective incentives in the form of direct or indirect subsidies.

The only real option therefore is to create an 'open systems architecture'-type environment in Mauritius that permits talent, ideas, capital, capacity and people to flow in and flow out without barriers in accordance with trends, technological changes, innovation and developments in global activities and markets. Resort to the previous methodology of attempting to pre-decide and over- determine what is good or bad may no longer work.

The round-table discussions at the 'Competitiveness Foresight' exercise concluded that Mauritius should focus on creating a platform that is conducive to all ideas being put into action, permitting them to succeed or fail on market terms, as long as the risks were being taken by those who could afford them and knew how to manage them. In the brave new world of information technology enabled services (ITES), Mauritian companies simply do not know enough nor are they sufficiently connected to emerging global business process outsourcing (BPO) networks. This is not an area of core competence as yet, rather it is one that will need to be developed. The easiest way to do so is to import that competence by the expedient of openness and a comparative 'platform' advantage.

For Mauritius to 'piggyback' on capturing a small fraction of the rapidly burgeoning global BPO market, it will have to be totally open and welcoming to firms that want to use Mauritius as a platform, without imposing any barriers to their entry, operation or exit. Yet to create the platform, Mauritius has to reconfigure its own 'systems architecture'. In fact, this is what it should concentrate on, rather than trying to come up with a detailed grand plan that again attempts to define specific industries to be attracted and incentives to be provided. There is no place for a pre-deterministic approach in a future of rising uncertainty. One has only to ensure that all the necessary conditions are put together so that opportunities – including those that are unexpected – can be taken best advantage of whenever they arise.

To make that move forward, the mindset that sees government driving development has to be changed. Instead, the role of government should be seen to be facilitating and supporting business, which should be the main engine of development and investment. Among the things that the government in Mauritius will have to do are the following:

- It must reduce its high overhead costs.
- Parastatals have to become efficient and results oriented, or else they should be privatised and subsidies to them removed so as to enforce market discipline.
- There should no longer be space for discretionary application of unnecessary rules and regulations. Mauritius needs to refrain from seeing every event as a special situation, then creating specific regulations, schemes and licences to manage that situation.

- To create the best operating platform for all kinds of businesses (manufacturing and services), Mauritius has to create the best regulatory capacity in each field and market. An open platform for manufacturing should be phased in.
- Mauritius has also to create the capacity and mindset to cope with occasional market failures, because markets will not always work as anticipated in Mauritius. Markets work best when risks are taken and managed. In Mauritius, there is too high a degree of risk aversion on the part of both domestic business and government. Failures are seen as something that should be avoided at all costs, rather than being seen as part and parcel of the process of 'creative destruction' through which markets enforce discipline and encourage optimal outcomes in terms of rewards for competitiveness and efficiency.
- Mauritius has to eliminate the protective nexus/collusive cartel to protect traditional domestic businesses and let them compete with other local businesses and foreign firms on level terms in all areas. Mauritius has to open up its land market and legislate to capture part of benefits of land development to go into a social fund and to create social housing.

The point was also made during the 'Competitiveness Foresight' exercise that local private-sector institutions will also have to restructure to respond to the new global situation. Furthermore, the concept of 'private sector' should not be restricted to local firms, but should also include foreign enterprises.

Such a shift in orientation would cause some internal hardships and the population would have to bear some transition costs. The discussions ended with a series of questions: What will the transition to openness entail? How will it be financed? How will domestic dislocations be taken care of? How will political support be garnered? How will the Mauritian electorate be taken on board, so that there is as a near universal consensus that this change is necessary and positive (i.e. to be embraced rather than resisted)? What future will Mauritius face if this transition is not made – i.e. what are the costs of inaction? The fundamental question was: **Will there be a government willing to undertake such drastic reforms?**

Bold reforms

A new government was voted into power in Mauritius in June 2005. The Minister of Finance, Hon. R Sithanen, started his second budget speech in 2006 with these words:

> **'We have reached the end of an economic cycle. A cycle based on trade preferences that has allowed our country to make significant progress since independence. We have used these trade preferences and also overseas development assistance well. However, the world has changed and we have not adapted. The preferences are now being swept away, but we have not reacted. We have been naïve in believing that these preferences would endure and that we could continue to obtain concessionary finance to sustain our now outdated socio-economic model.'**

He went on to outline the bold reforms that would be undertaken:

> **'... We simply cannot continue on the same path. It is the surest way to economic disaster and social upheaval. And those who will suffer most are the very people we want to protect: the poor, the vulnerable and the unemployed. We must charter a new course. Government is responding with boldness and imagination to create jobs, promote employment and return to high growth. Implementation of this plan will require discipline from all of us for the next two to three years. It is time for the nation to embrace radical change and build a new, open and competitive service platform that is fully integrated into the global economy, like Hong Kong, Singapore and Dubai. Moving in this direction would benefit all Mauritians. [...]This budget ushers in forty major reforms that sweep away a non-functional system which is very complicated, hard to understand and open to abuse and even corruption through excessive discretion. We want to make things simple, transparent and rule based.'**

Mauritius has thus embarked on a new path towards structural transformation. Success will eventually depend on the extent to which the new vision is internalised by the population as a whole and on the ability of the various drivers of the economy (especially the regulators) to create the right environment to lure foreign direct investment. The project to draw up a roadmap for the export of services from Mauritius, undertaken at the request of the government, was aimed at defining the milestones and the steps as seen by potential investors.

The remaining chapters of this book examine in detail four service sectors that appear to hold some potential for Mauritius and which were explored in depth at a series of symposia held in Mauritius in January and April 2008.[7]

Notes

1. In the 1982 general election the previous government lost all seats in the national assembly to the MMM/PSM Coalition, which split in 1983. The 1982 government was elected on a socialist platform, but ended up signing the second structural adjustment programme with the World Bank. Before 1982, the option of an alternative development path based on self-reliance was still thought to be valid. Since the 1982 elections, all parties have adhered to an export-led development strategy. See Cheeroo and Treebhoohun (1986) 'Development Planning in Retrospect' *Journal of Mauritian Studies*, No. 1.
2. Meade, *The Economic and Social Structure of Mauritius.*
3. IMF (2004).
4. In 1991, the share of foreign investment in the EPZ represented 43 per cent; in 2001, it was only 0.8 per cent.
5. Percy Mistry (1997) Mauritius: Quo Vadis?
6. NPCC (2005) *Competitiveness Foresight: what orientations for Mauritius?*
7. http://www.investmauritius.com/symposium/ [accessed 13 November 2008]

3 Exporting Financial Services

Mauritian international financial services industry: origins and evolution to 1992

The international financial services (IFS) industry in Mauritius was based conceptually on the export processing zone (EPZ), which was established in 1970 with tax concessions and exemptions, an export orientation and prohibitions on domestic market access. The creation of the country's offshore financial centre (OFC) some 20 years later applied the same basic idea to exporting international financial services (IFS). Although it actually materialised in 1992, studies on an OFC had been carried out by the Bank of Mauritius (BoM) at the request of the Prime Minister's Office a decade earlier. However, the idea was put on hold during the mid-1980s, a result of the debt crisis engulfing the developing world from 1982–1992 and the salutary experience of the Seychelles during the 1980s, when it became an offshore centre for unsavoury financial dealings. Mauritius's OFC came up again for public discussion in 1988/89, when the findings of a study commissioned from an international consulting firm became available and, concomitantly, the domestic financial sector was overhauled under an economic reform programme.

The first offshore banking and management company licence was granted in 1989, to Barclays Bank operating under a specially tailored tax regime. However, that experiment performed below expectations, triggering a review that led to the establishment of the Mauritius Offshore Business Activities Authority (MOBAA). The economic motives and objectives for establishing the OFC under the MOBAA were the same as for the EPZ: (i) economic diversification, (ii) inward transfer of know-how, (iii) expansion of services exports beyond tourism, (iv) high-value employment creation and (v) smoothing the path for the eventual integration of Mauritius into the global economy and financial system. In setting up the offshore regime, particular attention was paid to protecting the domestic economy, with a clear line being drawn between domestic and offshore activities (though such demarcation later proved to be partly illusory).

OFC operations were favoured with a flexible operational and legal environment. They had tax advantages, which the authorities were determined to prevent from spilling into the domestic economy in order to preserve the integrity of public finances and prevent them from deteriorating. Offshore finance was defined as: an activity carried out within Mauritius, but transacted with non-residents in non-Mauritian currency. In addition, an offshore entity registered in Mauritius could not 'deal or transact' with a Mauritian resident. In stipulating these conditions, the authorities were concerned about the possibilities of leakage and other risks under a regime of exchange control. They created an elaborate regulatory edifice within the BoM to ensure that the line between domestic and offshore business was not crossed.

During the 1990s, offshore business 'management companies' were incorporated by the Registrar of Companies on the filing of the usual company registration documents. However, the MOBAA was their regulator and licensor, issuing certificates authorising offshore operations after scrutinising the qualifications of applicants. This two-step incorporation and authorisation process, which took some time, was a bureaucratic irritant that made Mauritius uncompetitive with other OFCs that were able to issue administrative approvals for entities to begin operating within 24 hours. The overlapping institutional and legal framework was nonetheless thought necessary to prevent abuses of the OFC by money launderers and arms dealers, to which the MOBAA statute made specific reference.

Since its inception in 1992, this bureaucratic approach to IFS industry licensing and regulation has been challenged by management companies. There has been ongoing tension between the regulator and industry to achieve a better balance between the need for sound supervision to ensure the integrity of the IFS industry and prevent the line between domestic and offshore operations from being crossed on the one hand, and the need for operational flexibility and user-friendliness on the other. That tension was heightened with the establishment of the Financial Services Commission (FSC) ten years later and the ensuing avalanche of additional regulatory demands, making the argument about more balanced and appropriate regulation as current and relevant as ever.

Creation of the OFC in Mauritius did not result in immediate demand for international financial services from around the world: Mauritian firms did not have any domestic experience or capability in offering IFS. The island opted to have its IFS industry develop indigenously and organically, rather than opening up to experienced exponents from abroad. However, in fairness, better-known foreign corporate/bank providers of IFS had already established themselves in European 'offshore' jurisdictions (viz. Switzerland, Luxembourg, Lichtenstein and Monaco) as well as in Bermuda and the Caribbean (Bahamas, Cayman Islands etc.) to service their EU/US clientele. In Asia, OFCs like Singapore and Hong Kong had emerged rapidly to service clients from Japan and the ASEAN. At the time, South Africa was still a closed economy under apartheid with sanctions imposed upon it. Established global providers of IFS were not interested in offering IFS out of Mauritius, therefore. There was no critical mass of clients from another part of the world that the Mauritians could tap.

Reciprocally, typical OECD clients for IFS would not come to Mauritius unless established firms were operating out of there. Extant offshore banks, even foreign bank branches, did not attract business except for intra-bank, cross-border transactions aimed at achieving tax efficiency. For a nascent OFC it was a catch-22 situation. In other jurisdictions, the local legal establishment had been at the forefront of offshore business development. Yet in Mauritius, legal practitioners kept aloof. They had neither the experience nor the interest in offering IFS; their client base was primarily domestic. It was mainly local and foreign accounting firms, networked internationally, with access to global contacts and clients, who nurtured the incipient IFS industry at the outset. They were ready when Mauritius's OFC was suddenly catalysed by economic reforms in India in the early 1990s. These reforms brought to life the provisions of the double taxation agreement (DTA) between India and Mauritius, which was signed in 1982 and ratified in 1985.

When the DTA (treaty) was ratified, the beneficiaries were mainly Indian companies doing business in Mauritius, for example, New India Assurance, Life Insurance Corporation of India, Bank of Baroda and Air India, as well as Indian expatriates working in Mauritius. However, the treaty remained dormant until 1992–93 because: multinational corporations were sceptical about its efficacy; the lack of necessary infrastructure in India inhibited foreign multinationals from entering that market; and foreign investment in the Indian capital market had not been sanctioned before then.

Owing to the perceived anti-foreign investment stance of the Indian government at the time, foreign direct investors were reluctant to venture into India using Mauritius as a gateway. However, in 1993, the DTA came alive when India allowed foreign institutional investors to invest in the Indian secondary market. Conterminously, Mauritius was promoting use of its OFC with the MOBAA Act of 1992 and the International Companies Act of 1994. The benefits arising from the DTA with India – mainly exemption from capital gains tax on gains derived from stock market transactions – were beneficial to both signatories. Investment flows routed through Mauritius became a significant driver of foreign portfolio capital flows into India, while the Mauritian OFC gained new business and employment opportunities.[1]

Mauritian IFS industry in the 1990s

From 1992–98, Mauritius was among the fastest growing OFCs in the developing world. It built up a reputation as a treaty jurisdiction for channelling investments from institutional and high-net-worth (HNWI) clients in the US, EU and South Africa into the rapidly growing economies of India, China and the ASEAN. Tailored incentive regimes were created for attracting specialised offshore activities, such as ship registration, aircraft leasing and other similar industry specific, cross-border financial arrangements. Yet Mauritius was unsuccessful in attracting a share of these global activities away from established centres like Liberia (for ship registration). The most important attraction of Mauritius became its tax treaties with third countries. Administering (rather than actively managing) global investment funds that benefited from tax reductions/exemptions under treaty arrangements became the mainstay of the Mauritian IFS industry. Local expertise emerged for investment fund administration by management companies as a result of a requirement that funds in Mauritius had to have a local administrator and a cash custodian.

Such funds focused mainly on investment in listed and exchange-traded securities of neighbouring emerging markets and developed markets. However, offshore financial services offered by Mauritian management companies also involved direct investment through special purpose vehicles and joint ventures by Indian and ASEAN clients in China, South Africa and Indonesia. Apart from these corporate services, Mauritius attracted a small share of the market for private wealth management undertaken by portfolio managers on behalf of high-net-worth individuals (HNWIs), with the proceeds parked in Mauritius and administered by management companies.

In other Commonwealth OFCs, tax-exempt trusts were the favoured vehicles for managing private wealth. However, in Mauritius the trust industry did not take off because it had no history of trust-law application. For that reason, there was an absence of lawyers trained in trust law and local accounting firms had no experience in that area.

At the same time, there was no world-class global fund or asset manager located in Mauritius, with real-time access to global market information and with direct trading ability on the world's principal securities markets. Yet many HNWIs (including a substantial number of non-resident Indians – NRIs) and offshore commercial businesses (OCBs, now known as global business licence [holders] or GBLs) were content to hold portfolio investments in Indian and ASEAN equities and bonds held by passive investment companies that benefited from advantageous tax treatment. This explains the rapid growth of licensed offshore companies – from 2000 in 1992 when the industry was set up, to 8,000 in 1998. Of these, the overwhelming majority were tax exempt and not reliant on treaty provisions. At the time of writing, there were over 27,000 such global business licensees, although not all of them are completely tax exempt.

Though tax treaties were the foundations supporting the IFS industry in Mauritius, local management companies had to compete with other OFCs as well as financial centres in home jurisdictions for business generated by such treaties. That competition led them to expand their knowledge base by recruiting from abroad, sending their staff for training/secondment to foreign firms and investing in ongoing programmes of 'on-the-job' training and professional development for their human resources.

Meanwhile, better, more tax-efficient use of tax treaties was made in designing outward Mauritian foreign direct investment in Africa and the Indian Ocean, for instance, in Madagascar and Mozambique. Financial engineering and structuring by Mauritian management companies and banks has also become more sophisticated as IFS knowledge has spilled over into the local capital market. Local investment fund products have become more effective and asset management techniques have improved considerably. The rules of the Stock Exchange of Mauritius (SEM) have been revised to encourage offshore fund listing, with the SEM working toward adopting global best practices (e.g. those of the Dublin Stock Exchange) in its listing rules and protocols.

Offshore vs. domestic financial market demarcation

The demarcation between onshore and offshore jurisdictions was severely tested from 1998 onwards, as Mauritian companies and professionals began to demand tax benefits granted to non-residents. The IFS industry has been pressing the government to migrate from a dual (offshore-onshore) tax regime toward a single low-tax regime, and to relax supervisory rules to enable the industry to conquer new markets, sharpen its global profile and increase its global market share. The argument for a single tax regime has the added attraction of averting the opprobrium and over-intrusive attention from OECD members (on exchange of tax information and harmful tax practices) that a dual-tax regime inevitably attracts. Dual regimes often seem to home countries (especially in high-tax environments such as those of OECD countries) to be designed to exploit inter-jurisdictional tax arbitrage opportunities created artificially at their expense.

More relaxed regulation would theoretically attract a greater number of company incorporations, while rules requiring more substantive value-addition and employment in Mauritius, with closer regulatory oversight, were traditionally thought to be indispensable in strengthening the capability of domestic firms. However, such rules are now being looked at with disapproval under the WTO regime for global trade in financial services, as being unacceptably protectionist in nature. Such rules are also seen by potential foreign investors in the financial services industry as an antediluvian deterrent restricting operational choice and flexibility.

Types of offshore entities/licensees

There are now two types of company incorporation in the Mauritian offshore sector:

- Offshore companies with regular company law features, qualifying for tax-treaty access but being subject to domestic tax. Mauritian residents investing abroad are allowed to set up or to hold a shareholding interest in such companies; and
- International companies exempt from taxation, which are more flexible than mainstream companies.

Trust settlements are open to foreign nationals when they have no Mauritian resident beneficiaries and no assets in Mauritius. Partnerships are rarely used. Special legislation for protected cell companies was adopted in 1999 to house 'fund-of-funds' structures, multi-class funds and the captive insurance business. Mauritius has not attracted much offshore insurance or reinsurance business except for some from South Africa. To accommodate the needs of a wide variety of global clientele, tax rules once provided for myriad tax structuring possibilities. Between 1993 and 1998, for example, a voluntary option was available that allowed offshore companies to choose a rate of tax along a scale from 0 per cent to 35 per cent. At the time of writing, all global business company (GBC) licensees are subject to a low 15 per cent rate of domestic tax which, by taking advantage of double tax avoidance agreements, can be reduced to 3 per cent on corporate income in many cases.

One of the hallmarks of the Mauritian IFS industry was total protection of confidentiality, safeguarded by legislation that prevented information relating to offshore clients from being disclosed (except by court order on specified grounds of suspected money laundering and arms dealing). However, that legislation did not bar domestic regulators from conducting investigations and exchanging information with their foreign counterparts. Nor did it prevent foreign authorities from obtaining rogatory commissions or other forms of permission for disclosure of information on local management companies and offshore or international companies.

The Mauritian IFS industry is now well established, but the country has yet to attract well-known foreign firms in the global investment or advisory business. Nor has it attracted well-known international law firms with global corporate and HNWI advisory practices. This is because of a legal framework constraint: the Mauritius Law Practitioners Act does not yet permit international firms to enter, although a study was carried out in 2006 that recommended amending the Act to make such entry possible. (Despite the current situation, one law firm has been operating from Mauritius for the last 12 years providing services to its Swiss-based clients).

As a result, IFS space has been left uncontested to local management companies with comparatively limited global experience and few international connections, especially in terms of dealing with OECD clientele. This may be because of invisible barriers – for example, excessive red tape in the granting of operating licences and not granting resident visas to managers and staff of foreign firms quickly and easily. The general complaint of foreign IFS firms seeking to locate in Mauritius is that the jurisdiction is far more protectionist in practice than it is in theory, and much more so than its legislation suggests. For that reason, despite its rapid growth in 1992–98, the Mauritius IFS industry continues to suffer from geographic concentration risk in its dependency on clients from the US/EU investing in India, Indonesia, Greater China and Africa, and excessive functional risk in being dependent on a limited range of products and services.

Post-1998 developments affecting the Mauritian IFS industry and its regulation

Growth of the IFS industry in Mauritius stalled when the OECD released its report on *Harmful Tax Competition* in April 1998. That report passed part of the burden of solving a problem created by OECD countries themselves on to offshore financial centres. Since then, OFCs like Mauritius have been under constant pressure from the Financial Action Task Force (FATF), the OECD, IFIs and the G7's Financial Stability Forum (FSF) to improve the transparency and accountability of their operations. The accompanying threat of blacklisting and applying sanctions to jurisdictions deemed non-compliant with OECD demands has strained international relations. Institutions and countries with asymmetric power have attempted to exercise extraterritoriality on questionable grounds over many small jurisdictions without countervailing power.

Fear of being blacklisted, with an ensuing loss of credibility and reputation, prompted OFCs around the world into taking disproportionate measures. OECD countries seem concerned about the proliferation of smaller OFCs offering services based on confidentiality; this was perhaps in part because of the competition offered to their own IFS industries in centres such as London. OFCs have been automatically, and in most cases quite wrongly, equated with the facilitation of money laundering and providing a safe haven for illicit tax-evading capital flows. When the 1998 report was released, Luxembourg and Switzerland, two OECD members, objected to the bank secrecy and confidentiality provisions it contained. After all, their financial services industries had been based on providing those two rights. However, these countries were not included in the 'tax haven' list, although non-OECD jurisdictions were faced with that stigma.

Harmful tax competition

The OECD report was published with the aim of countering tax practices deemed harmful to the interests of high-tax OECD economies. It took a prejudiced view of tax competition and set out criteria for identifying tax havens, which included inter alia, a nil or nominal tax regime, legalisation of entities with no substantial business activity, lack of transparency and no or little provision for exchange of tax information.

In May 2000, the Mauritian government made a set of commitments to eliminate tax practices deemed harmful by the OECD Fiscal Committee. It committed to a programme of tax information exchange, transparency, the elimination of provisions aimed at attracting offshore businesses with no substantial domestic activities, and to phasing out any practice deemed harmful by end-2005. In parallel, changes were made to remove the ring fencing of the offshore sector. From 1998 onwards, offshore companies (deemed 'incentive companies') were taxed at a flat rate of 15 per cent, although that rate could be brought down to a maximum of 3 per cent under domestic foreign tax credit regulations. The final list of 'tax havens' published by OECD on 26 June 2000 contained 35 jurisdictions. Mauritius was removed from the list for having committed to eliminating harmful tax practices. OECD has since monitored Mauritius's compliance with commitments and has conducted surveys to check adherence with its principles of international taxation. Mauritius was later given 'participating partner' status at the Global Tax Forum.

The Financial Stability Forum (FSF) report on OFCs

The Report of the FSF Working Group on Offshore Centres (2000) contained a list of OFCs categorised in accordance with perceptions about their quality of regulation/supervision, degree of co-operation with other jurisdictions and compliance with international standards. Category I included jurisdictions perceived as having supervision of a high quality. Category II included OFCs with procedures for good supervision in place, but weak in implementation, while category III jurisdictions were defined as having supervision of a low quality, with little or no attempt to meet international norms. The unjustifiable classification of Mauritius in the third category led to an official protest by the government. The FSF was criticised because it had not given Mauritius an opportunity to make any representations on the findings of its Working Group on OFCs. Nevertheless, desperate steps were taken to meet the highest international standards at considerable domestic financial and political cost. The Mauritius government made forceful attempts to remove the country from the third category, but without success; this was in spite of a favourable Financial Sector Assessment Programme (FSAP; see below) assessment on its banking and anti-money laundering regulation.

The FATF-NCCT list

To avoid being blacklisted by the FATF, Mauritius pushed through a series of measures, tightened disclosure requirements of offshore companies and reduced its protection of confidentiality. The February 2000 FATF report on Non-Cooperative Countries or Territories (NCCT) established procedures and criteria for identifying jurisdictions that failed to co-operate in implementing effective anti-money laundering (AML) regimes. To compel compliance, FATF compiled a list of non-co-operative countries or territories (the infamous NCCT list) that failed to meet its criteria for 'co-operation'. When Mauritius enacted its Economic Crime and Anti-Money Laundering Act of 2000 (ECAMLA), the FATF excluded Mauritius from the list. ECAMLA was the forerunner to the Financial Intelligence and Anti-Money Laundering Act (FIAMLA) of 2002, which consolidated existing legislation on AML measures, although certain concerns regarding the identity of directors and beneficial owners of offshore trusts were raised.

By 2002, reacting to pressure from international bodies, Mauritius compromised the legitimate long-term expectations of its IFS industry and offshore clientele by reversing earlier policies and curtailing tax privileges provided to offshore entities. It whittled down confidentiality protection, increased regulatory scrutiny and imposed substantially heightened, costly compliance requirements over the IFS and domestic financial services industries. Government policy was to: (i) avoid confrontation with IFIs, FATF and OECD on OFC issues; (ii) make externally mandated changes at almost any cost short of closing down the IFS industry; and (iii) implement international standards and core principles set out in the modules of the IMF/FSF Compendium, regardless of whether they were contextually appropriate to Mauritius. That policy begs the question as to whether government made the right trade-off in accommodating the extraordinary demands of OECD countries and international agencies, while risking the IFS industry's business competitiveness. The conclusions of another Commonwealth Secretariat study provide an answer to that question.[2]

Major regulatory developments occurred after the Report of the Steering Committee on Financial Services Sector Reform in Mauritius (February 2001). That report recommended: (i) regulatory and industry consolidation and integration of the financial services sector; (ii) establishment of the Financial Services Commission (FSC) as a unified regulator for all non-bank financial institutions (NBFIs) and for licensing global business entities, formerly known as offshore entities; and (iii) adopting a functional, rather than product-based, approach to regulation. The FSC was supposed to be the first step towards creating a single regulator for all financial services and was intended to bring about eventual integration of offshore and domestic financial services.

Prior to the establishment of the FSC, the regulation/supervision of financial services and institutions was carried out by several different institutions. In addition to its responsibility for the conduct of monetary policy, the BoM was responsible for the supervision of banks. Insurance companies and brokers were regulated and supervised by the Controller of Insurance in the Ministry of Finance. The Stock Exchange Commission (SEC) regulated the securities market, while the offshore sector was regulated by the Mauritius Offshore Business Activities Authority (MOBAA). This fragmented approach resulted in some key financial service providers escaping regulatory oversight. Effectively unregulated entities included, inter alia, leasing companies, commercial credit institutions, pension funds, asset management companies and investment advisory services. Moreover, the legislative foundations for financial regulation and supervision were not updated regularly. In many areas, current law inhibited supervisory authorities from taking timely action to prevent financial entities from becoming illiquid, insolvent or engaging in malpractices.

The industry impression was that supervisory authorities were vulnerable to inappropriate political pressure exerted to prevent them from taking necessary actions, so protecting privileged private interests. Because regulation was product based and sector based, the patchwork institutional framework supporting it was ill equipped to deal with the rapid changes sweeping through the financial services industry worldwide. Growing linkages between banking, insurance and securities activities, coming together under the umbrella of large, complex financial holding companies on the one hand, and the proliferation of hybrid financial products and derivates on the other, posed a serious challenge to a fragmented group of regulators, especially against the backdrop of ongoing globalisation and the development of e-commerce.

Under those evolving circumstances it was found that segregation between domestic and offshore business activities was no longer tenable. The division created too much opportunity for arbitrage and led to external misperceptions about how the system operated in Mauritius. The OECD, FATF and IFIs continued to challenge these artificial divisions established to exploit tax arbitrage. More importantly, such segregation was a handicap in the future development of the financial services industry in Mauritius. Accordingly, the island's OFC was abolished in favour of a single low-tax regime and the International Companies Act was repealed. That was not a condemnation of the offshore regime, which had been successful until 1998. Instead it suggested the need for a different response to changing circumstances triggered by OECD's 1998 broadside and subsequent developments.

It was thought that a unified single regulator for financial services, applying the highest international standards, would alleviate external perceptions about regulatory gaps and shortcomings in Mauritius. A two-phase process for regulatory unification was envisaged. The first was the establishment of the FSC as a single regulator for all NBFIs. It subsumed SEC, MOBAA and the Insurance Division of the Ministry of Finance under a single umbrella. The creation of the FSC was also intended to facilitate smooth integration of the onshore and offshore regimes. MOBAA's promotional functions were devolved to a new Financial Services Promotion Agency. The second phase involved the FSC merging with the regulatory part of the BoM to form a single regulator for all financial services. With the FSC's establishment in 2001, the first phase was completed. However, the second phase appears to have been dropped from official consciousness.

Since 2001, there has been a continual stream of legislative changes governing financial services in Mauritius including the Companies Act of 2001, the Financial Services Development (FSD) Act of 2001 and the Trusts Act of 2001. The Insurance Act of 1987 and the Stock Exchange Act of 1988 were maintained until 2005 and administered by the FSC. This arrangement was kept in place until the enactment of further special legislation (in 2005, see below) to consolidate the regulatory framework and harmonise the regulatory approach.[3]

The Companies Act of 2001 eliminated ring fencing between the offshore and domestic sector by providing for incorporating domestic and offshore companies under a single piece of legislation, with the incorporation process being streamlined. It also repealed the International Companies Act of 1995, while the FSD Act repealed the Mauritius Offshore Business Activities Act of 1992, which had provided the legal regime for offshore companies. It introduced the term 'global business' and expunged the word 'offshore' from the statute books. The Trusts Act of 2001 repealed the Trust Act of 1989 and the Offshore Trust Act of 1992. It added to the *Code Civil Mauricien* in order to integrate the fiduciary concept into domestic law. Broadly speaking, the Trusts Act of 2001 extended features previously available to offshore trusts to all trusts created under the Act, with certain limitations on trusts set up by a Mauritian resident.

The distinction between domestic and offshore banks was removed under the Banking Act of 2004 and replaced by a two-tier licensing regime. Class A licences permitted banks only to conduct domestic banking and open branches in Mauritius. Class B licences permitted transacting with non-residents and dealing in foreign currencies.[4] This was the first step towards further integration to be achieved through a single licence for providing banking services to domestic clientele and to non-residents and global businesses. However, an accounting distinction was still maintained between these two activities for determining the tax to be levied on the net income generated by each.

The supervisory regime for global business has changed from 'registration' to 'licensing', with the name change supposedly heralding closer monitoring of permitted activities in that area. There are now two types of global business company (GBC) licences, viz. GBC-1 and GBC-2. Both draw on the Companies Act of 2001. A GBC-1 licensee can undertake prescribed activities in Mauritius, but is also permitted to transact business with non-residents in foreign currencies and is subject to Mauritian corporation tax. As a resident, it can avail of double tax treaty provisions entered into by Mauritius with other countries. GBC-1 licensees are subject to annual reporting requirements under the FSD Act. A GBC-2 licence is issued to a private company that conducts approved global business only with non-residents and only in foreign currencies. As a GBC-2 licensee is non-resident and tax exempt, it cannot avail of the benefits of the double tax treaties and is not subject to annual financial reporting obligations.

The enactment of the FSD Act was the first stepping stone towards meeting international standards. It aimed at improved supervision of the sector as a whole and at providing a building block for eventually embracing other specialised pieces of legislation covering various financial services. In 2005, the new Insurance Act and the new Securities Act were passed to modernise the approach to regulation in both sectors respectively by adopting international standards. Both statutes provide for domestic and global business in their respective sectors under the same unified legislation. The FSD Act was later amended to provide for more comprehensive enforcement powers of the FSC, establish a right of appeal against its decisions and the imposition of penalties and to require greater transparency on the part of the regulator in explaining its decisions.

Financial Sector Assessment Programme

In 2002–2003, a joint IMF/World Bank mission under the Financial Sector Assessment Programme (FSAP) on the observance of standards and codes for the FATF 40 recommendations on money laundering and eight (now nine) special recommendations on terrorist financing, reported that Mauritius had made progress in implementing a comprehensive AML/countering the financing of terrorism (CFT) regime. The mission applauded the government's efforts to enhance the AML/CFT legal and enforcement framework by introducing new legislation, including: the Dangerous Drugs Act of 2000, the FSD Act of 2001, the Prevention of Corruption Act of 2002, the Prevention of Terrorism Act of 2002 and the Financial Intelligence and Anti-Money Laundering Act of 2002. It found that enactment of these laws represented key advances in bringing Mauritius toward full compliance with international standards, but identified areas where further effort needed to be made. These included:

- modifying confidentiality provisions that hampered information sharing on suspected money laundering cases between supervisory authorities and the Financial Intelligence Unit (FIU);

- expanding the scope and focus of AML/CFT reviews during onsite inspection of financial institutions in line with the guidelines issued by the supervisory authorities; and
- improved co-ordination of law enforcement efforts.

The mission also recommended that financial institutions should: strengthen internal AML and CFT programmes by developing adequate internal policy/procedure frameworks to reflect guidelines issued by regulators, increase compliance testing and ensure that front-line and compliance staff received adequate training. These recommendations were implemented immediately, with supervisory bodies over-emphasising AML/CFT in monitoring their licensed population.

Where does the Mauritian IFS industry go from here? The challenge of diversification, expansion and growth

As the previous sections establish, Mauritius has exported international financial services (IFS) since the early 1990s. The value of such exports has grown nearly fifteen-fold: from barely MRs60 million in 1994 to over MRs875 million in 2006. This growth has not been linear. IFS exports were set back in 2001–2004 when issues arose with the OECD on harmful tax practices. OECD countries and international financial institutions unilaterally blacklisted what were deemed to be 'tax havens'. Externally imposed requirements on IFS transparency – monitored by the IMF and World Bank on behalf of the Financial Action Task Force (FATF) and Financial Stability Forum (FSF) – were accepted without much protest by the Mauritian authorities.

Consequently, new restrictions came into force involving 'know-your-client' and due diligence requirements for IFS transactions. Anti-money laundering (AML) and countering the financing of terrorism (CFT) requirements were the stated raison d'être. Yet the real underlying concerns seemed to be tax leakage and the competition provided by Mauritius to financial centres in OECD countries. These developments had a deleterious impact on Mauritius's IFS exports for three years until 2004. The legitimacy of the post-2001 regulatory restrictions, and the manner in which they were imposed on the local financial services industry, have been evaluated in another study undertaken under the Commonwealth Secretariat aegis.[5]

At the same time, while Mauritius's IFS exports have grown over the years, they have not diversified vertically into different IFS domains (although there has been some geographic diversification). The bulk of IFS exports are still attributable (directly or indirectly) to low value-added, passive administration of foreign accounts established to benefit from double taxation treaties and agreements (DTT/DTAs) with a number of countries. Most such accounts are related to tax benefits conferred by the DTT with India.

Under its terms, Mauritius has become a favoured way station for flows of foreign portfolio investment (FPI) from institutional and high-net-worth individuals (HNWIs) in the US, EU, Australia and the UK into India. These flows, and the investments to which they relate, are booked, administered and audited in Mauritius. They involve mainly account-management services. However, they generate a significant volume of connected offshore banking transactions as well.

Although there was little concern about that DTT in the late 1980s and 1990s, FPI flows into India exploded in the early years of the new millennium and especially after 2004. Confronting such large, almost unmanageable, inflows of FPI in 2005–07, the Indian authorities felt that the tax benefits/concessions provided to foreign investors through Mauritius were too generous. They exacerbated growth in FPI of a volume that threatened to destabilise monetary policy and India's macro-economy. The government of India felt that the treaty favoured, if not encouraged, round-tripping of resident and non-resident Indian investment – veiled as investment from other countries – into India via Mauritius. Although evidence in support of that was tenuous, circumstantial and speculative, the issue remains contentious, as are other provisions of the DTT.

India is now trying to standardise its DTTs with all other countries and has renegotiated its treaty with Singapore. However, the clauses renegotiated in that DTT cannot come into effect until the treaty with Mauritius is brought into alignment. The Indian tax authorities believe that they need to prevent domestic tax revenues (from FPI transactions) from haemorrhaging as a result of offshore tax treatment conceived 20 years ago. This backdrop, and the serious intent with which the Indian authorities are pursuing renegotiations, make Mauritius's current IFS exports seem dangerously concentrated and overly dependent upon its DTT with India. To avoid the adverse consequences of over-concentration, Mauritius urgently needs to expand and diversity its range of IFS offered to global clientele.

International financial services diversification/expansion was the subject of a symposium organised by the Commonwealth Secretariat in partnership with the Mauritian Board of Investment (BoI) from 22 to 26 January 2008. That symposium provided an overview of rapidly evolving global markets for IFS exports, clarified the role that Mauritius might play and dealt with IFS domains in which globally competitive capabilities could be developed.

Individual symposium sessions focused on: (i) private banking and wealth management (PBWM); (ii) asset management; (iii) insurance and re-insurance; (iv) transfer pricing and tax management (TPTM) for transnational corporations; (v) risk management services accompanied by local exchange traded risk management derivatives contracts; and (vi) complex financial engineering services for regional and global corporations in areas such as mergers and acquisitions (with an Africa focus) and public-private partnerships for infrastructure financing (mainly in Africa). The conclusions reached at the symposium and the observations and recommendations flowing from them are elaborated upon in the remainder of this chapter.

Table 3.1: Crude illustrative dimensions of international financial services (US$ trillions)

Year	2005	2010	2015	2020
World output	44	63	88	122
Global IFS revenue	1.1	1.9	3.6	6.9
World equity market capital	39	61	85	115
Global bonds outstanding	40	65	93	120
Global assets under management	45	64	98	125
Private wealth under management	33.3	44.6	>70	>95
Global recorded mergers and acquisitions	0.812	0.915	1.3	>2

Source: Capgemini, Boston Merrill Lynch, Consulting, Financial Times, Wall Street Journal, Business Standard India

Private banking, wealth management and asset management

The sense emerging from the Commonwealth Secretariat–Mauritian Board of Investment symposium of January 2008 was that Mauritius needed to make a strategic shift from **passive, low value-added** account management to **proactive, substantive high value-added** international financial services on an accelerated basis. To do so, the government and the financial services industry needed to work jointly on a programme aimed at developing policies, alleviating systemic constraints of

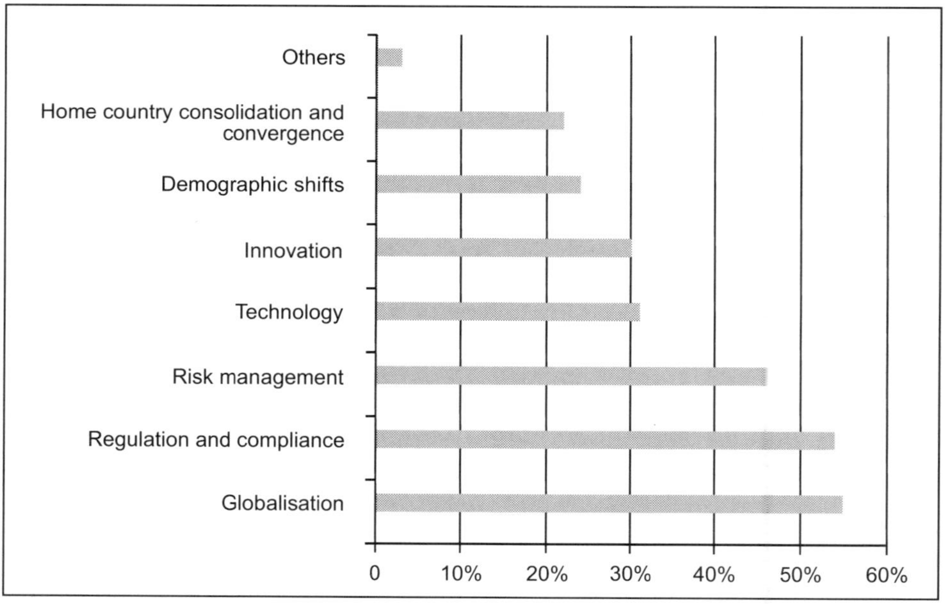

Figure 3.1 Catalysts estimated to have the highest impact on transformation of financial firms

manpower and infrastructure, and developing business plans, to exploit rapidly growing global opportunities for services exports in these domains.

In particular, Mauritius needed to develop **private banking, wealth management and asset management** capabilities as a matter of urgency. Its management companies are already serving an established base of HNWI clients in India and Asia. Mauritius is well located to provide private banking, wealth management (PBWM) services to emerging entrepreneurs from India, the rest of South Asia, South-East Asia (ASEAN) and China (whose HNWIs are also being served by Hong Kong and Singapore). HNWIs from the Arabian Gulf were more likely to be served by global banks operating from Abu Dhabi, Dubai, Bahrain, Kuwait, Muscat and Doha. However, unlike other centres, Mauritius could specialise in creating African investment portfolios for these clients, especially as Africa now provides the last emerging market frontier that has not yet matured.

The large and rapidly growing pool of HNWIs in Asia[6] would be easier for Mauritius to tap than HNWIs in OECD countries, which represent 'old wealth' serviced in other established IFCs. PBWM as a business relies on trust, strict observance of privacy, discretion, a firm's reputation for global investment knowledge, proficiency and probity. Firms with established global brands to whom clients feel they have recourse tend to dominate, while small domestic firms and banks unknown to HNWI clients offshore are unlikely to make significant inroads into developing such business without international partnerships.

The bulk of global PBWM business is concentrated in the 20 largest global financial firms.[7] Such firms/banks have to be attracted to Mauritius and offered assurance that it is a safe, attractive (in terms of tax, security, privacy and country/political risk) centre in which to locate (and from which to have actively managed) a part or the bulk of their wealth.

PBWM activity is consonant with Mauritius's efforts to market high-value properties developed under its specially legislated Integrated Resort Scheme (IRS) to a global

Table 3.2: Dimensions of private wealth management: number of HNWIs (net worth > US$1m) and their wealth

	1996	2000	2005	2010
Number of HNWIs global (millions)	4.5	7.2	8.7	10.5
Value of their wealth (US$ tr.)	16.6	27.0	33.3	44.6
Number of Asian HNWIs (millions)	0.9	1.5	2.4	5.0
Value of Asian HNWI wealth (US$ tr.)	2.8	4.2	7.6	14.2
Value of Indian HNWI wealth (US$ tr.)	<0.1	>0.1	0.3	1.1
Annual growth in global HNWIs			6.0%	5.7%
Annual growth in Asian HNWIs			6.4%	6.7%
Annual growth in Indian HNWIs			19.3%	12.5%

Source: Capgemini/Merrill Lynch World Wealth Reports for 2005–06.

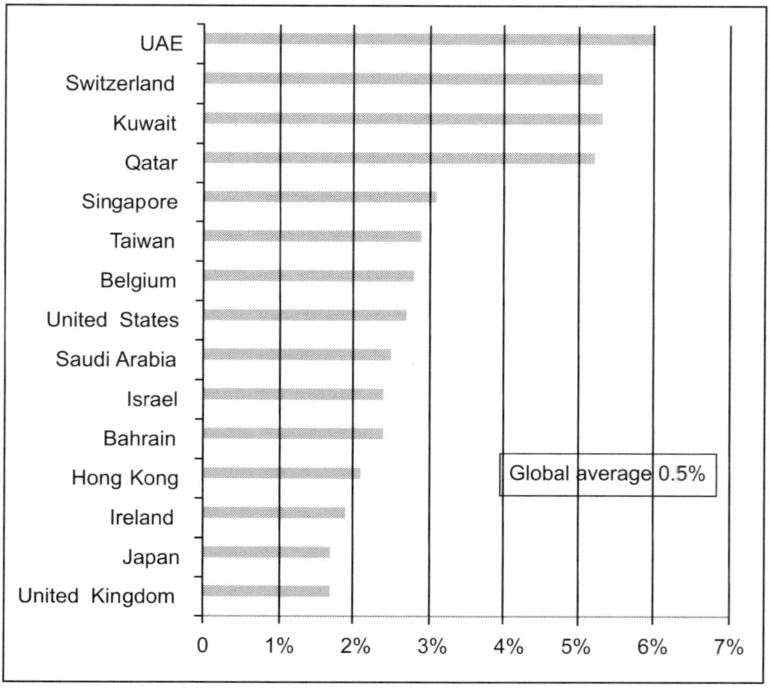

Figure 3.2 Millionaire households as percentage of total households

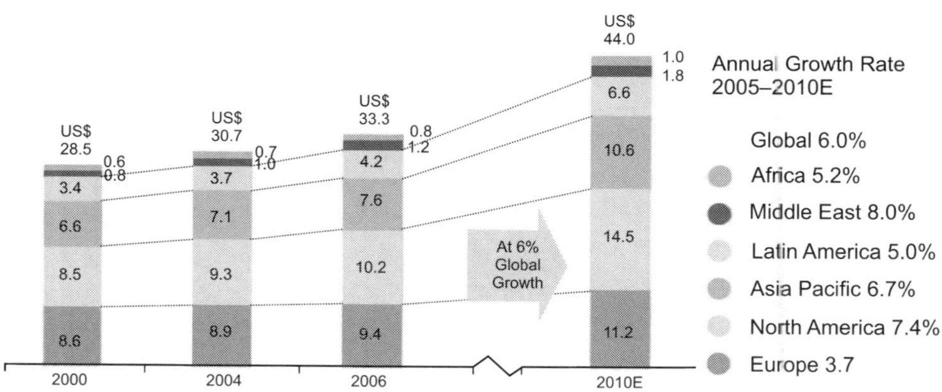

Figure 3.3 High Net Worth Individual wealth forecast by region, 2003–2010 (US$ trillions)
Source: Capgemini Lorenz curve analysis, 2006.

HNWI clientele. Such clients are likely to be more comfortable having investment portfolios managed where they are residing on a part- or full-time basis. That synergy needs to be exploited through joint marketing efforts by IRS developers with the local financial services industry to attract HNWIs into IRS investment **and simultaneously** into FBWM services.

Thus, a natural entrée would be for financial firms to work with IRS developers in offering financing and insurance packages (in foreign currencies with instruments allowing value fluctuations to be hedged) for the acquisition, maintenance and (possibly rental) of IRS properties and their contents. Marketing efforts for IRS properties, in conjunction with efforts to attract PBWM business, need to be refocused from targeting potential IRS buyers from the 'old' European Union, to targeting HNWIs from the 'new' EU, as well as the Gulf emirates, India, China and the ASEAN.

Partnerships with established IFCs specialising in PBWM

Some established IFCs that had specialised in providing PBWM services to a global clientele for decades (e.g. the Channel Islands, the Isle of Man and Ireland) are now running out of human resources, space and infrastructure. Their costs have escalated and they are becoming uncompetitive. As a result, opportunities are emerging for firms/banks located in Mauritius to 'partner' with PBWM firms in these jurisdictions. Appropriate partnership arrangements need to be devised that aim at relieving the constraints of the latter, while attracting a growing volume of PBWM business into Mauritius, along with the knowledge/expertise that exists in these IFCs.

PBWM services are usually provided successfully in financial centres that also have asset-management capabilities. Mauritius would be unable to offer PBWM credibly

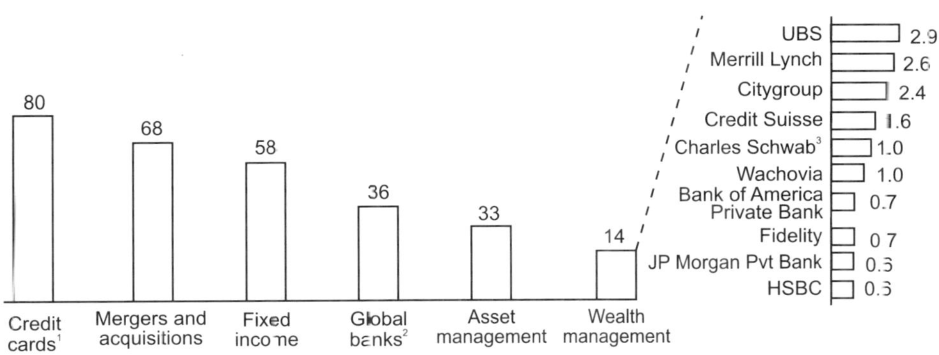

Figure 3.4 Global market share of top ten players, end 2004 (percentage)

[1] US market only

[2] top fifteen, based on market capitalisation

[3] includes US Trust

Source: Percy Mistry, Presentation at Symposium on the Export of Financial Services

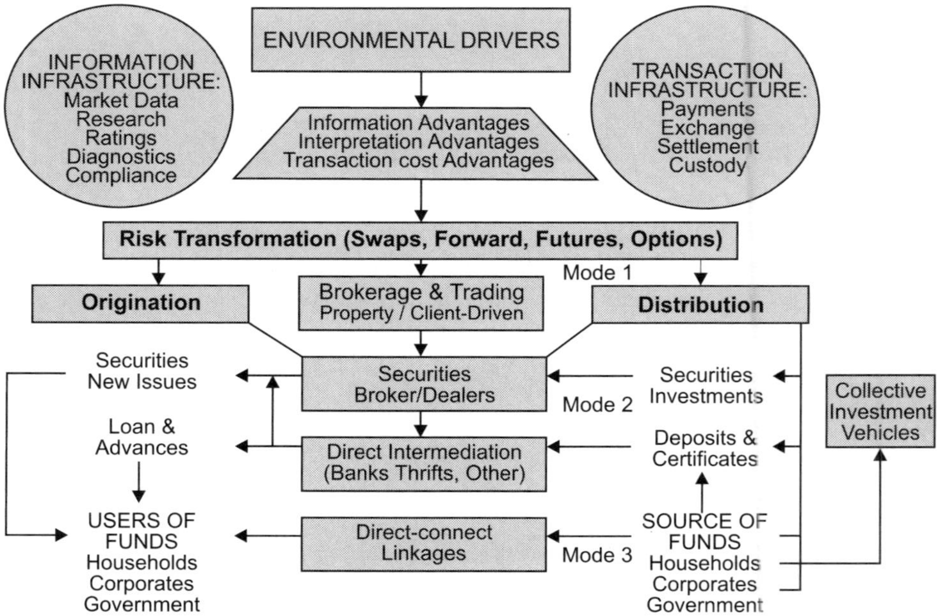

Figure 3.5 What drives asset management?

Source: Asset Management and Investor Protection: An International Analysis by Julian Franks, Colin Mayer and Luis Correia da Silva, New York: Oxford University Press, 2003. Presentation by Percy Mistry at Symposium on the Export of Financial Services.

without developing a local asset-management industry at the same time. Such an industry has to be capable of managing **global** assets in equities, fixed-income, derivatives, as well as in art, real estate, gold, commodities and so on. It is imperative for Mauritius to attract asset-management companies capable of handling global and African portfolios of HNWI clients. It is also necessary for the Government of Mauritius to consider repatriating the asset management of Mauritian public and private pension funds, so as to provide a boost to the local asset-management industry.

With full capital account convertibility, Mauritius offers an advantage to asset managers constrained in providing similar services from India. The Reserve Bank of India (RBI) recently liberalised capital outflow for investment abroad by **resident** Indians through established Indian and global asset management vehicles.[8] This relaxation provided an opportunity for Mauritius to attract global fund management business by having Indian asset managers operating from the island. Simply put, such firms need to be persuaded to use the same operating and account management platform created for directing foreign portfolio investment (FPI) flows into India via Mauritius, by facilitating a symmetric reversal of flows of outward FPI from India to the rest of the world.

A similar opportunity has emerged since April 2008, when the UK levied a tax on non-domiciles (unprecedented in two centuries) who have resided in Britain for more than seven years. There is expected to be an exodus from the UK of 'non-doms' betrayed by this retroactive punitive tax action. Mauritius could benefit by targeting PWBM and asset-management services to non-domiciles seeking to exit the UK, by emulating financial services providers (as well as lawyers and accountants with HNWI clientele) from the Channel Islands, as well as jurisdictions like Switzerland and the Netherlands.

For the foregoing reasons, PBWM and asset-management activities need a policy-cum-implementation push **jointly** from **government**, which needs to take policy measures to facilitate the rapid emergence of specialised firms, private banks and asset managers; and **private** foreign and domestic firms in the IFS industry to upgrade and transform presently limited capabilities. It requires a concerted industry effort to realise the potential that exists.

A promising start could be made if the fragmented sub-industry associations in the financial sector (i.e. for insurance, banking and management companies, not to mention brokerages) were to merge voluntarily into a single financial services industry association under unified leadership, while keeping their sub-industry focus intact under a single umbrella.

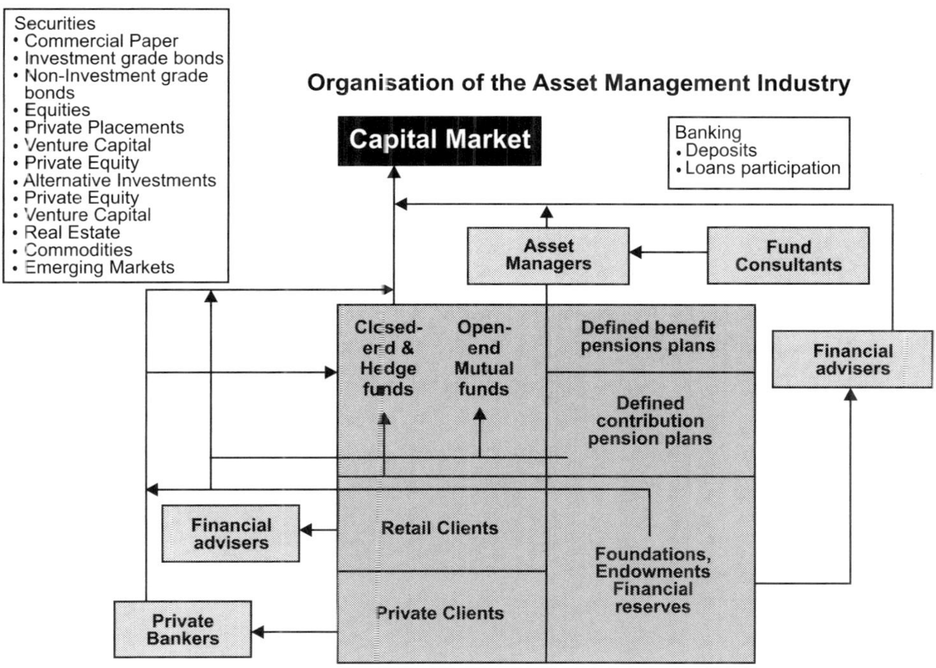

Figure 3.6 The asset management industry

Source: New York: Oxford University Press, 2003. Presentation by Percy Mistry at Symposium on the Export of Financial Services.

Insurance and re-insurance[9]

For insurance and re-insurance to become important areas for international financial services in Mauritius, established local companies would need to operate in the African and Indian Ocean regions more aggressively. Concomitantly, they would need to de-concentrate their over-exposure to domestic risk and domestic investments.

It is unlikely that global insurance companies would use Mauritius as a regional insurance centre for Africa or for asset-liability management. They are more likely to gravitate to South Africa for that purpose. Nonetheless, there is scope for Mauritius to emulate the success of Bermuda and some Caribbean islands as a regional or global **re-insurance** centre. That would, however, imply providing specifically tailored tax advantages for this industry, which might cause problems with other African countries and possibly even with some OECD jurisdictions.

As two-way trade between India-Africa and China-Africa grows, it is bound to create more insurance opportunities (for goods and the vessels they are being carried in) to be captured by insurance companies based in Mauritius (whether locally, regionally or globally owned) for tax as well as operational reasons. New products (such as catastrophic risk, cyclone risk and weather insurance) also offer opportunities for IFS growth by insurance companies based in Mauritius, working in tandem with international counterparts to undertake the associated actuarial risk analysis and to offer insurance products tailored to African markets and for exploiting insurance opportunities created by rapidly growing Afro-Asian economic interaction.

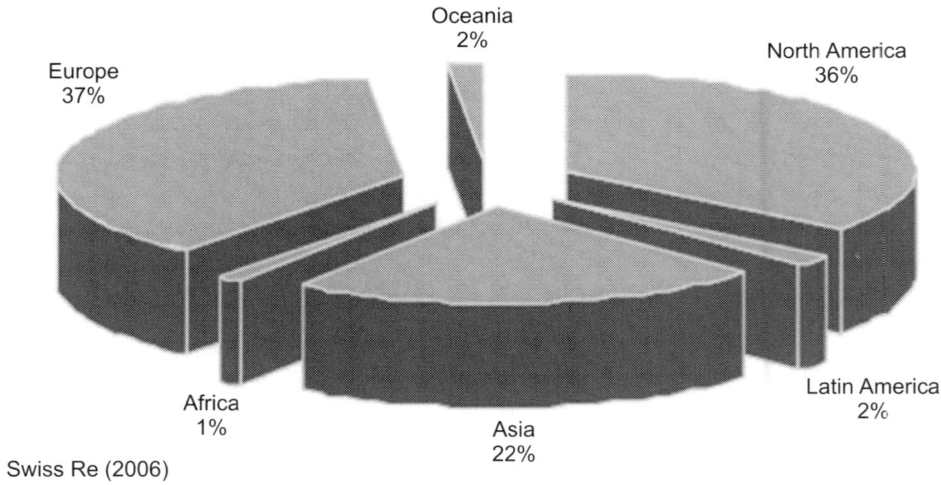

Figure 3.7 Distribution of insurance premiums

Source: Presentation by Mr Anthony Pedersen at the Symposium on the Export of Financial Services

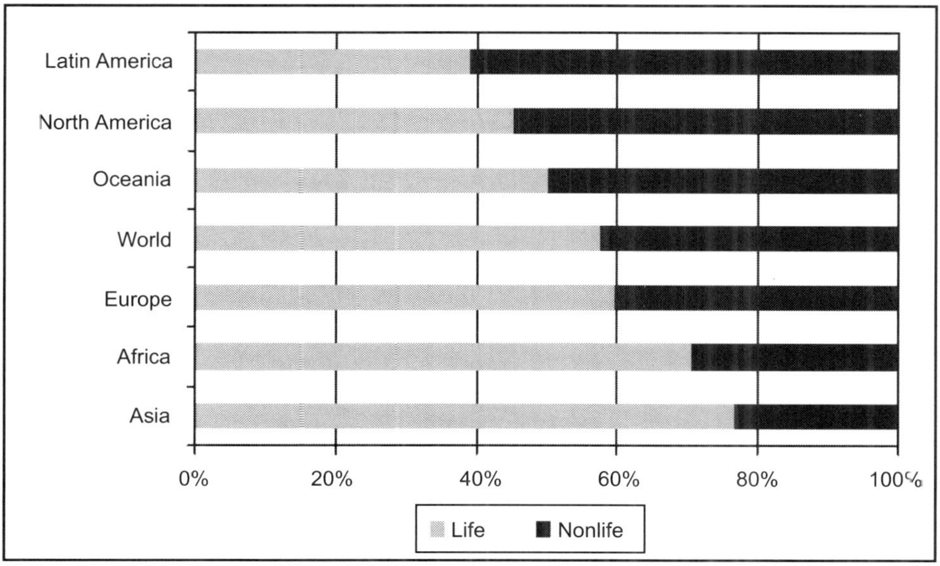

Swiss Re (2006)

Figure 3.8 Share of insurance premiums
Source: Presentation by Mr Anthony Pedersen at the Symposium on the Export of Financial Services

Transfer pricing and global tax management

Discussions at the Commonwealth Secretariat–Mauritian Board of Investment symposium of January 2008 also established that there was unexploited potential in Mauritius for offering a range of transfer pricing and tax management (TPTM) services to a larger universe of transnational corporations (TNCs) than is presently imagined by local management companies, given the flexibility and amenability of global business licence (issued by the Financial Services Commission of Mauritius) tax treatment. What seemed to be lacking was sufficient domestic knowledge and experience in TPTM for the global market.

To develop such expertise quickly, Mauritius needs to make itself more attractive for the world's major tax and accounting firms to relocate TPTM business from other centres. While Mauritius has over 33 double taxation treaties/agreements negotiated on a bilateral basis, it remains too dependent on routing FPI investments to India. For TPTM business to grow, tax-related IFS must be provided over a wider canvas. Local management companies, as well as tax accountants and tax lawyers, need to develop skills in offering TPTM services as a specific area of IFS business opportunity.

By the same token, a larger number of TNCs (in manufacturing, financial services, transport services and other areas) need to operate out of Mauritius to avail of TPTM benefits and services, so lowering their global tax liabilities. The objective of attracting such TNCs into Mauritius, in turn, would be easier to achieve if Mauritius could be developed into a more attractive location for the regional headquarters of TNCs involved in growing Asia-Africa trade, or even as the administrative or treasury headquarters of emerging TNCs from Asian-source countries, particularly India and China, which have the largest future need for African resources, commodities and markets.

To prevent tax leakage from their own jurisdictions, large countries are refining and tightening their approaches and laws to deal with TPTM. They require more 'substance' to be demonstrated in offshore locations of TNCs where TPTM services are being availed of. These requirements do not pose insuperable obstacles to the potential growth of TPTM-international financial services from Mauritius. With the growing importance of TNCs from Asia in world trade, and particularly trade/investment interaction between India/China and Africa, Mauritius is well positioned to develop this business successfully. To do so, it needs to ensure that the tax treatment of global business licence (holders – GBLs) remains favourable and competitive by global standards, taking into account changes occurring elsewhere.

Given the highly specific, tailor-made nature of TPTM services offered to individual client firms (as well as to HNWIs) it is difficult to advocate generic solutions and prescriptions. Different management companies need to devise specific strategies (including strategies for acquiring the necessary skill sets) for developing such business, beginning with their extant client base in particular geographies. However, the Government of Mauritius and the Financial Services Commission need to be made aware on a real-time basis of TPTM issues and opportunities, to ensure that continual changes in tax and regulatory policy/practice do not compromise the steady development of this line of business.

Risk management and capital market activity

In contemplating the provision of risk-management services[10] from Mauritius, it is important to distinguish between: (i) specialised **financial** risk management – i.e. a narrow concept employing financial, traded derivatives to manage specific types of country, political, credit, currency, interest rate and equity price risk; and (ii) a wider notion of risk management, which embraces virtually every corporate asset and activity. The Mauritian IFS industry should focus on the narrow concept for IFS. However, such services are unlikely to develop apace if the Stock Exchange of Mauritius (SEM) and local firms are confined and geared exclusively to meeting the needs of a small and inherently unviable (from a volume and transaction-cost viewpoint) domestic capital market.

In view of the state of development of Mauritius's capital and derivatives markets, local participants believe that risk management employing derivatives is likely to be a distant development in the context of the island. Yet foreign interlocutors think

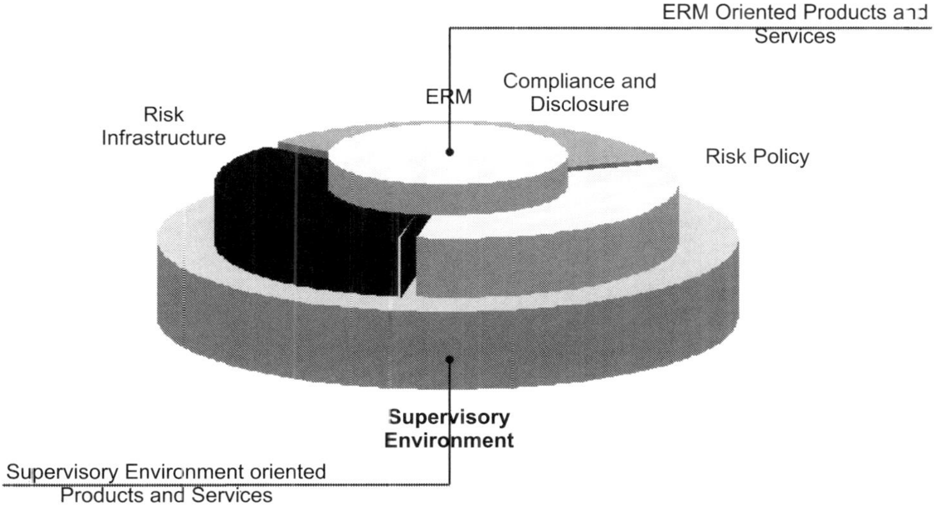

Figure 3.9 Risk management industry
Source: Presentation by Dr Manoj Vaish at the Symposium on the Export of Financial Services

the opposite. They believe that, despite the existing limitations of the SEM, Mauritius already offers a valuable incubation site for innovating specific risk management (derivative) contracts relating to Indian currency and securities markets (in which Mauritius plays an important pass-through role). Over time, such products and services could be extended to African markets as well.

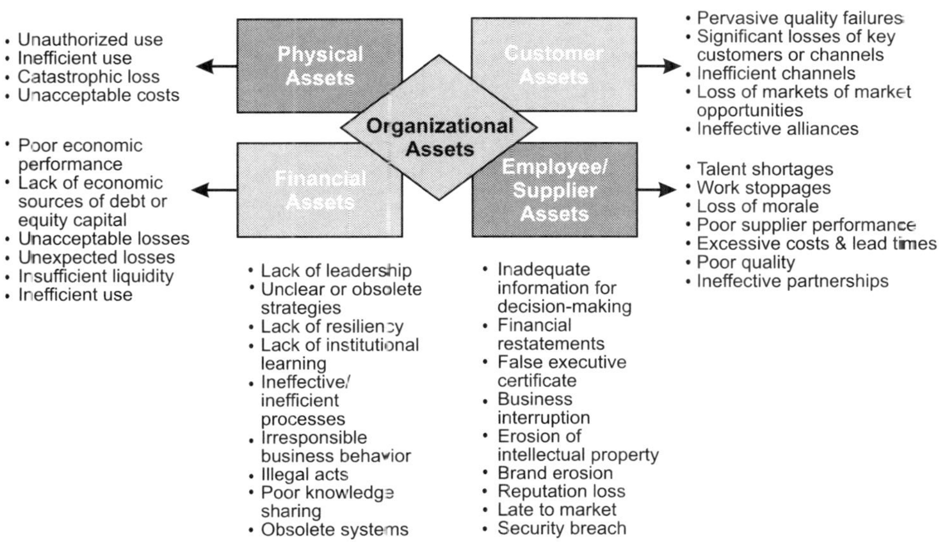

Figure 3.10 Risks associated with the sources of value

Resident and foreign investors in Indian securities presently confront restricted possibilities for portfolio risk management. Remaining restrictions on Indian rupee convertibility and the absence of standard derivative instruments traded in India hinder them in managing currency, interest rate, duration and country risk, as well as hedging against market movements in either direction. The development of such possibilities in India is likely to be much slower than growth in demand. The same is true of China.

Yet there are no similar restrictions on innovating and trading such instruments in Mauritius in real time. There is a large latent market for such services, which is being imperfectly catered to in Singapore and Dubai. However, to successfully develop and trade appropriately structured derivative contracts in Mauritius for Indian currency and securities markets, and to make them available to a global investor base, the SEM needs to be linked (through ownership) to Indian exchanges (particularly the National Stock Exchange of India – the NSE). Moreover, constructive and co-operative regulatory arrangements with Indian regulatory authorities need to be devised to ensure that the services offered in Mauritius do not circumvent key (and justifiable) Indian restrictions. Investment banks in India need to offer such services to their extensive client base from Mauritius, thus requiring them to establish a presence on the island for providing India-related risk-management services, as well as other investment banking and corporate finance services.

It should be a priority for Mauritius to attract such business as quickly as possible. The window that is now open will probably close within the next four to five years (i.e. by 2012 or 2013), when full Indian rupee convertibility becomes inevitable, and as non-equity derivative markets in India develop more rapidly with the extant regulatory chokehold over them being gradually relaxed. Mauritius needs to establish a first-mover advantage in key risk-management contracts before then. Such an advantage would enable it to retain a large share of the business so created, as the example of Singapore with Nikkei Index (spot and derivatives) trading amply demonstrates.

Developing the ability to provide such specialised international financial services will provide Mauritius with the knowledge and skill sets necessary to give it an added advantage in developing suitable financial derivative (risk-hedging) contracts for African securities markets (and commodities) as well, at a later stage. Over time, Mauritius might be able to develop the ability to offer and trade more sophisticated derivative contracts: for example, for country and political risk in Africa (if such a contract were available today, it would be heavily traded) and for weather risk, as well as for cyclone and catastrophic risk.

The role of the Stock Exchange of Mauritius (SEM)

In addition to risk management, formal and informal discussions at the symposium suggested that the Stock Exchange of Mauritius has a wider regional (and global) role to play than its current offering of capital market related IFS. The SEM is, after

Johannesburg, the most technically proficient and capable securities exchange in Africa. It operates in a jurisdiction with sound regulation, in conformity with international standards and with an established reputation for transparency and probity. It has established **commercial** viability servicing its limited domestic market. However, the SEM is too small an operation to be **economically** viable in global terms, unless its scope expands. Remaining confined to the domestic market, or to the limited eastern African regional market in the near future, will provide the SEM with little room for growth and diversification.

The trend worldwide is for bourses to ally themselves through cross-ownership holdings in two or three emerging **global** securities markets networks. That trend will encourage **globally seamless** trading in all 'national' securities in a phased manner over the next decade. The most liquid and heavily traded securities (equities, bonds and associated derivative contracts) will be cross-listed on multiple exchanges (some already are) and traded on a 24 hours a day, 365 days a year basis around the world as the future unfolds. Once that is done, the next tier of securities will be similarly globalised in a linked single market space.

Given the gradual emergence of such a world, the SEM has three strategic options: (i) remain independent with its present shareholding and attempt to grow using its own resources outside the domestic market to exploit opportunities wherever they present themselves; (ii) enter into an alliance with a premier exchange in Africa – most probably the Johannesburg Stock Exchange (JSE) – to form the foundations of a strong **regional or continental** African exchange; or (iii) enter into a similar alliance with an established Indian exchange – with the NSE probably offering the best partnership potential.

Conceptually, it might be thought that the same arrangement might apply with China. However, that is unlikely for a number of reasons. **First**, in comparison with India, the Chinese capital market (indeed its whole financial system) is relatively undeveloped in operational and regulatory terms. **Second**, China is too remote compared to the proximity of India, despite its obvious interest in Africa. **Third**, the benefits to the SEM from an alliance with Shanghai are much less obvious than a similar alliance with the JSE (option ii) or the NSE (option iii), while the complications involved are greater.

The first of the SEM's strategic options would stretch its resources and cap its future prospects. It could not compete effectively with the JSE as a credible exchange either for the regional Community of Eastern and Southern Africa (COMESA) or continental Africa. The domestic market is too small (in comparison with other African markets) to provide the SEM with significant leverage capacity. The second option would embed the SEM firmly in Africa. Over time, it might create opportunities for the SEM to 'bring Africa to the global capital market'.

The third option would permit the SEM to develop regional capabilities by leveraging and enhancing its resource base (in terms of financial, human and technical resources). At the same time, it would allow the SEM to: (i) develop India-related risk management business in the near future; and (ii) link small African capital markets (in COMESA) with the larger, more rapidly growing Indian capital market. The latter option would permit Mauritian and growing African firms to access the Indian (and through it the global) capital market for funding. It would enable a greater number of firms (from Africa and India) to be cross-listed with their shares being traded in Mauritius for global buyers.

The Mauritian authorities and the SEM need to work together in formulating and co-ordinating a clear business strategy for securing its future. That needs to be done in a manner that enhances Mauritius's opportunities for expanding/diversifying its IFS exports. All three options outlined above need careful consideration. A clear business strategy needs to be decided upon and pursued. That should be done not on the basis of a 'beauty contest' to see which partner would offer the most for the SEM's shareholders and stakeholders. Instead, it should be done recognising that only one of these three options is optimal. Once that option is decided, the SEM should pursue the alliance most favourable to its prospects, for growth and diversification in the short and long term, on the basis of a specifically **targeted merger**. It should not open itself to being acquired through 'competitive bidding', which may not turn out in its own interests. That process is not appropriate under the circumstances.

If the right decision about the Stock Exchange of Mauritius is made, capital market and securities trading activity may provide a new area for the country to exploit, providing international financial services to a far greater degree than has presently entered the consciousness of either its capital market players or its authorities.

Complex financial engineering: mergers and acquisitions and public-private partnerships[11]

There has to be some immediate doubt about Mauritius's ability to evolve into a centre for IFS involving complex financial engineering, such as: (i) mergers and acquisitions (M&A) activity, which is staple of most investment banks around the world; and (ii) the growing global (and regional) interest in putting together more public-private partnerships (PPPs), especially for financing infrastructure. Mauritius does not lack the basic ingredients needed for such activities to be undertaken: i.e. a combination of financial-engineering skills, along with specialised skills in corporate legal work, familiarity with cross-border tax issues, complex corporate accounting skills and so on, and (for PPP activity) skills in large project construction, public-service delivery on a cost-recovery basis and project/service monitoring.

However, what Mauritius does lack is a universe of institutions (investment banks) with sufficient experience and credibility in these areas; a sufficiently large universe of private firms that engender M&A activity on a significant scale; and the necessary experience (and skills) in government and the private sector with successful public-private partnerships operating on the ground in Mauritius.

As far as M&A activity is concerned, Mauritius can only develop the capacity for providing IFS if Mauritian firms (i.e. banks, investment banks and corporate finance boutiques) are operating credibly across Africa. Alternatively, it requires capable investment banks operating in Africa to locate in and operate from Mauritius. Most investment banks with such capabilities are based either in South Africa or in North African countries (Morocco and Egypt). It would be difficult to attract these institutions to Mauritius unless there was a particularly strong reason. A possible reason might be the prospect of accessing a wider universe of potential suitors (or acquirers) for African enterprises through M&A deals than they might from their extant operating bases. Such acquirers could be from Gulf oil-surplus countries with a strategic investment interest in Africa (although Egypt and Morocco would have an advantage over Mauritius in this instance) or from India, ASEAN countries or China.

However, Mauritius would need to demonstrate the capacity for clearly superior access to Asian and other sources of funds and acquisition interest in Africa. Conversely, to make Africa-related M&A activity sustainable over the long term, investment banks operating from Mauritius would need to make strategic investments in developing a credible knowledge base and operating capacity across the continent. These considerations suggest that the development of M&A activity as a source of IFS exports might pose greater difficulties and take more time than other areas of IFS activity.

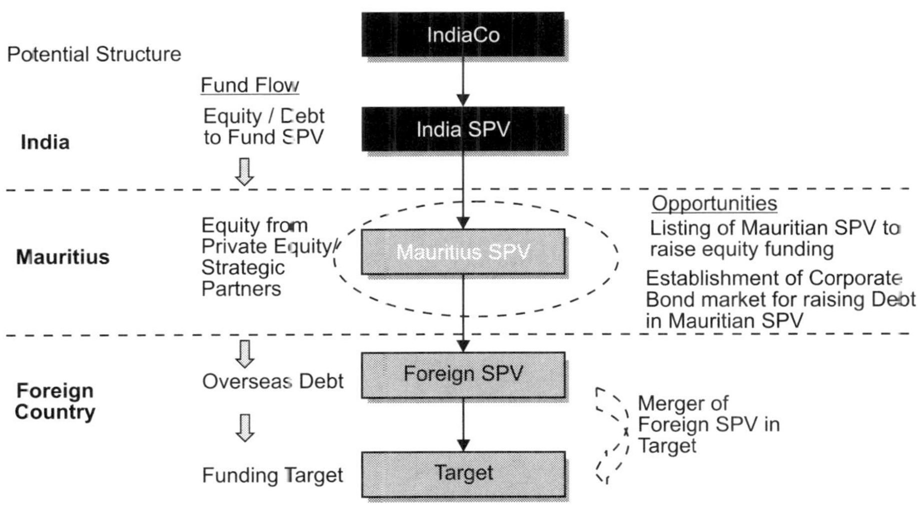

Figure 3.11 International Acquisition Structure

Source: Presentation by Mr Nimesh Kampani at the Symposium on the Export of Financial Services

Moreover, the African corporate landscape is inhabited largely by state-owned enterprises (SOEs) that are not subject to normal market-driven takeovers and acquisitions. SOE-dominated corporate environments are infertile for M&A activity (which flourishes mainly in a private sector dominated economy) to take off and be sustained. Large-scale privatisation of SOEs across Africa is a necessary pre-requisite for future market-driven M&A activity to be sustained in that region. One approach to kick-starting such a process on the continent would be for Mauritius to trigger exemplary privatisations of its own (e.g. of Air Mauritius, Mauritius Telecom, the State Bank of Mauritius) to attract global investment banking interest in Mauritius and get the ball rolling.

As far as PPP activity is concerned, the obvious drawbacks notwithstanding, the pipeline of infrastructure projects for Africa amounts to $300–400 billion over the next 10 years.[12] The infrastructure pipeline for India is about $500 billion for the period 2007–2012.[13] In both cases it is estimated that between half and two-thirds of these projects would be PPPs.[14] In Africa and India the 'demand' side of the equation for PPP skills and services far exceeds known sources of supply. As a result, the rate of implementation of PPP infrastructure financing has been slower than anticipated. Such services are intrinsically of a very high value-added genre. They are of a kind that Mauritius is suited to providing, if it can put the right ingredients (i.e. human resources, financial capital and knowledge/experience/expertise) together and use a recipe that works.

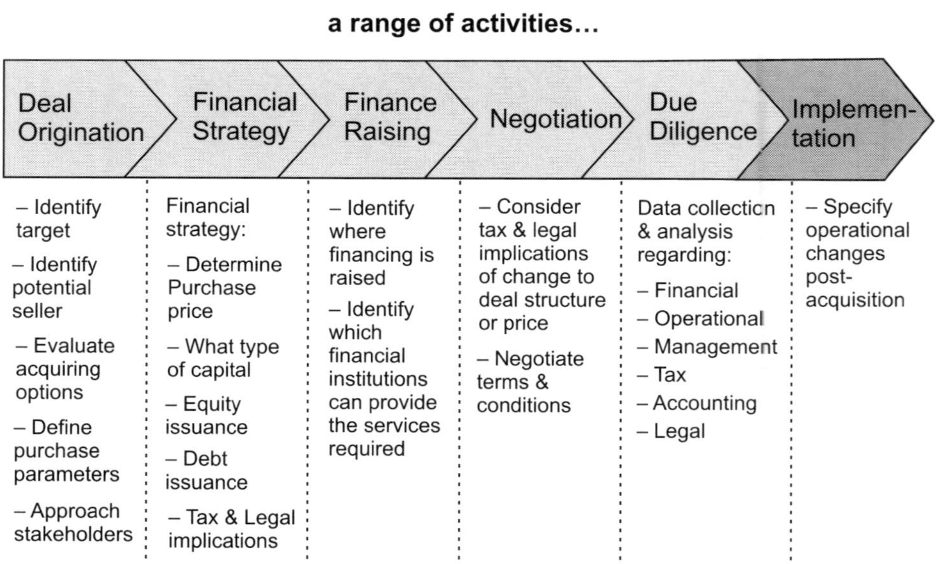

Figure 3.12 Mergers and acquisitions transaction flow

Source: Presentation by Mr Raymond Bourdeaux at the Symposium on the Export of Financial Services

	Global	Regional	Local
Tax Advisors	✓✓✓ ☺	✓ ☺ ☺ ☺	✓✓✓ ☺ ☺ ☺
Management Consultants	✓✓✓ –	✓✓ ☺ ☺	– ☺
Industry Experts	✓✓✓ –	✓ ☺ ☺	– ☺
Lawyers	✓✓✓ ☺	✓ ☺ ☺ ☺	✓✓ ☺ ☺ ☺
Accountants	✓✓✓ –	✓ ☺ ☺	✓✓ ☺
Investment Bankers / Financiers	✓✓✓ ☺	✓✓ ☺ ☺ ☺	– ☺

Figure 3.13 Essential Services Matrix

Note: ☺ refer to expertise required for medium-sized deals (*Scale:* ☺ ☺ ☺ (critical for success), ☺ ☺ (good to have, but not critical), ☺ (good to have)
✓ refer to expertise required for large deals (*Scale:* ✓✓✓ (critical for success), ✓✓ (good to have, but not critical), ✓ (good to have)

Source: Presentation by Mr Raymond Bourdeaux at the Symposium on the Export of Financial Services

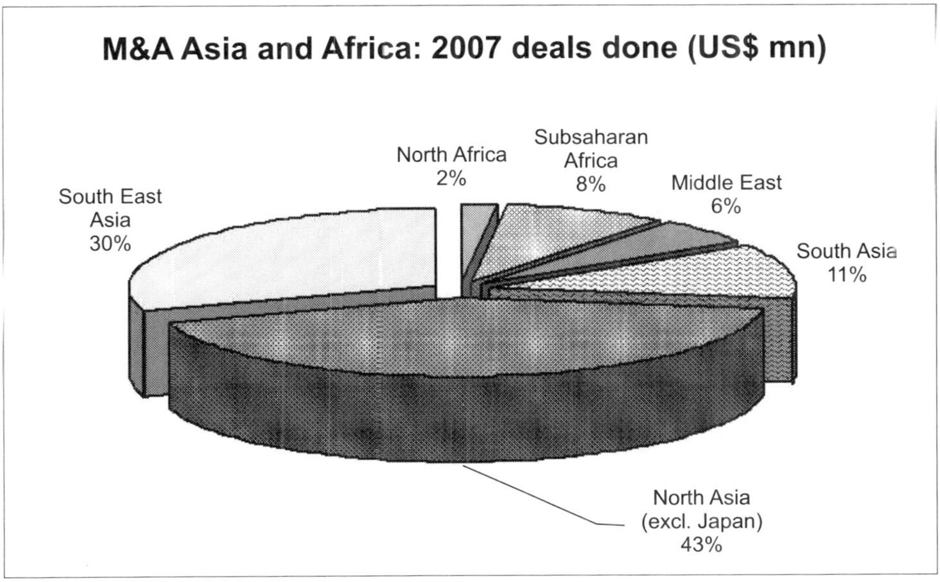

Figure 3.14 2007 Asia and Africa transaction value

Source: Presentation by Mr Raymond Bourdeaux at the Symposium on the Export of Financial Services

To do that, the Government of Mauritius and key players in the private sector need to exert joint efforts to acquire the requisite knowledge–skill mix quickly from abroad. The most advanced institutions with PPP skills and experience are based in the UK and continental Europe. The World Bank has also acquired a large database about what works and what doesn't.[15]

Tapping into these reservoirs of knowledge, the Government of Mauritius and the local financial services industry need to develop jointly a strategy to ensure that Mauritius acquires the image and credibility it needs as a purveyor of sophisticated PPP services. The potential pay-off of making Mauritius a centre of excellence for this particular high value-added service is extremely high. Both the public and private sectors need to make the upfront investment required to capitalise on the opportunities that are available.

Table 3.3 Examples of PPP projects in the SADC region funded by the European Investment Bank

Country	Project Name	Sector	Nature of PPP
Madagascar	Réseau nord des Chemins de Fer (Madarail)	Transport	Concession
Madagascar	JIRAMA	Water and electricity	Management contract at utility level (more than five active EIB projects in the water and electricity sector)
Mauritius	Harel Belle-vue Bagasse Energy	Energy	IPP concession
Mozambique	Maputo Water Supply	Water	Lease
South Africa	N3 Toll	Transport	Concession
South Africa	N4 Platinum Toll Highway	Transport	Concession
South Africa/ Mozambique	Mozambique-South Africa Natural Gas	Energy	Special purpose entity with public equity contribution

Source: David White, Regional representation for Southern Africa and Indian Ocean, European Investment Bank

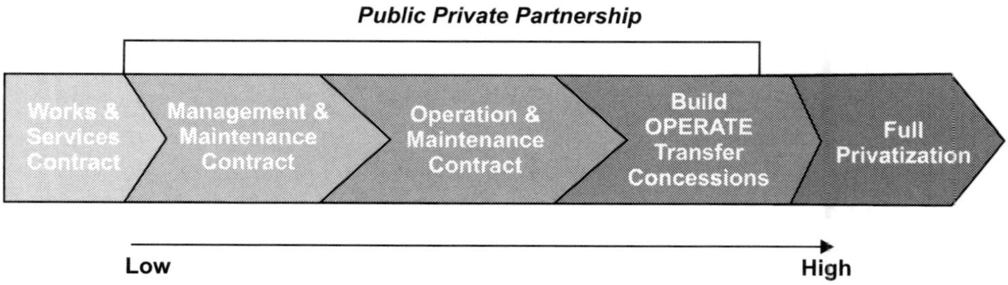

Figure 3.15 PPPs: A spectrum of options

Source: Presentation by Mr Raymond Bourdeaux at the Symposium on the Export of Financial Services

	Global	Regional	Local
Financial advisors	√√√	√√	√
Lawyers	√√√	√√	√√√ –
Technical advisors	√√√	√√	–
Lenders	√√√	√√	√
Tax and Accounting advisors	√√√	√	√√
Financial investors	√√√	√√	√

Figure 3.16 Expertise required

Source: Presentation by Mr Raymond Bourdeaux at the Symposium on the Export of Financial Services

Issues arising from the Symposium on the Export of Financial Services

Themes that arose when contemplating the evolution of the IFS industry in Mauritius – especially with respect to the constraints to capturing growing global IFS opportunities – are outlined below.

First, there is a counterproductive propensity for generating new laws, rules and regulations governing financial sector activity, as if that has become an objective in its own right. The financial services industry believes it is suffering from acute regulatory overload. At the time of the symposium, the industry felt that a pause was needed to digest regulations issued in the preceding two years. The implication is that there should be a moratorium on new regulatory initiatives, until the IFS industry has developed the absorptive capacity to cope with those already in place.

Second, there are concerns about the implicit conflict of interest between the roles of the FSC as a principal regulator as well as the prime promoter/marketer of IFS from Mauritius. Most private-sector players felt that playing both roles assertively compromised the external image of the FSC as an impartial, dispassionate, arms-length regulator; this is especially the case when it is seen by foreign governments and firms to be aggressively lobbying for business as well.

There are also concerns that governments of the day do not display sufficient political maturity when deciding on chief executive officers, senior executives and staff of regulatory, and other quasi-governmental, agencies (quangos). These agencies are supposedly independent, but are subordinated to ministries for budgetary convenience. Most providers of IFS believe that the Government of Mauritius displays a disconcerting tendency to change top regulators after each election, subordinating economic regulation to shifting political fortunes and convenience. Worse, quangos have been shunted around between ministries to suit temporal political convenience or display prime ministerial displeasure with a particular minister. That practice conveys a poor impression to global interlocutors (and clients of the financial services industry) about whether the Government of Mauritius understands what good governance is, especially in terms of the independence, impartiality and probity of key regulatory agencies.

Ongoing concerns about an absolute shortage of qualified staff for the financial services industry remain. However, the industry had taken some self-help measures to remedy the situation in the months leading up to the symposium. Financial firms and associations were working with the universities and the Empowerment Programme[16] to upgrade the quality of the graduate intake at the industry's own expense, by providing remedial and inductive pre-training courses for school and university leavers, as well as on-the-job vocational training. This action is still not sufficient to remedy the problem.

The IFS industry in Mauritius was also concerned about the declining quality and dysfunctionality of output from the education system. School leavers and university graduates lack the basic attitudes, as well as literacy, numeracy and interpersonal skills, needed to make them employable in a rapidly changing labour market. It was felt that Government of Mauritius needed to review this situation (along with education policy, curricula etc.) urgently and to take swift remedial measures. The declining quality of human resources is incompatible with labour market needs, and this cannot continue without severe consequences for the future competitiveness of Mauritius.

Another area of concern was the extent to which the Mauritian financial services industry would need to depend on foreign staff and investment to develop the capabilities it needed to avail of global IFS export opportunities. Given the lacunae that exist in the domestic IFS knowledge and skills base, a larger foreign presence is a *sine qua non* for the expansion and diversification of IFS exports from the island. However, there is disquiet about the delicate balance between domestic and foreign firms being disturbed – for instance, by an overwhelming dominance by foreign companies, or by the possible disappearance of local IFS firms. While, in economic efficiency terms, the distinction between local and foreign players in IFS should not matter, the fact remains that as a socio-cultural-political issue it does. For that reason, the foreign-domestic firm balance in the financial services industry needs to be watched carefully and dealt with sensitively to avoid an anti-foreign backlash.

Finally, the financial services industry expressed concern about its ability to expand and diversify IFS exports when handicapped by poor physical and electronic connectivity with the rest of the world. It was emphasised that it is difficult for Mauritian financial firms to present themselves credibly to Asian or European firms as experts on Africa, when flight connections to African capitals other than Pretoria have to be made via Europe or the Middle East. Similarly, Mauritius Telecommunications Ltd. (MTL) made strong representations at the Financial Services Symposium (FSS), and at the ICT-BPO Symposium as well, to the effect that it had reduced bulk-connectivity costs dramatically. Yet electronic connectivity costs are still too high by international standards, although MTL compares itself with African standards. Moreover, the critical issue of back-up redundancy is yet to be properly addressed, resulting in the financial services industry (and the ICT-BPO industries as well) being disadvantaged, if not compromised, in their efforts to compete effectively in global markets.

A post-script acknowledging the events of September 2008

Much has happened in the world of global finance since January 2008 when the Symposium on Financial Services was held and the contents of this chapter were written. The global crisis that broke in August 2007 entered a new and dangerous phase, resulting in the swift obliteration of many institutions and the demise of the independent investment banking model on which the bulge bracket investment banks – like Goldman Sachs, Morgan Stanley, Merrill Lynch, Lehman Brothers and Bear Stearns – were based. Only the first two of these are left standing, and they too have become deposit-taking banks. Two of these names have been absorbed into larger universal banks, while Lehman Brothers no longer exists.

The crisis is still unfolding and will take a greater toll on the global financial landscape. In the US, financial assets are being consolidated around three major universal banking groups and in the UK in five similar groups. Bank consolidation will probably gather force in most countries, resulting in fewer, larger institutions that could develop oligopolistic characteristics and tendencies if left undisturbed when things return to normal.

Despite the tectonic changes that have occurred abruptly in a very short time span, all of what has been said in this chapter about the export opportunities for Mauritius in higher value-added financial services and new markets remains valid. It may well be that, with confidence having been severely shaken in the banking systems of the US and Western Europe, but less so (if at all) in the economies of Asia, Africa and the Middle East, the locus of global financial services provision will shift gradually, but inexorably, from western financial centres to centres that are more proximate to emerging countries. These centres could then create new wealth more rapidly in the coming decades than the established ones.

The current situation may provide Mauritius with even greater opportunities for exporting a wide array of financial services than presently envisaged, providing it positions itself, and opens itself up quickly enough, to capitalise on these trends. To do so successfully, it will need to make the necessary changes at the **macro** (economy-wide governance), **meso** (in the financial services industry) and **micro** (in the structure and competitiveness of its financial firms and the human capital deployed in the industry) levels. Nowhere is that likely to be more true than in the areas of private banking, wealth management and asset management.

Notes

1. The authors are grateful to the CEO of the Mauritian Bankers Association (MBA) and the CEO of Multiconsult for clarifying issues regarded the DTA with India, and explaining how the situation evolved between its signing/ratification in 1985 and its coming alive in the early 1990s with the launch of Indian reforms.
2. J Sharman and P Mistry (2008). See http://publications.thecommonwealth.org/considering-the-consequences-556-p.aspx [accessed 14 November 2008].
3. The new Securities and Insurance Acts were enacted in 2005. New legislation covering pension funds as well as trust and corporate service providers was in the pipeline at the time of writing.
4. The Class A and Class B terminology was subsequently replaced by the Finance Act 2002, becoming Category 1 and Category 2 banking licences, without any fundamental change in the regime.
5. J Sharman and P Mistry (2008).
6. See tables entitled: Number of millionaires (source: BCG Global Wealth 2006, Mr Sanjeev Bhasin); Estimated growth of HNWI wealth (source: Mr Percy S Mistry taken from Cap Gemini and Merrill Lynch annual reports for 2005 and 2006); and HNWI population growth, 2005–2006 (source: Mr Sanjeev Bhasin). All tables presented at Symposium on the Export of Financial Services.
7. See table: Main players – fragmented market, presented by Mr Percy S Mistry at the Symposium on the Export of Financial Services.
8. Resident Indians are now permitted to invest US$200,000 annually per capita abroad in financial securities or real estate. That is equivalent to about US$1 million per family. There are estimated to be over three million families in India that can afford such an outflow representing a major market for PBWM services from Mauritius.
9. See also presentation by Mr Anthony Pedersen at the Symposium on the Export of Financial Services, especially diagrams: Distribution of insurance premiums and Share of insurance premiums.
10. See diagram presented by Dr Manoj Vaish at the Symposium on the Export of Financial Services, entitled: Risk Management Industry.
11. See also presentation by Mr Raymond Bordeaux at the Symposium on the Export of Financial Services, especially diagrams: The global M&A market; M&A transaction flow; Essential services matrix; 2007 Asia and Africa transaction value; PPPs: spectrum of options; Expertise required; and PPI projects in developing countries by region, 1990–2006.
12. See various World Bank and AfDB reports on infrastructure in Africa as reported in: the FT Special Report on African Infrastructure, 16 November 2006; World Bank Africa Action Plan (available: http://web.worldbank.org/WBSITE/EXTERNAL/COUNTRIES/AFRICAEXT/0,,contentMDK:20641976~menuPK:258658~pagePK:146736~piPK:146830~theSitePK:258644,00.html [accessed 5 January 2009]); Infrastructure Consortium for Africa, Annual Report, 2006, etc.
13. See the 11th Five Year Plan prepared by the Planning Commission, Government of India, for the period 2007–2012.

14. See diagram: Observed PPP trends worldwide, 1990–2005, presented by Mr Percy S Mistry at the Symposium on the Export of Financial Services.
15. The World Bank PPI Project Database is accessible through www.worldbank.org [accessed 14 November 2008]
16. The Empowerment Programme was set up by the Government of Mauritius in late 2006. It aims to 'empower' young Mauritians, as well as employees displaced by structural change in industries such as textiles, to upgrade and change their skill sets through public grant support for specialised vocational training. The programme works with firms, trade unions and industry associations to adapt the skill sets of Mauritian labour with the changing needs of the Mauritian labour market. See: http://pmo.gov.mu/portal/site/Mainhomepage/menuitem [accessed 5 January 2008].

4

Exporting ICT and Business Process Outsourcing Services

The Mauritian information and communications technology industry: contours and growth characteristics

The export of information and communications technology (ICT) services – including business process outsourcing (BPO) and information technology enabled services (ITES) – is the fastest growing industry in Mauritius. ICT, BPO and ITES are collectively abbreviated to IBI in this chapter.

Annual growth of the island's IBI industry (i.e. in terms of revenues) has averaged at over 25 per cent since 2004. However, growth in the number of IBI firms has been closer to 37 per cent annually. That is remarkable for an industry established principally to serve domestic market needs in the mid-1990s, an industry that was almost invisible until around 2003–04. Yet, employment in IBI increased from 2,100 in 2004 to over 8,000 at end-2007. The National Computer Board (NCB) expected such employment to climb to over 11,000 in 2008. From fewer than 50 firms in 2004, there were more than 380 firms in IBI at the time of writing, of which about 50 per cent are in the BPO and ITES segments, with the other half being involved in ICT

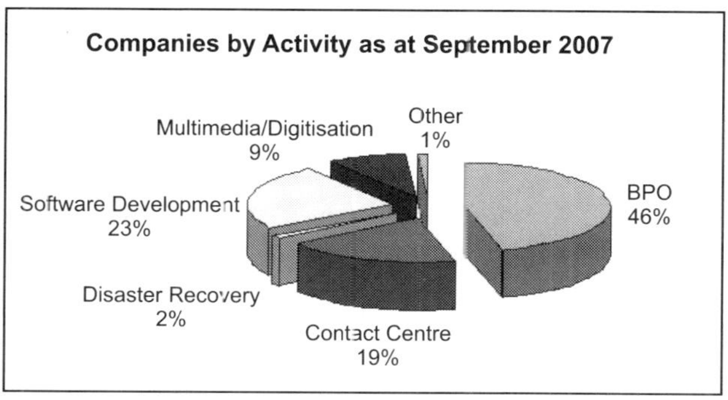

Origin	No. of companies
Mauritius	75
France	63
UK	13
India	13
Other EU	6
Benelux	5
South Africa	4
Regional	3
USA	3
Asia Pacific	3

Indicators	Jan-06	Sep-06	Sep-07
No. of Companies	107	148	188
Employment	4,332	5,513	8,000

Figure 4.1 Mauritius ICT export sector

Source: Presentation by Mr Vidia Mooneegan at the Symposium on the Export of ICT-BPO-ITES Services, and Mauritius Board of Investment

work. Nearly a fifth of the BPO-ITES firms in existence by mid-2008 had been formed after October 2006.[1]

With a few exceptions representing local operations of global firms (e.g. Accenture, Infosys, Oracle etc.) the present ICT-BPO-ITES industry structure in Mauritius is fragmented and disjointed, comprising mainly a host of small, opportunistic firms operating in highly specific niches. Aggregate IBI turnover was estimated to exceed MRs25 billion in 2007 (about US$1 billion), with exports approaching a tenth of that, i.e. US$100 million. A handful of large ICT and BPO firms accounted for the bulk (over 60 per cent) of total employment, revenues and exports of the combined IBI industry, while a much larger number of small firms accounted for the minority share of all these measures.

To put that situation in context, the **global** IBI industry turned over more than an estimated $450 billion in 2007 with outsourcing exports of over $120 billion. **Thus the revenues of the Mauritian IBI industry represent less than 0.2 per cent of world IBI revenues and its exports represent less than 0.08 per cent of global IBI exports.** According to the National Association of the ICT-BPO Services Industry (in India – NASSCOM), India accounts for total IBI turnover of over US$45 billion and exports exceeding US$20 billion (with BPO and ITES accounting for $11 billion). It is obviously misleading to compare Mauritius directly with India for this (or any other) purpose. However, what the relative difference in size highlights is that Mauritius can make an adequate (and rapidly growing) living from IBI by earning an infinitesimal fraction of what India needs to earn. If the estimates above are taken at face value, with Mauritius's IBI exports accounting for less than 0.1 per cent of global IBI outsourcing exports, there is considerable room for their expansion and diversification to ten times that size.

Unlike India's NASSCOM, the IBI industry in Mauritius does not yet have a representative association acting in the industry's wider collective interests (assuming it has identified those interests), either for market-scanning and dealing with constraints or for capturing regional and global opportunities, since fewer than 15 per cent of the firms in the industry are members of the relevant trade association. This also seems characteristic of Mauritian private firms at large in any industry, which appear to be myopically preoccupied with their own immediate firm-specific concerns and interests, rather than with wider, long-term competitiveness and the collective interests of the industries to which they belong.

Nonetheless, the Government of Mauritius has taken a more systemic perspective in considering the future of the industry, with the Ministry for Information Technology & Telecommunications (MITT) commissioning a comprehensive plan for the industry's development over the next five years.[2] That plan – known as the National Information & Communications Technologies Strategic Plan (NICTSP) – aims to make IBI the fifth pillar of the Mauritian economy and the premier African ICT hub.

The plan's strategy for attracting inward foreign investment in IBI is not based on tax incentives. It relies instead on providing a high degree of economic freedom for firms, combined with a low and competitive tax regime, a benign and positive business climate, and an openness that permits firms to have considerable operational and financial flexibility in conducting their affairs. Yet, NICSTP seems over-prescriptive, over-programmatic, detailed and deterministic in suggesting how the Mauritian IBI industry should develop in a top-down fashion. It embraces 15 programmes and 124 projects requiring a budget of over MRs2 billion, a part of which MITT hopes will be financed by the World Bank.

By 2011, the NICTSP intends to achieve: (i) IBI services exports of US$800 million (or 0.25 per cent of global exports in that year), which would be equivalent to 7 per cent of national GDP; (ii) employment for 29,000, of which 13,000 will be non-nationals; (iii) an increase in household personal computer (PC) penetration of 20,000 – for an island with over 300,000 households; (iv) an increase in school penetration by PCs of about 12,000 – for what purports to be a cyber-island; and (e) broadband penetration of 250,000, for a population of over 1.3 million. What is remarkable about these targets is that they seem unusually modest, given the potential that exists for IBI exports from Mauritius. In contrast, the five strategies, 15 programmes and 124 projects identified for financing under the NICTSP seem over-ambitious.

If experience in other countries is a guide, such a plan must be regarded with scepticism, especially in a rapidly changing and fluid industry, where global market developments and niche opportunities are likely to be less clear, less predictable and more volatile, and with products and services being more temporally vulnerable (i.e. having a shorter shelf-life) than such plans anticipate.

What should the Mauritian 'model' be?

With the background described above in view, a symposium on ICT, BPO and ITES was held in January 2008 to consider the likely future evolution of the industry and the scope for expanding IBI exports rapidly. It brought together local industry leaders with carefully selected foreign participants in domains where global outsourcing was established and burgeoning. These verticals included: (i) **financial services**; (ii) **design and architecture**; (iii) **accounting and business consulting**; (iv) **legal processes**; (v) **hospitality, airlines and travel**; (vi) **human resources recruiting and training**; (vii) **media, entertainment and animation services**; and (viii) **business process outsourcing for Africa**.

The symposium attempted to identify appropriate 'partnership models' for Mauritius, particularly with established ICT-BPO firms in countries like India and France. On all key indices (e.g. network readiness digitalisation etc.) Mauritius ranked between first and third in Africa.[3] South Africa was its only competitor on any of the relevant measures. The question was whether Mauritius should be comparing itself with Africa or with countries that have carved out a more solid and significant niche for themselves in the global IBI space?

If global experience is a reliable guide, IBI exports from Mauritius would need to be differentiated and unique. Given Mauritius's characteristics and attributes, its IBI development and export model has to be different from models pursued by other larger, established IBI services exporters. Unlike India or China (if it overcame its lack of English-fluency) or countries like the Philippines and Malaysia, it would be unrealistic and unviable for Mauritius to export IBI services in activities/domains that require a large supply of low-cost labour with unexploited potential for continuous back-filling from an even larger, under-utilised national labour pool (as in India). Mauritius does not have those endowments, nor does it possess the immigration or accommodation potential for that purpose.

Neither does it have sufficient investment capital available domestically from public or private sources. For that reason, Mauritius cannot emulate the Dubai IBI export model either. That emirate is attempting to create an entire IBI industry via the import and transplantation of skilled human resources from India and South-East Asia. To these it is adding state-of-the-art infrastructure, financed by a state with a great deal of surplus resources, complemented with executive management, capital investment and cutting-edge IBI technologies imported from the EU, Japan and US. The Dubai model provides a no-tax regime and extraordinary infrastructure incentives to attract every global IBI firm to locate a part of its operations in that city, using a package of inputs that it can provide on a 'ready-to-go, plug-and-play' platform.

Mauritius cannot afford such luxuries. To succeed, it needs to rely on a different model that first focuses on a highly qualified, but small labour pool, allowing for significant immigration, second is targeted at specific, lucrative vertical niches and third has high, specialised knowledge-content, unique firm-to-firm relationships/partnerships, aimed at exploiting Mauritius's multilingual and creative skills. The Mauritius IBI export model needs to be flexible in combining the resources of:

- Global firms like Accenture, Infosys, TCS, Oracle, SAP etc., which are already located on the island, to service traditional verticals (financial services, business support, accounting, auditing, payments processing, back-office customer care etc.) requiring multilingual skills; with the
- Flexibility and adaptability of **smaller specialist niche domestic and foreign firms** utilising creative human resources to develop non-traditional verticals in BPO for: design and architecture, legal processes, media, entertainment and animation services, research and knowledge processes.

It could build such a model by forming partnerships with ICT firms, as well as BPO-ITES firms, in India, France, the UK, Canada and the US that have an established client base, but can use Mauritius's capabilities to extend into new geographies (Africa?) and jointly exploit high-value niche opportunities. These considerations become clearer when viewed in the context of specific-niche BPO verticals, which Mauritius should look to exploit more fully; these are discussed in greater detail below.

Banking and financial services outsourcing

Banking and financial services (BFS) comprises the single largest outsourcing sub-domain, accounting for a 38 per cent share (4 per cent being insurance) of global BPO-ITES business, which amounted to about US$45 billion in 2007.

In this highly competitive arena, the main outsourcers are the large global banks. Most BPO (>60 per cent of the total) is carried out by US banks (such as Citigroup, Bank of America, Morgan Stanley, JP Morgan-Chase and Goldman Sachs) primarily to India, but also to other English-speaking countries in Asia. India has a 50 per cent market share in the BFS outsourcing domain. Banks from Britain (e.g. Lloyds TSB, Barclays and HSBC), continental Europe (ABN-Amro, ING, CSFB, UBS and Deutsche Bank) and Australia (National Australia Bank and ANZ-Grindlays) account for another 30 per cent of BFS outsourcing to India and the Philippines. The principal BFS offerings by outsourcing destinations include: processing of payments transactions and handling customer account queries; mortgage back-office document processing and checking; back-office processing of leasing activities; credit card transaction processing and customer queries; managing customer contact for front- and back-office demands; managing customer contact for collection of arrears; customer origination processes, such as solicitation for credit card applications, mortgages, car loans, personal loans, direct debit payment orders etc; software systems development for IT applications support; and maintenance of banking IT networks and support infrastructure.

BPO requirements of the major banks (with millions of customers) in the above areas demand large, low-cost, labour pools, which countries like Mauritius cannot provide but India and the Philippines can. What Mauritius, with its attributes and limitations, needs to focus on is:

- Becoming a BFS regulatory centre of excellence for Africa that specialises in assisting regulators with monitoring the quality and probity of outsourced processes and activities in BFS;
- **Smaller and medium-sized** banking and other financial services players (e.g. securities brokerages and boutique corporate finance units), especially in non-English speaking Europe, which need to outsource a plethora of functions and processes to reduce their costs in order to compete with larger banks;
- Targeting private banks around the world and particularly in high-cost private banking and wealth management jurisdictions, offering tailored BPO-ITES services for their HNWI clientele;
- Providing high value-added knowledge process/research process outsourcing (KPO/RPO) activities, such as detailed corporate, credit, industry and country research and analysis that smaller banks need;

- Offering outsourcing services for managing the IT/ASP (applications service provider) functions of smaller banks in high-cost locations; and
- Offering regulatory expertise in outsourcing for smaller, less-capable regulatory institutions in Africa.

Such BFS outsourcing offerings are unlikely to be feasible for small firms specialising in particular niches of this large market. Smaller banks/financial firms interested in outsourcing to Mauritius are more likely (and have an easier time convincing their regulators) to outsource:

- To established global BPO firms (such as Accenture, Infosys, TCS, Wipro, SAP, IBM, EDS etc.) already located on the island; or
- To global accounting and auditing firms (such as DTT, PWC, EY, KPMG etc) with a local presence, which may be able to undertake some but not all of this work, due to constraints on auditors becoming involved in conflicts-of-interest by providing what might be construed as integral services; or
- To their own fully- or majority-owned subsidiaries set up specifically to undertake 'insourcing' in locations like Mauritius, managing their business processing under the same corporate umbrella; for example, Deutsche Bank is now doing this in Mauritius and expanding its intra-group BPO business rapidly.

As far as BFS outsourcing for **French** banks is concerned, Mauritius faces competition from Morocco, Tunisia and Romania. However, banks in *Canada* requiring bilingual capabilities, which are outsourcing a limited amount of work to the Caribbean, could outsource to Mauritius. Smaller banks in a number of EU countries (e.g. Ireland, the Netherlands, Germany, the Channel Islands, Portugal, Scandinavia, Italy and in 'new' Europe) could also benefit from outsourcing to Mauritius. To access such customers, the Government of Mauritius and the country's Board of Investment need to support larger Mauritian firms (e.g. Accenture) to compete for such business on a targeted basis. Alternatively, they may need to partner with established Indian, South African, French or Canadian firms to provide assurance to customers that Mauritius can deliver what it promises by way of banking and financial services outsourcing.

Engineering design and architectural services outsourcing

Global spending on engineering services in 2007 was about US$750 billion, with only US$10-15 billion (or 1–2 per cent) of that being outsourced. This suggests enormous potential for the growth of engineering services outsourcing (ESO) in the coming years. Industry estimates are that, by 2020, the ESO market – driven by firms in the US, EU, Middle East and Japan – could grow to **US$150–225 billion**. The major beneficiaries of this shift to ESO are expected to be India, Canada, and Mexico (for the US and Middle East); China (for Japan, Korea and Taiwan) and Eastern Europe (for the EU).

A survey conducted in 2004[4] suggested that only 11 per cent of US architectural firms had outsourced work on one or more projects, with the cost savings realised being 40–70 per cent of total project costs. By 2007, that figure had increased to 25 per cent of US architectural firms resorting to outsourcing, indicative of the considerable future potential for architectural service outsourcing (ASO) that exists.

Up to now, ASO has comprised: automated mapping and facilities management; layering; conversion services; space planning; digitisation; and 3D-rendering with virtual room design. Core work outsourced involves schematic design and design development work, while non-core work comprises pre-design, model/presentation, construction document or computerised working drawings for client preview.

The main reasons cited for resorting to ASO are to alleviate unmanageable office work loads, achieve significant cost savings and achieve faster production to meet tight client deadlines for viewing alternatives and options. Research on ASO undertaken by the American Institute of Architects and Harvard University[5] suggested that:

- ASO depended critically on confidentiality and transparency in relationships between the outsourcer and the ASO service provider;
- Higher productivity and shortening of project development time spans was the main motivation;
- Process customisation for individual clients and individualised service was the principal focus;
- ASO was particularly effective either for basic services or for highly specialised services;
- Overcoming the learning curve drove success for adoption of outsourcing as a practical and desirable alternative to in-house work with high-cost and long-time implications; and
- ASO facilitated the emergence of global networks of knowledge and expertise that fed back into strengthening the overall capacity of the worldwide architectural industry.

A recent Booz Allen Hamilton study,[6] conducted in conjunction with NASSCOM, suggested that India was likely to be the main beneficiary of rapidly growing ESO/ASO, capturing 25–30 per cent of outsourcing work in these areas in 2007 from 12 per cent in 2004. This is because India has the largest pool of engineering talent required for ESO (graduating from world-class Indian Institutes of Technology, IITs) among emerging countries, more than Russia and China combined. The current graduate talent pool suitable for ESO/ASO work in India represents 28 per cent of the total estimated technically qualified resource pool in low-cost (i.e. developing and transition) countries. The next largest sources of such labour are in Russia (11 per cent) and China (10 per cent).

Mauritius has much to offer Indian firms specialising in this domain in terms of extending their reach into francophone and African markets. However, the island needs a larger number of qualified and trained engineers and architects to capitalise on this opportunity, opening itself to immigration by people with these skills from other parts of Africa. Triangulation with South Africa would enable Indo-Mauritian firms to cater to Dutch, German and other non-English speaking European markets.

Apart from partnering with specialist Indian firms working in ESO/ASO to enable them to extend their market reach (into the francophone and African countries), Mauritius also needs to attract onshore:

- specialist and innovative space development firms like Technopolis of Finland;
- major global architectural and engineering **consulting** firms (e.g. Ove Arup & Associates, WS Atkins etc.) from the developed world; as well as
- construction firms that have embedded pools of architectural and engineering staff – e.g. Shapoorji Pallonji, Tata Realty & Infrastructure, Reliance Infrastructure, Larsen & Toubro, DLF and IVRCL Infrastructure from India.

These firms need to locate in Mauritius to serve the large continental African market for construction and infrastructure, and to lower their costs for undertaking global ESO/ASO by enabling them to hire Mauritian, African and Asian engineering and architectural talent. The African market could be a magnet to attract such operations into Mauritius.

Those familiar with ESO/ASO potential, suggest strongly that a 'technical ecosystem' is needed for exporting such services. In this context, while not perfectly endowed, Mauritius seems to have a number of inherent advantages:

- An open economy with ease of entry and few restrictions on doing business
- Reliable infrastructure – six internet providers, connectivity through SAFE
- A base of skilled human resources – two universities; close to 70 per cent of the working population being bilingual; and a literacy rate of 88 per cent (this skills base still needs to be expanded organically and through immigration to exploit ESO/ASO opportunities with sufficient critical mass)
- A vibrant local industry, with 49 architectural firms and nearly 200 BPO companies
- Ranking of 25th out of the top 50 offshoring locations for Mauritius in an AT Kearney survey
- Supportive government policies that are amenable to encouraging ESO/ASO growth
- A good location for niche knowledge-based operations, offering an attractive lifestyle to highly skilled human capital

However, some interesting dimensions and imbalances need to be appreciated. *First*, there is an obvious global asymmetry driving ESO/ASO. While 75 per cent of the world's engineers/architects are located in **developed** countries, 67 per cent of the world market for engineering services and architecture is now located in the **developing** world. India has a million qualified engineers, but only 35,000 architects. Africa has fewer than 400,000 engineers and 50,000 architects, of which 25 per cent are in South Africa. Mauritius has barely 2,000 qualified engineers and 120 architects. Europe has over 8 million qualified engineers and 500,000 architects, while the US has over 15 million engineers and over 700,000 architects.[7]

These asymmetries suggest that the availability of technical/professional skills is now concentrated in a different geography to the location of most future engineering and architectural work. That imbalance will drive the growth of ESO/ASO, as surplus engineering and architectural talent in OECD countries is deployed to meet the needs of the developing world. To lower their costs, engineering consulting and architectural firms will need to outsource more work. Somewhere in between, there are opportunities for Mauritius to play a specialised niche role in bridging the gaps. However, to do so it will need to expand its output of technically qualified engineers and architects dramatically.

The **second** dimension/imbalance exists in that there are different policies and standards governing ESO/ASO in the developed and developing worlds. BPO service providers need to contend with different design standards for public health and safety, building design standards, environmental protection and climate-change standards, materials-handling standards, codes of professional ethics, social responsibility and so on.

Third, architectural firms that outsource have more than 100 professionals with multi-disciplinary skills. As of 2008, that figure represents nearly the entire architecture profession in Mauritius.

These dimensions illustrate the challenges that Mauritius faces in developing even a small niche capability for exporting ESO/ASO services. It is unlikely that such capability can be developed, or sufficiently well directed, to address the needs of the emerging global market for ESO/ASO without carefully conceived and intelligently structured **partnerships**.

Nonetheless, the size and attraction of the African market for construction and infrastructure provides an opportunity for Mauritius to open the door in developing its capabilities in this specialised, high-value market with potential for explosive growth in 2008–20. Clearly the Government of Mauritius, MITT, the two universities, the engineering and architectural professions, and local IBI firms need collectively to formulate ways in which this emerging outsourcing market can be exploited to Mauritius's advantage, through carefully targeted niche-service offerings to potential outsourcers.

Accounting and business support services outsourcing

Accounting and business support services outsourcing (ABSO) is the best-established BPO domain after BFS (with which it is often combined). Such outsourcing started the late-1980s with TNCs in financial services, airlines and manufacturing (e.g. General Electric) from the US and the UK outsourcing accounting functions and processes to India. However, it has spread rapidly to other industries and countries, and is still expanding as outsourcing from Europe, other parts of the OECD and the Middle East catch up with levels of outsourcing undertaken by US and UK firms.

Growth in this area is therefore being driven by geographical **and** sector (or vertical) diversification. Most ABSO business is dominated by large firms such as Accenture, IBM, Infosys, TCS, Wipro, EDS etc. These firms have established a large and growing presence in low-cost countries to undertake outsourced work. However, a significant amount of ABSO is also carried out by smaller, specialised firms servicing particular clients and industries.

In Mauritius, the continued expansion of ABSO exports will depend largely on the growth of firms like Accenture, which offers an instructive case study.[8] This business was established in 2002, and has grown rapidly since. Accenture is a **global** market leader (one of the top five global TNCs in outsourcing), with over 625 clients in more than 30 industries and 45 countries. Its outsourcing revenues in FY2007 were US$7.84 billion or 40 per cent of its total revenues. Accenture offers a full range of outsourcing services from BPO to applications outsourcing (AO) and infrastructure outsourcing (IO) as well as systems integration (SI). In 2007 it had more than 75,000 outsourcing employees worldwide, of which 750 (or 1 per cent) were in Mauritius.

Accenture accounts for 11–12 per cent of total employment in the Mauritian IBI industry. Of its 750 staff, 550 work on BPO (with 400 dedicated to ABSO) and 200 for AO/SI. Its Mauritius centre is expected to double from 750 to more than 1,400 employees by 2010; BPO employment will grow to 1,000 employees and AO/SI to 400. These numbers could be larger, if more qualified labour was available. This example demonstrates the potential that still exists for ABSO exports from Mauritius.

Typically, ABSO exports include: managing and recording accounts payable and receivable; billing; general ledger recording and maintenance; treasury transactions recording and management; tax transactions management; risk management transactions recording; and a variety of payment and collection services, including arrears notification and management. These activities fall into three groups classified as: (i) procure to pay (PTP); (ii) order to cash (OTC); and (iii) record to report (RTR).

Global firms specialising in ABSO work have assessed Mauritius (in terms of its capacity to expand ABSO exports) (see table 4.1).

The advantages Mauritius has to offer include a sound economic performance over a sustained period of time, a track record of relative political stability, with respect for democratic processes, institutions and rule-of-law and a relatively good legal

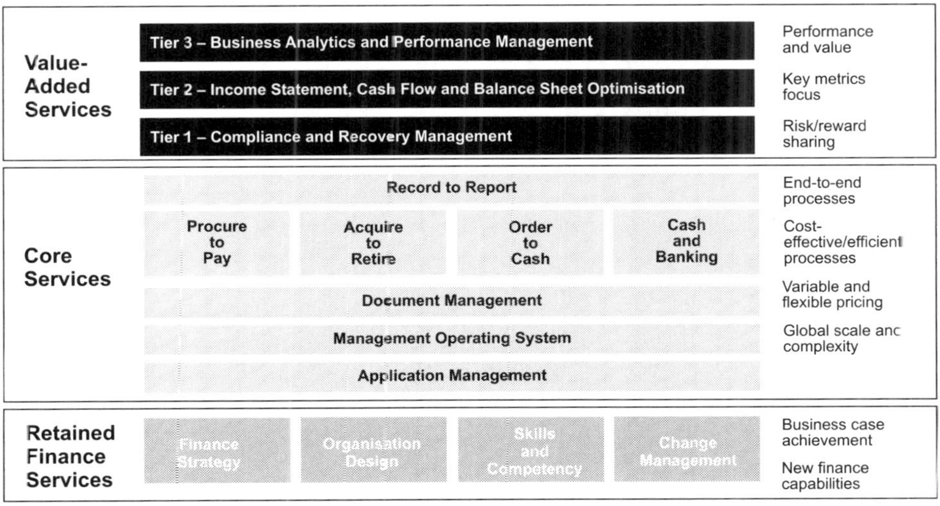

Figure 4.2 Accenture – finance and accounting BPO scope of services
Source: Presentation by Ms Josie Lapierre at the Symposium on the Export of ICT-BPO-ITES Services

Table 4.1 Mauritius's capacity to expand ABSO exports

Criterion	Rating: South Africa	Rating: Mauritius	Mauritian L-T Advantage
Multiple language skills	Excellent	Excellent	(French)
Government support for IBI	Fair	Good	Good
Intrinsic quality of labour pool	Fair	Fair	Fair
Quality of infrastructure (ICT + other)	Fair	Good	(ICT ok)
Educational system	Good	Good	Fair
Labour and other costs	Fair	Good	Deteriorating
Political & economic environment	Good	Very good	Low risk
Cultural compatibility with clients	Very good	Very good	Very good
Rule-of-law & legal maturity	Good	Good	Good
Data and IPR security and privacy	Very good	Good	Good

framework for rule-of-law, data protection etc. Additional advantages are its a limited pool of talented, tactile, trainable people, bilingual advantage of functional literacy in English and French, relatively good ICT-telecom infrastructure when measured against African standards and a business-friendly environment, especially post-2005, with ease of entry and exit and diminished obstacles to inward/outward movement of key managers and staff. The island also: has a favourable time zone vis-à-vis Europe for undertaking outsourcing work outside core working hours, with a 3–4-hour working daytime overlap; provides a gateway for the African regional market; has strong ties with India, which is the global bastion of BPO in general and ABSO in particular; provides cultural understanding of and compatibility with European clients; and is adaptable to rapidly changing global and market circumstances, which characterises the global BPO industry in terms of demand and supply factors.

In addition, as far as ABSO exports are concerned, Mauritius already has:

- A strong existing BPO-ITES sector, which is growing rapidly
- A strong presence of international players like Accenture
- A strong accounting profession, with globally recognised qualifications
- An adequate educational set-up, although this needs further strengthening
- An international financial service centre, although this needs to become more active

By the same token, the constraints operating on Mauritius's growth as an ABSO centre are: its limited ability to scale-up operations quickly in terms of staff numbers, thus making investment by global majors in BPO subject to a finite cap in growth potential; insufficient skills in the right areas, the result of a mismatch in human resources between what the educational system produces and what the labour market demands; the relatively low priority that appears to be given by government and the population at large to the IBI industry, compared to other priorities like the financial services sector, construction etc; and high connectivity costs, coupled with a lack of redundancy and service reliability standards that need substantial improvement, despite the progress made by MTL so far.

The main challenges to be addressed from the experience of firms like Accenture, in terms of bolstering the ability to expand and diversify ABSO exports from Mauritius, include the following:

- Change the mindset/culture of the Government of Mauritius and the population through PPPs
- Educate the population at large on BPO career opportunities
- Target information campaigns at parents, students, potential employees, the business community at large and government
- Operate in a globalised world by facilitating access to key services outside core working hours
- Remember that Mauritius is competing globally in every time zone, not locally
- Close HR skills gap through customised training programmes for the IBI industry
- Training programmes need to be intensive, short term and delivered through PPPs (like, for example, the private IBI industry working with the Empowerment Programme)

- Improve bilingual skills (English/French)
- Increase proficiency in other global languages
- Improve core technical skills (finance, accounting, computer skills and business processes)
- Improve soft communication and interaction skills through exposure to the global environment
- Tap directly into the school certificate/higher school certificate school-leaving pool – short-term access to 12–15,000 per year
- Facilitate diplomas/degrees for people who work – short term, through PPPs
- Provide continuous classroom, on-the-job and online training in IBI
- Provide training from recognised, accredited institutions outside core working hours
- Review the national secondary education programme to match it to labour-market demand (for languages, technical and soft interpersonal and communication skills)
- Focus on quality of delivery – build BPO expertise and reputation through PPPs
- Scan the global business environment for emerging opportunities in new BPO areas
- Focus on sustained economic development across key sectors of the economy
- Pay particular regard to accelerated infrastructure development and improved security
- Establish an amenable regulatory environment, one that adapts quickly to changing global demands

Mauritius's ability to increase ABSO exports would be bolstered if it acted as hub to triangulate Indo-Mauritian-South African partnerships. At the symposium, ABSO exporters from all three countries felt that such a troika would be 'unbeatable' in developing a globally dominant profile for ABSO work, because of the advantages that would accrue from exploiting/leveraging language skills, geographical affinities (to particular customer bases) and the technical capabilities of each country. However, such triangulation could best be experimented with under the organisational umbrella of a single global firm like Accenture or Deloittes, rather than being left to independent firms unaccustomed to working with such an organisational culture and operating processes and protocols.

For the Mauritian IBI industry to develop a recognised and distinct brand image in the outsourcing world (as India has), it would need to form a more effective industry association to project such an image, and learn lessons from the Mauritian tourism industry, which has succeeded in developing a unique brand image as an exotic, high-value destination that is globally recognised.

Legal process outsourcing

In 2005, worldwide expenditure on legal process outsourcing (LPO) was estimated to be US$20 billion and was growing at 8 per cent annually. Of this figure, about US$6bn was related to 'legal' services comprising: litigation support (US$4.9bn or 82 per cent of total expenditure); customised legal research (US$0.62bn, over 10 per cent); and patent and trademark prosecution ($0.4bn or nearly 7 per cent).[9]

Most LPO work is outsourced by US and (to a lesser extent) UK law firms that operate globally. A small but rapidly increasing amount of LPO work is shifting from onshore to offshore, with India being a favoured destination. The current activity breakdown of the Indian LPO market shows a bias towards International Patent Review (IPR) solutions. Current LPO revenues in India are about US$100 million, with US$42mn being earned from patent and trademark filing support services; another US$32mn from customised legal research and the remaining US$26mn from litigation support.[10]

As with ESO/ASO, the LPO business is in a nascent stage with enormous future growth potential. In advanced, high-cost, English-speaking countries, for example, the legal industry is structured as follows: (i) **the US** has over 231,000 law firms, employing one million attorneys and five million support staff; (ii) **the UK** has over 9,000 legal firms and chambers, employing some 100,000 solicitors, 13,000 barristers and 22,000 paralegal staff; (iii) **Australia** has over 35,000 solicitors and barristers and 57,000 other legal staff; (iv) **Canada** has about 16,800 registered law firms, with over 36,500 lawyers; and (v) **New Zealand** has over 9,050 barristers and solicitors.

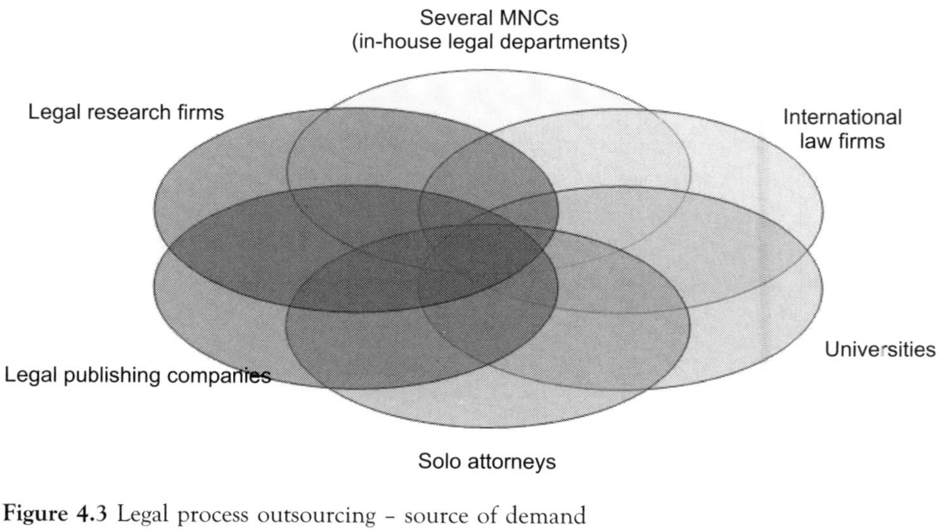

Figure 4.3 Legal process outsourcing – source of demand
Source: Presentation by Mr Pankaj Parnami at the Symposium on the Export of ICT-BPO-ITES Services

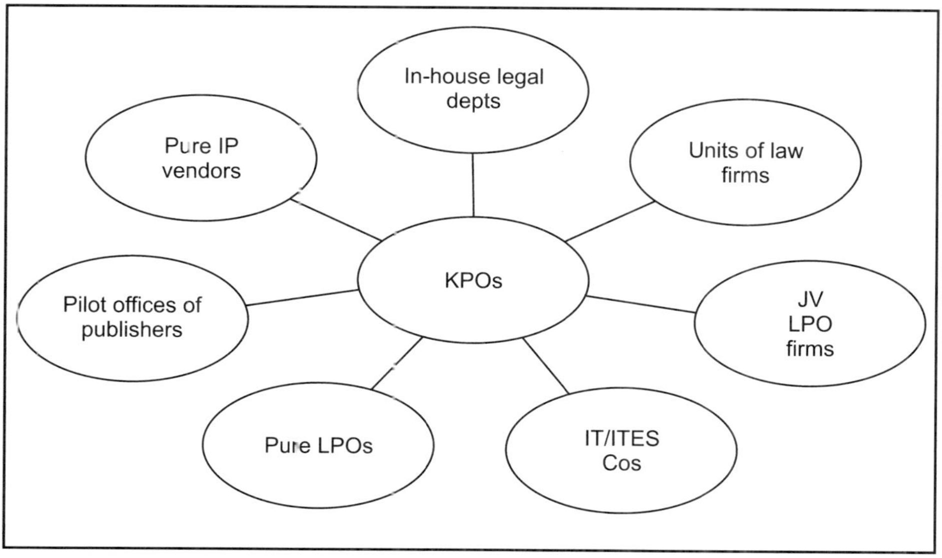

Figure 4.4 Legal process outsourcing – source of supply
Source: Presentation by Mr Pankaj Parnami at the Symposium on the Export of ICT-BPO-ITES Services

On average, professional fees for qualified lawyers in these countries range from US$500–2,000 per hour. Paralegal billing rates vary between US$200–800 per hour. Given growing client resistance to these high rates, law firms in the developed world are under pressure to reduce costs. With the advent of corporate law firms that are public and listed on stock exchanges, these cost-cutting pressures will increase. LPO is likely to be resorted to a great deal more in future.

This will happen simply because of the substantial cost differentials between similarly qualified legal professionals in the developed and developing worlds. The latter's hourly costs are a fraction (between 15–25 per cent) of those in the former. Table 4.2 provides an indicative picture of the total amount of spending by the top 200 US law firms (out of a total of 231,000) by category of activity undertaken.

Table 4.2 Spending by US law firms by category of activity

Expenditure of top 200 US law firms Category	Annual spend (US$ bn)	Share of total spend (%)
Office operations	6.2	31.1
Litigation support	4.9	24.6
Word processing & secretarial support	2.9	14.6
Information systems	2.5	12.6
Marketing & legal research	1.5	7.5
Support functions & HR	1.6	7.6
Patent prosecution	0.4	2.0
Total	19.9	100

Based on table 4.2, it would be reasonable to estimate total expenditures by the top 5,000 US law firms as being $200 billion, with their counterparts in the rest of the developed world (EU and Japan) together probably spending a similar amount. Compared to that expenditure, extant LPO amounts to barely 5 per cent of the total (probably less, as only the largest law firms are included for the total spend estimate).

There are over 1.7 million patents filed around the world each year (with 90 per cent of these being filed in OECD countries), with the cost of processing each exceeding US$2,000 on average. A classic LPO function, for example, would be to carry out the patent art search involved as a first step and to prepare documents for filing the patent as a second.

Extrapolating from crude figures, and cutting across the functions listed in the table above, the LPO market could easily exceed US$100 billion in size within the next five years. **This is a highly specialised market, within which Mauritius could service a significant niche in the English-speaking and francophone worlds.** Table 4.3 shows the services offered under legal process outsourcing.

The pricing trend analysis emerging from Indian billing rates for LPO is shown in table 4.4, below.

Mauritius could levy a premium on these billing rates and still attract LPO business from the US and developed Commonwealth countries, as well as from the EU with

Table 4.3 Services offered under legal process outsourcing

Litigation support	International patent review services	Paralegal support
• Contract review • Memo & brief writing • Legal research • Drafting • E-discovery • Business research	• Prior-art search • Freedom-to-operate research • Patentability search • Product clearance investigation • Patent & technology landscaping • Patent data mining services • Patent watch services • Trademark & copyright	• Image scanning • Document coding, indexing & tagging • Legal transcription • Archiving • Deposition summary • Document/evidence review

Table 4.4 Pricing trends from Indian billing rates for legal process outsourcing

Services	Description of activity	Indian billing rates
Paralegal support	Document management: word processing, legal transcription, legal coding and document conversion	US$12–25/hr
Legal support	Drafting and proofreading contracts/agreements, legal research, including case and statutory law	US$30–125/hr or more for specific services
Patent services	Helping file patent applications, infringement studies and patent /trademark prior-art searches	US$25–80/hr

its language skills. Many of the factors that make Mauritius an attractive proposition for ABSO apply to LPO as well. Additional attractions include a nascent existing base of LPO and law firms exposed to the operation of global business activities, and amendments in the Law Practitioners Act by the government to open entry, enable large multi-disciplinary law practices to be set up and permit the pooling of skills and resources that would enable LPO to be undertaken. The island has a hybrid legal system, which enables familiarity with both British Common Law and the French Napoleonic Code, and steps are also being taken toward data protection and confidentiality via the Data Protection Act 2004, ICT Act 2001, Copyright Act 1997, Computer Misuse and Cyber Crimes Act 2003, among others.

However, the constraints that affect other outsourcing domains also restrict opportunities for LPO. These include limited prospects for upward scalability, resulting from a small existing pool of legal professionals compared to competing countries like India and the Philippines,[11] and the absence of core local professional expertise needed for developing this domain, with most Mauritian law firms being 'one-man (or woman)' offices. At the same time, there is a lack of interest on the part of a myopic domestic legal profession, who are interested mainly in litigation (to deploy amateur theatrical skills, as one experienced practitioner put it) and inclined to erect protectionist barriers to competition from outside. The legal profession is also generally complacent/unwilling to consider new sources of revenue from global business activities like LPO and to become a Centre of Excellence for LPO work pertaining to the activities of TNCs and multilateral agencies in Africa.

Given the attributes and characteristics of the legal profession in Mauritius, it is unlikely that LPO will take off if it is left to the local legal community. For LPO

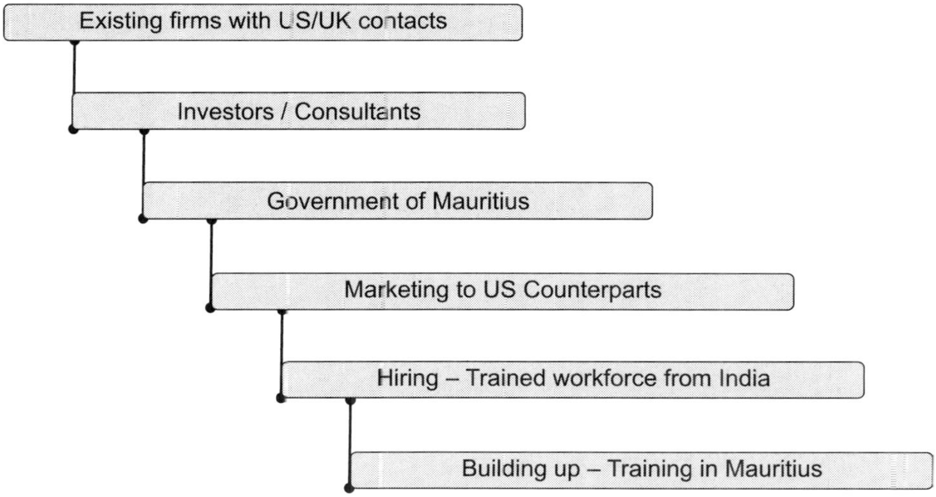

Figure 4.5 Strategies for developing a legal process outsourcing industry

Source: Presentation by Mr Pankaj Parnami at the Symposium on the Export of ICT-BPO-ITES Services

capability to materialise, Mauritius will require: (i) the entry of foreign firms specialising in LPO activity; (ii) interest on the part of locally established large BPO firms to enter LPO space through appropriate alliances with domestic and foreign law firms; and (iii) government-induced and sponsored large-scale import of qualified legal and paralegal professionals from India and Africa to staff the Mauritian LPO industry and help it to achieve take-off. However, like other areas of BPO activity, Mauritian legal process outsourcing will need to be geared towards special niches and client needs. It cannot be geared to 'mass production'.[12]

Hospitality, travel and tourism outsourcing

In 2006, the global hospitality, travel and tourism (HTT) industries added value of about US$1.76 trillion (or about 3.6 per cent) to world output. That amount is estimated rise to US$3 trillion (or 4 per cent of world GDP) in 2016. HTT is presently characterised by **in-country** outsourcing. However, as costs in OECD countries rise, and as new travel markets emerge (especially in India, China and ASEAN), there is ongoing customer demand for lowering the overall costs of HTT. The result has been **offshore** outsourcing increasing at an accelerating pace (from 10 per cent annual growth in 2006 to an estimated 15 per cent by 2010), although this still accounts for an insignificant proportion of HTT business.[13]

Global trends in HTT suggest that every segment of the industry faces:

i. **intensive global competition**, with large rates of attrition but also new entrants in new geographies and new niche areas emerging continuously – e.g. ecotourism, adventure tourism, knowledge tourism etc;

ii. **pressures to lower the cost of distribution** – on the part of the **hospitality industry, tourism-transport industry** (airlines, cruise ships, railways, coach tours, car rental firms etc.), the **restaurant industry**, the **tourism-dependent entertainment industry** and the **package-tour industry** – with a progressive shift to an internet-based, ITES-driven 'direct-to-customer' service replacing reliance on 'agents';

iii. **a higher degree of customer choice and empowerment**, permitting them to keep changing their preferences and their service providers at will and with speed;

iv. **demands for higher levels of individualisation and customisation**;

v. rapidly rising fuel and labour costs, which are triggering **pressures to lower all other operational costs**;

vi. **pricing pressures** from 'bulk HTT buyers' – such as major corporate travel accounts – on 'bulk sellers' of HTT services (e.g. airlines, car rental companies and hotel chains); and

vii. **rapid changes in technology** in every sphere of HTT operations, which is reducing the life cycles of products, services and tourism equipment, with customers demanding the 'latest' technology in every segment.

Confronted with such circumstances, and with potential for customer-centric market opportunities, it is surprising that the industry structure of hospitality, travel and tourism outsourcing (HTTO) service providers remains so fragmented. Specific BPO activities that need to be managed in the HTT domain are portrayed below. The universe of HTTO operators is specialised by activity (i.e. by hotel chain, airline or package-tour operator) with a bias towards promoting in-house brands/services rather than offering optimal price-and-quality customer solutions. As yet, no significant BPO player has emerged with a low-cost **global** delivery model, that is to say providing HTTO in all services areas (hotels, transport, food etc.) and in all major languages, including English, 'FIGS' (French-Italian-German-Spanish), Chinese etc. The services being offered by large players are often provided without segment-specific geography or domain expertise outside their own domains. Customer feedback from around the world suggests a lack of well-trained staff knowledgeable about all aspects of HTT, who customers can deal with online or by phone.

To put things in perspective, if just 1 per cent of the HTTO market in the EU were outsourced to Mauritius, HTTO firms in the country would need 5,600 direct-selling agents and 12,000 call-centre and other employees. Although Mauritius has developed a unique global image as an HTT destination, it does not have even a fraction of that kind of BPO employment in HTTO. Clearly, with its limited labour resources Mauritius cannot begin to handle HTTO business volume related to the **personal** travel market – i.e. the business associated with retail package-tour sales. What it must specialise in is HTTO for the corporate 'bulk buy' market in parts of the world that are, at present, being inadequately served.

Most service providers like airlines, hotels, car rentals and so on have already established vendor relations for (home) in-country and offshore outsourcing, which is why the HTTO industry is as fragmented as it is. Stand-alone, specialist HTTO vendors have little chance of survival. Success is likely to accrue to established group players already in the industry (like Indigo or other well-known HTT groups in Mauritius) branching out into the HTTO domain and partnering with an appropriate Indian BPO partner (like Quattro), which is experienced in setting up the right BPO service platform.

As a niche player, Mauritius needs to focus its HTTO capabilities on the corporate and 'bulk-purchase' travel market, especially in geographies where it has language, cultural and competitive advantages (for instance, in France and other non-English speaking countries in the EU) over other HTTO service providers (such as India). There is little point in Mauritius attempting to capture HTTO business from the US. The island is too remote, culturally incompatible and unfamiliar with the demands of that marketplace. Instead, it needs to focus on the continental (and especially southern and new) EU, as well as the growing Australian, Indian, Chinese and ASEAN HTT markets, especially as far as Africa-related travel is concerned. There are also HTTO opportunities to be exploited in cargo operations and in the non-tourism travel market. Ticket processing is unlikely to be profitable, however, because of IATA licensing/qualification barriers.

For Mauritius to achieve HTTO success, intensive staff training will be necessary in languages, geography, food, cultural preferences, airline and shipping schedules, travel, safety and security anxieties, and other intricacies of the HTT business. There is no large local skill base with naturally acquired experience in the global HTT industry, people who are familiar with its ever-changing, complex demands. Given its middle-income status, and its relatively high employee cost structure, Mauritius cannot be a lost-cost, volume supplier of HTTO services. Nonetheless, it still needs to reduce costs in every other area that it can.

From that point of view, the cost of bulk connectivity and the absence of redundancy feed into the overall BPO cost chain counterproductively. Such costs might not be 'deal breakers' for firms aspiring to exploit the HTTO market, but they must, nevertheless, be lowered further. Moreover, it is important to realise that while connectivity costs might not be deal breakers, they are still sufficiently high to deter potential customers for HTTO services from considering Mauritius as a BPO location. The number of customers/BPO investors who stay away because of their own analysis of how Mauritius performs on key cost parameters, is unknown.

Triangulation involving Indian-Mauritian-South African partners might make sense in developing an HTTO capability in Mauritius. Such a partnership would widen the market that could be exploited if such resources were combined, and would lower overall operating costs as well. Yet bilateral deals are difficult enough to construct; trilateral arrangements would be even more complex. What is clear is that in this space, Mauritian firms will not be able to 'go it alone'.

Human resources recruitment, training and development outsourcing[14]

Recent research[15] undertaken to examine how the human resources (HR) function was being performed in the Fortune Top 500 companies suggested that, even as costs continue to rise, HR staff spend 56 per cent of their time on programme delivery and transactional activities. Only 32 per cent of their time is spent on value-added activities such as recruitment, monitoring benefits and compensation, HR performance and arranging appropriate HR training/development.

There has been rapid growth in human resources outsourcing (HRO) since 1998, with total contract value of HRO transactions projected to reach US$25.4 billion in 2007.[16] There are a variety of corporate needs driving the transformation of the HR function, including the need: (i) for HR to be more global and strategic; (ii) to find ways to significantly reduce the functional costs of HR-related activities; (iii) to improve service and quality to the HR base of a corporation; and finally (iv) to minimise or avoid repeated large capital investments in HR. Often, major companies resort to

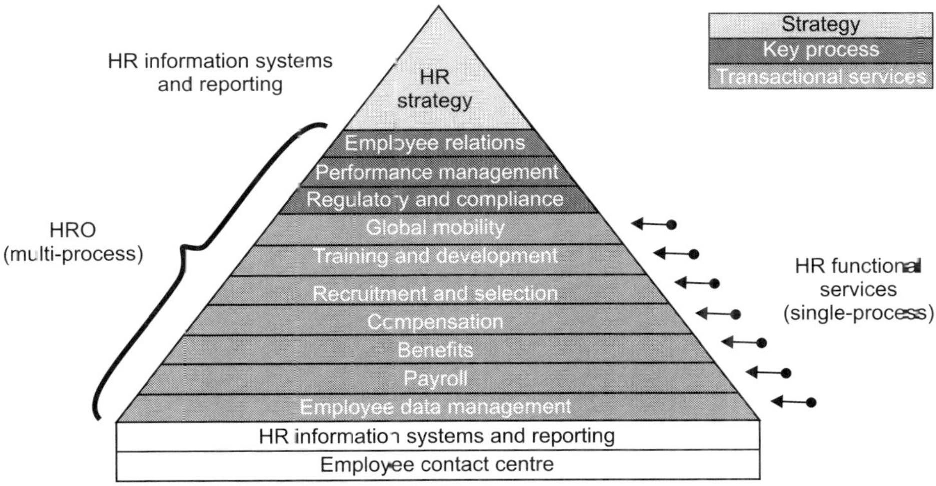

Figure 4.6 Multi-process human resources outsourcing versus single-process human resources functional services

Source: Presentation by Mr Vidia Mooneegan at the Symposium on the Export of ICT-BPO-ITES Services

outsourcing the HR management function when driven by a significant compelling event such as a merger, takeover or shift of geographic location. Alternatively, the function may be outsourced as a spin-off of the extant HR department to make it independent and enable more aggressive timelines to be achieved in delivering HR services. Often, given their core competencies (e.g. in IT or logistics) companies lack the specialised people, technology and processes needed to support HR in-house. Other reasons for outsourcing include:

- The need to completely transform the HR function in a particular context
- The need to improve service levels
- The need to lower the administrative cost of delivering HR services
- The need to increase business focus with retained organisation and to raise productivity
- Cost-cutting considerations, by replacing expensive managers
- Capital-cost avoidance
- Access to the latest technology at lower costs
- Compliance
- The need to comply with the Sarbanes Oxley Act (passed by the US Congress after the Enron debacle), EU directives and/or other regulatory mandates.

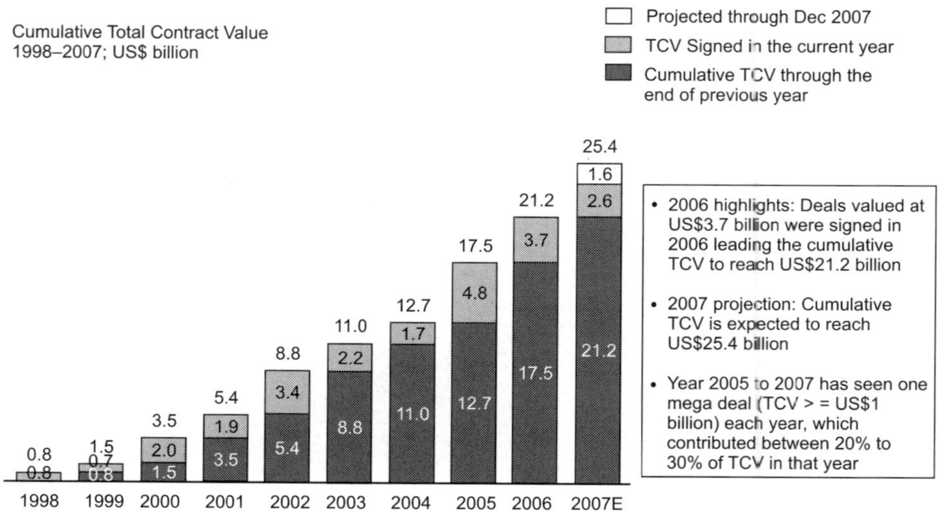

Figure 4.7 Cumulative total contract value of human resources outsourcing transactions
Source: Presentation by Mr Vidia Mooneegan at the Symposium on the Export of ICT-BPO-ITES Services

There are a variety of approaches to this transformation including: greater use of technology to execute HR transactions more efficiently, greater scale leverage and **HR business process outsourcing (HRO)**, defined as outsourcing of three or four transactional services, including but not limited to payroll, benefits, workforce administration and so forth.

The dominant companies operating in the global HRO space include Hewitt, Convergys, IBM, Accenture, ACS, ADP, ExcellerateHRO and Northgate ARINSO. For geographic and functional share the major companies in the HRO space see Everest Research Institute (2007).[17]

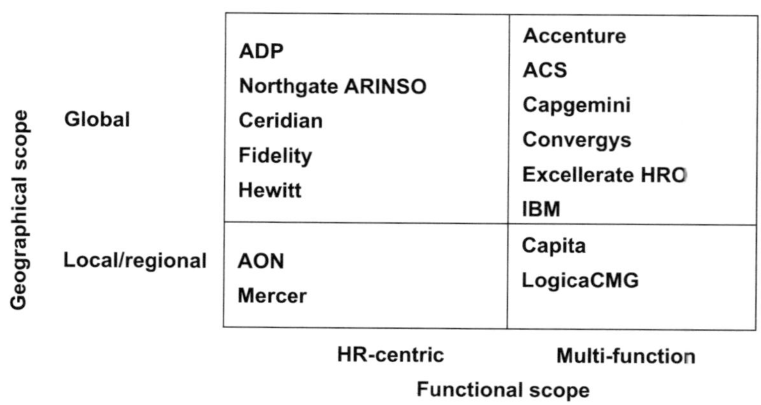

Figure 4.8 Global human resources business process outsourcing market 1
Source: Everest Research Institute

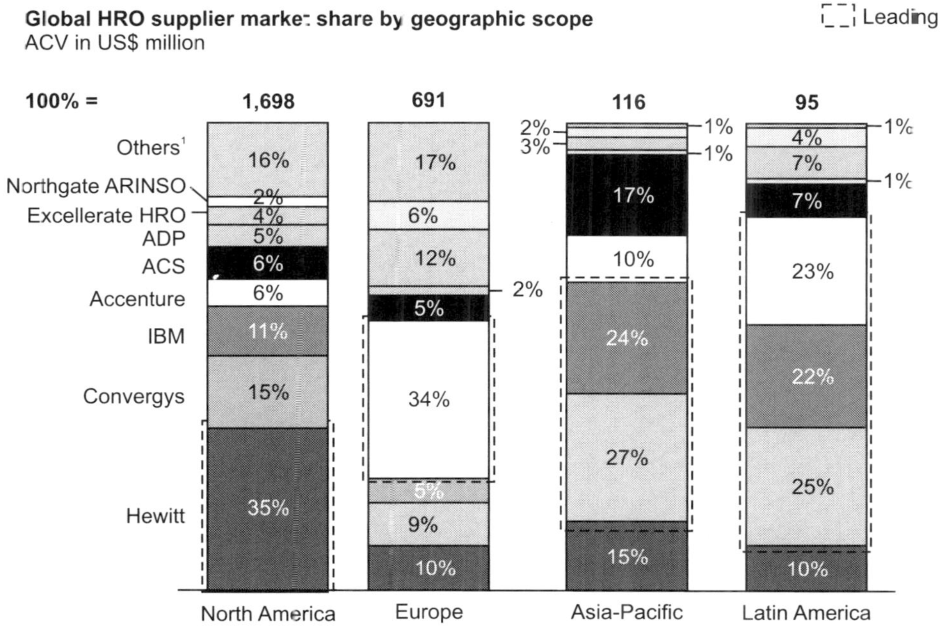

Figure 4.9 Global human resources business process outsourcing market 2

[1] Others include AON, Capita, Ceridian, Fidelity, Fujitsu, LogicaCMG, Mercer, Xansa, and Xchanging

Sample size: 207 HRO transactions signed as of July 2007

Note: We apportioned the revenues of global deals based on number of employees served in each geography

Source: Everest Reaserch Institute (2007)

The projected breakdown of HRO revenues (in US$ billion) between 2007 and 2010 can be found in table 4.5.

Table 4.5 Projected breakdown of HRO revenues, 2007-2010[18]

Service	CAGR*	2007	2008	2009	2010
Total HRO revenues (US$ billion)	13%+	35-38	40-42	45-47	48-54
› Payroll	10%+	18-19	20-21	22-23	23-25
› Benefits	11%+	10-11	11-12	13-14	14-16
› Talent management	20%+	2-3	3-4	4-4	4-5
› Other HR BPO**	15%+	4-5	5-6	6-7	7-8

* Compound Annual Growth Rate

** HR BPO is defined as outsourcing 3-4 transactional services, including but not limited to payroll, benefits, workforce administration etc.

HRO involves a multiplicity of functions, of which the most commonly outsourced are (in terms of frequency of inclusion within HRO transactions): employee contact centre (92 per cent), payroll (90 per cent), employee data management (85 per cent), benefits and compensation (77 and 60 per cent respectively), recruiting and selection (63 per cent), training and development (52 per cent), regulatory and compliance (51 per cent), performance management (35 per cent), global mobility (20 per cent), employee relations (7 per cent) and HR strategy (5 per cent).[19]

In terms of **future growth, trends and directions** for the **global** HRO industry, the following picture emerges:

- Market size is increasing at a more moderate pace than over the previous decade, with annual revenue growth of about 14 per cent in 2007;
- Global offshoring of HRO will continue to increase, with the main HRO service suppliers continuing to build global delivery networks to leverage capacity, capabilities and competitive pricing;
- The comfort levels of HRO buyers with offshoring is continuing to increase with experience, as offshoring emerges as one of the key value levers;
- An increasing number of smaller HRO deal sizes are being agreed and HRO services are becoming less packaged and more **'componentised'**;
- The EU market is seeing increased activity – it accounted for only 16 per cent of global HRO business in 2000, but for 26 per cent in 2007 – with regional and emerging HRO suppliers in 'new Europe' growing rapidly;
- Technology is becoming an increasingly critical component of the HRO evaluation and decision;
- HRO will become an increasingly attractive option for mid-size TNC and small and medium-sized enterprises (SME) buyers, especially as there is considerable untapped demand, given the low penetration of only 1.5 per cent of potential HR business being outsourced in the mid-size market;
- Under-served and under-outsourced segments of the HRO market are likely to be penetrated systematically over the next decade, resulting in global transformation of the HRO industry; and
- The trend toward HRO becoming an integral part of the multi-functional BPO market will accelerate, with established large firms (i.e. Accenture, Infosys, TCS etc.) absorbing more of that space.

Given this scenario, what niches can Mauritius exploit in this large, growing global service market? Mauritius has a track record with key HRO suppliers (Ceridian and Accenture), which have already established core competence with process expertise. This BPO segment offers considerable scope for Mauritius to move to higher-value activities by attracting as many of the principal global HRO vendors as possible to

Table 4.6 Global human resources outsourcing market size by service (US$ billion)

Service	Compound annual growth rate	2007	2008	2009	2010
HRO		35–38	40–42	45–47	48–54
Payroll	>10%	18–19	20–21	22–23	23–25
Benefits	>11%	10–11	11–12	13–14	14–16
Talent management	>20%	2–3	3–4	4	4–5
HR BPO[1]	>15%	4–5	5–6	6–7	7–8

[1] HR BPO is defined as outsourcing of generally three to four transactional services including but not limited to payroll, benefits, workforce administration, etc.

Source: Rajeev Grover, Hewitt, presentation at symposium on the export of ICT-BPO-ITES services

expand their global delivery models from a Mauritian centre. The island is ideally positioned to serve the growing European market, because it is more competitive than Eastern European locations and can exploit its bilingual capabilities to better advantage.

What Mauritius needs to do is upgrade its existing HRO centres to offer better-priced HRO services, such as employee contact and employee data management services. The mid-size company market has the highest growth potential. This is because HRO covers a wide spectrum of functions, making it possible for small-size service providers to develop a niche approach. Mauritius needs, therefore, to pursue a strategy of encouraging – through direct and indirect support – large multi-function BPO service providers to expand and grow into HRO and, at the same time, encouraging the emergence of small-niche players to exploit specialised corners of the global HRO market that are not yet being fully exploited by the global majors.

The particular challenges Mauritius faces are that: (i) the bundling of IT into BPO is higher in HRO compared to other outsourced functions; (ii) the confidentiality and security of personal data, of HR processes and the integrity of people employed are critical for customer confidence; and so (iii) Mauritius needs to have a stronger Data Protection Act in force as soon as possible.

Media, entertainment and animation services

Media, entertainment and animation (MEA) services is a rapidly growing segment of the information technology enabled service (ITES) industry, yet it is a difficult one to encapsulate as easily as other BPO segments. The structure, dimensions and rapidly expanding contours of MEA outsourcing embrace several segments, many of which are still nascent. It includes outsourcing for: the print and electronic media, both general and specialised (technical/professional) media; the conceptualisation, design and production of hard and soft audiovisual content for the global and local advertising industries; media companies engaged in producing or altering for different markets (i.e. through translation, dubbing etc.) any conceivable form of hard or soft audio, visual or combined audiovisual content (music, games, interactive situations, documentaries, reality shows, entertainment, drama, theatre, opera, ballet, educational or information) for television, cinema or the web; and increasingly animation. There are no overall industry studies available that provide a sense of the dimensions of this aggregated grab bag of creative and highly skilled technical services.

The kind of service opportunities that exist in the media, entertainment and animation outsourcing (MEAO) domain are perhaps best exemplified by:

- A specialised publishing/digitisation enterprise headquartered in France, but with most of its people and production located in Bucharest, Mauritius and Madagascar
- A film studio operating from Germany and Mauritius
- A rapidly growing animation company from India, which is considering locating in Mauritius

These vignettes are perhaps more evocative and illustrative of the possibilities that exist for Mauritius in this particular creative domain than any reiteration of statistics might be.

Diadeis

The first of these case studies concerns **Diadeis**, a French company established in 1676. It is a highly specialised **precision engineering** company dedicated to the production of data and documents through two divisions: publishing and data digitisation. Both divisions process, industrialise, harmonise, manage, structure and deliver highly detailed, precise, sophisticated material of different types published with very short lead times. It does this at lower cost than would normally apply in the OECD world through **in-sourcing** from wholly owned **offshore** locations. To manage and update in real time its customers' large databases, Diadeis processes and digitises the proprietorial data upon which they rely. The publishing division's outputs include: printed material and information disseminated on CD-ROMs and on the web. Its publications are multilingual and highly technical (e.g. manuals and legal reference books). For example, Diadeis publishes the official *EU Journal*, which requires the production of 133,000 pages annually in 23 languages using 38 processes (27 automated and 11 manual); produces technical and marketing brochures for Renault (25,000 pages annually used in 15 countries); and produces over 1,000 different types of packages for Nestle foodstuffs in seven different languages for global use.

The digitisation division uses manual inputs, optical character recognition (OCR) technology and XML structuring to vectorise and scan vast quantities of data and to organise the output into usable information. This division has undertaken, for example: the digitisation of French land registry archives (GILFAM), a task that involved digitising eight million pages using 16 automated and nine manual processes, which took more than three years; and the creation of a geographical reference index of French cadastral surveys, which involved 200,000 detailed cadastral maps providing 3,000,000 national co-ordinates and 9,000,000 local references, with 160 operators undertaking 42 tasks (25 automated and 17 manual). These maps were developed using four principal data sources: topographic, ortho-photographic, parcel maps and individual addresses.

Organising itself on an **'offshore in-sourcing'** model, Diadeis has 70 staff in France and 40 in Romania, complemented by 780 employees in Madagascar and Mauritius. The Paris HQ has 35 people who manage the company, undertake major project management, R&D and technical consultancy functions. A satellite unit in Nancy has 35 people undertaking scanning, automatic page layout and R&D functions. In Bucharest, Romania, 40 people carry out multilingual proofreading, page layout and quality control. These EU-based skills are leveraged by a larger employee base in Mauritius, where 180 people undertake highly skilled work involving DTP, publishing, geographical referencing and packaging artwork and reproduction. Diadeis has an even larger base in lower-cost Madagascar, where 600 people undertake work related to XML inputs, file conversions, cadastral map conversions and automatic page layouts.

Having established itself in Mauritius in 1996, on the basis of its experience, Diadeis ranks the island highest as an outsourcing destination for a French employer in the MEAO domain for the following reasons:

- It is located in a convenient time zone, with a two or three hours difference from Paris time
- It is bilingual, making it possible to employ people fluent in French and English
- It is familiar with sophisticated IT technology
- The working environment is similar to that of Europe, but expensive compared to other offshoring locations
- Its educational system is good, but nonetheless produces limited qualified human resources; as a result, scalability is focused in Madagascar rather than Mauritius
- Its society and culture are more occidental, rather than African or Asian in nature
- Confidence in its political system and adherence to rule-of-law is relatively high
- Compared to the EU, its labour costs are competitive and flexible (although not compared to Asia).

A comparison provided by Diadeis of a number of possible outsourcing destinations, indicating the level of attractiveness, is given in Table 4.7.

Table 4.7 Offshore countries comparison by level of attractiveness

Country\Criteria	Labour cost	Time zone	Language	Technology	Education	Culture	Political confidence
Mauritius	high	high	high	high	medium	medium	high
Romania/Poland/ Bulgaria	medium	high	medium	high	high	high	high
Tunisia/Morocco/ Senegal	high	high	high	medium	medium	medium	medium
Madagascar	high	high	medium	medium	medium	medium	low
India	high	low	low	high	high	low	high
China/Indonesia/ Vietnam	high	low	low	medium	medium	low	medium

Source: Presentation by Mr Eric Legent at the Symposium on the Export of ICT-BPO-ITES Services

Yet Diadeis has found that locating in Mauritius is not problem free, challenges being that (i) the output of the local education system is insufficient in both quantitative and qualitative terms for the needs of this industry; (ii) consequently, Diadeis has had to create its own school of design and training, which is a high-cost activity for a small, specialised company; (iii) the '*pena problema* syndrome' (i.e. the automatic 'no problem' response resulting in everything becoming a problem), which requires intensive management and control procedures to ensure that things get done when they should, deadlines are met and quality control is not compromised; (iv) telecom costs limit the firm's global competitiveness. These constraints result in Diadeis not recruiting as many Mauritians, nor locating as much activity in Mauritius, as it would ideally like to do.

Under its tailored, offshore in-sourcing model, Diadeis does not see Mauritius as a BPO/MEAO destination where low value-added processes can be externalised. Instead, Mauritius is a place where highly specialised SMEs like Diadeis can invest and locate skilled EU managers and professionals (because of an amenable environment, climate and lifestyle) to achieve global standards of productivity and competitiveness in a win-win deal. Mauritius leads in attracting similar French firms. However, the Government of Mauritius should understand that this leadership position is not embedded nor guaranteed for all time. In fact it is quite precarious, with a balance that can tip the other way at any time. Despite this, Diadeis' dealings with the authorities have engendered considerable confidence that issues will be dealt with efficiently and with flexibility in policy-making and action.

Eruption Studios

The second case study involves a production studio (Eruption Studios) that carries out the following tasks.

A. Audio work using Pro-Tools configurations and related audio software to do:

- Production of commercial spots for TV and radio advertising
- Sound designing
- Audio conception for video games and/or related projects
- External sound recording for TV and film production
- Audio-dubbing for TV and film production
- Conceptualisation and production of corporate 'jingles' for TV/radio commercials
- Audio post-production on video
- Advertising spots conceptualisation
- Pre-production for radio programmes, theatrical shows etc.

B. Video work using Avid Xpress and Beta SP DVPro to undertake:

- Film editing on outsourced TV productions and language dubbing
- Video post-production and video animation
- Commercial advertising spots and corporate films

C. Multimedia work using Flash MX, Dreamweaver MX and Adobe Suite CS2 to do:

- Web designing, hosting and maintenance
- Flash animation
- Graphic design
- Corporate ID
- Music and video online
- CD ROM/Interactive etc.
- Programming: Action Script, PHP, CSS, Javascript, XHTML, DHTML

In its specialised domain, Eruption employs top-level skills from abroad to acquire contracts and undertake production for its EU and global clientele. These include **sound engineers and designers** for creative audio and video work, including experienced specialists from France for audio engineering and sound-editing for films; **IT developers and Web designers** to run the company's multimedia facility and train local staff, as well as to develop the company's service export markets by sourcing foreign clients; and **experienced film editors** from the EU who have edited prime-time movies made for TV, to outsource film editing contracts (mainly from Germany) and to train local staff.

With its expatriate and local staff base, the studio has: carried out radio and TV commercial work for global clients (including Coca Cola, Pepsi Cola, Orangina, KFC, Nestle's HSBC, Barclays, Renault, Nissan and IBL Products) as well as regional/local clients such as (MCB, Chantecler, BAI, Emtel, Cellplus, Canal Sat, Parabole Maurice & Reunion); produced corporate films for local groups such as Beachcomber, Bois Cherie, Floreal and Novel); and has carried out a host of miscellaneous productions, such as musical conception/production of the AAA awards, musical productions of theatrical and comedy shows, dubbing for Bollywood films and son-et-lumiere productions.

Maya Entertainment

The third case study for entry into Mauritius is that of a rapidly growing Indian animation company, Maya Entertainment. A recent NASSCOM Report (2007)[20] estimated the value-added of the global animation industry at US$70 billion, with Indian animation value-addition at US$900 million by 2010. Animation production services generated revenue of US$350mn in 2006 and the Indian animation industry will employ more than 30,000 professionals by 2010. Animation is an ITES activity particular suited to Mauritius because it is:

- A niche domain with specialised training needs
- Independent of geography, source or ethnicity
- Characterised by somewhat high barriers to entry
- An industry where firm size matters less: a studio with 50 people is mid-sized; one with 250 people it is large (Pixar was sold for US$7.5bn with less than 1,500 employees)
- An ITES service area that provides opportunities to move up the value chain rapidly

Animation verticals comprise: films, TV series, e-learning, video games, corporate videos, scientific visualisation, social networking and Web content. The value-chain in animation includes: infrastructure services (game hosting, grid computing clusters); localisation services (subtitles, dubbing, menus); production services (work for hire, WFH); design and creative services (WFH); co-productions; intellectual property (IP) creation; and distribution and merchandising. The degree of specialisation involved has led Maya Entertainment to establish its own academy for training in response to a shortage of talent, even in a vast labour pool like India's. The Maya Academy has grown from one in-house centre in 2002 to over 60 centres (directly owned and franchised) in six years. It teaches industry standard courses certified by Cambridge University Exams and has graduated more than 10,000 animators since its start up.

With its considerable artistic and creative talent, Mauritius is an ideal location for establishing a number of niche firms in the growing area of animation services, starting by encouraging proven firms like Maya to locate in the island. The government, BoI and Enterprise Mauritius need to prioritise animation services as a key thrust area for future development and explore what needs to be done to make that happen. Specifically, the following objectives have to be achieved:

- Promoting creative and fine arts as commercial, not just cultural, activities;
- Promoting awareness in local industry and the community at large of the commercial potential that media and animation services have;
- Setting up training programmes for media outsourcing specialists and animators;
- Establishing an ASIFA (*Association International du Film d'Animation*) chapter in Mauritius;
- Attracting captive offices of animation production studios from India, the EU and North America (especially Canada);
- Encouraging local industry and government to commission animated content as part of their own promotional and advertising programmes on TV and the web;
- Negotiating co-production treaties for media services and animation with key countries (e.g. the UK, France, Canada, the US, India, China, Singapore and South Africa); and
- Framing strong intellectual property rights (IPR) laws for the protection of content.

Mauritius as an African outsourcing gateway

In attracting FDI – whether in financial services, establishing regional headquarters, creating an African transport hub and so on – Mauritius has invariably been represented by Board of Investment (BoI) to, for example, Indian and Chinese investors, as an ideal entrée into Africa (particularly into francophone Africa, i.e. Madagascar and Central/West Africa). This has been done with global ICT firms as well. Is such representation myth or reality? Where ICT is concerned, four questions relating to Africa are critical: (i) Does Mauritius have privileged access to the regional market in Africa? (ii) What is the state of Africa's ICT industry, which reflects its absorptive capacity to handle outsourced services? (iii) What is the width and depth of the African outsourcing market? and (iv) Are African countries sources of ICT skills that Mauritius does not have **in the quantity it needs** to achieve minimum critical size in many of the specific outsourcing segments identified above?

Mauritius may appear to outsiders to have good access to the **sub-regional** COMESA market, and beyond that to the continental and francophone African markets. That impression is fortified by membership in a number of regional arrangements, i.e. COMESA, SADC, the Francophonie, the African, Caribbean and Pacific (ACP) group of states, the Commonwealth, the Indian Ocean Rim, the African Union (AU) etc.

Asian and EU citizens often feel more comfortable living in Mauritius to carry out African business, than to live in Africa, other than perhaps in South Africa (which itself has security, political and ethnic problems to deal with).

In reality, it has proven difficult to convert the superficial **'notion'** of Mauritius as a gateway to Africa into a practical business reality, except to say that Mauritius has access to opportunities in Madagascar and, possibly Mozambique, because its sugar and tourism (and to a lesser extent textiles) industries have established business beachheads in those countries. Mauritius's access to Africa is arguably worse than that of South Africa or other countries on the continent. Intra-regional investment and trade in Africa, or in any of its sub-regions, is minuscule. Mauritius's membership of COMESA, SADC and the AU give it no particular advantage. The island's air and telecom connectivity to Africa is worse than Nairobi's or Johannesburg's; indeed, Dubai has better air and shipping connections to African capitals than Mauritius, as do London, Paris, Frankfurt and Rome. Thus the notion that Mauritius has privileged access to Africa – however often repeated – may be no more than a self-serving, but erroneous, mirage.

When it comes to the state of ICT, it has to be accepted that outside of Mauritius, South Africa, Botswana and Namibia, ICT infrastructure in Africa is undeveloped. As at November 2007, Internet penetration in Africa was only 5 per cent, although 'use growth' in 2000–2007 was 879 per cent compared to 214 per cent for the rest of the world. African communications infrastructure is extremely weak, but major projects are being undertaken that will change that situation over time. The regional African outsourcing market for Mauritius is almost non-existent at present, with the only serious market prospect being South Africa. Yet South Africa is also Mauritius's strongest competitor in Africa for the outsourcing business.

Prima facie, there might be opportunities to undertake outsourced work for national or sub-regional companies operating transport services (especially airlines and shipping companies); financial services (such as banks, exchanges, brokerages and insurance companies); media services (such as production of content for TV stations in anglophone and francophone Africa); HR services; and possibly for e-government. There might be isolated opportunities for capturing BPO from **foreign** companies (e.g. mining companies, as well as manufacturing and services firms) operating in all or parts of Africa, which might want to have back-up and security in a location that is commercially viable and politically stable. There may even be unexplored opportunities for BPO and KPO from **regional institutions** like COMESA, SADC and the AU (e.g. for ABSO, LPO, HR, media services etc.) not to mention **multilaterals** like the African Development Bank (AfDB), World Bank and the European Development Fund (EDF), as well as **bilateral aid agencies** operating across the continent.

However, 'conceptual possibility' is far removed from practical achievability. Most African companies in areas that offer the largest BPO opportunities are **parastatals.** They are subject to public procurement rules (and inhibitions), which are open to corruption to secure contracts. Their proclivity to outsource offshore (even if lower cost, greater efficiency and better quality might be achieved) is limited. Outsourcing decisions are not made strictly on commercial criteria.

Taking all that into account, it becomes clear that exploiting BPO opportunities from Africa will need substantial front-end investment, i.e. investment of a kind that global companies like Accenture, Infosys, TCS etc. can afford. But can local Mauritian ICT services companies invest in this way without public support? In addition, outsourcing contracts in domains like ABSO, E/ASO and LPO, will require larger numbers of low-cost workers than Mauritius has. This situation might require: importing skills from Madagascar, Mozambique or other low-cost countries and coping with the immigration consequences; Mauritian ICT companies investing in Madagascar to acquire a low-cost workforce; or working with Indian partners that have the low-cost processing capacity, but need to use Mauritius as a front-end interface for dealing with African and French clients.

Finally, are African countries a potential source of critically needed HR in the IBI industry? If instructive examples like Diadeis are to be taken seriously, the answer has to be affirmative. It is possible that, relying on its own limited base of human resources, Mauritius will not be able to exploit BPO opportunities in areas where rapid scalability is important, i.e. to attract and retain core clients around the world whose needs will expand. That constraint can be relieved if Mauritius can access qualified labour (e.g. accountants, lawyers, engineers, architects etc.) from South Africa, Madagascar, Mozambique and other East African countries, or countries like Zimbabwe, which has experienced mass emigration of highly qualified professionals in the last few years.

By the same token, Mauritius can attract the HR it needs from the EU, South Asia and ASEAN. Although this would perhaps be at a higher nominal cost, it may not necessarily be at a higher 'risk-adjusted' overall cost (including the cost of training, local absorption and/or possible eventual repatriation). The issue is one of **optimising** HR sourcing, given what the Mauritian labour market might need and what Mauritian society is prepared to absorb, as the IBI industry develops.

There, will, of course, be consequences for immigration and absorption into the local economy, regardless of the sources from which HR is attracted. Mauritian policy-makers and society at large will need to take these into account, and adjust labour market and immigration policies to accommodate and ameliorate (rather than exacerbate) local socio-cultural and politico-ethnic sensitivities. However, the **realpolitik** of increased immigration aside, in an overall sense there can be no doubt that Africa, along with the EU and South Asia, is an important source of HR to meet Mauritius's IBI labour market needs, as that industry grows and becomes more specialised and sophisticated.

Based on that overall assessment, Africa as a **market** for BPO provides relatively infertile ground as far as immediate opportunities are concerned. Yet it may be essential for Mauritius to exploit first-mover advantage in developing African BPO opportunities for the **medium and long term**, if only because Africa is the next major emerging market frontier. The continent may provide Mauritius with a useful source of IBI opportunity growth beyond the next decade, if local firms have the foresight and resources to look beyond the horizon.

Nonetheless, if Africa is to be developed as a future BPO source market, some key challenges will need to be addressed. These include, *inter alia*: (i) close collaboration between the IBI industry and government, with both being required to understand properly the precise nature of each client industry's focus, its costs, constraints and pattern of evolution, and where BPO might help that industry to transform its prospects; (ii) much larger amounts of public and private investment in strengthening and expanding communication gateways, i.e. air, sea and wavelengths; (iii) investment in a larger pool of qualified, professional staff; (iv) substantial product/service knowledge about the unique BPO needs of each industry being targeted as a possible source market; and (v) bringing to bear an extraordinarily high level of technical competency, along with professional ethics and integrity.

There are four main constraints to developing African BPO opportunities: technical, governmental, structural and socio-political constraints. To elaborate, the **technical** constraints concern: the limited availability of reliable/efficient world-class port and airport services; the high-cost, limited reliability and indifferent quality of communication gateways with no back-up redundancy; and insufficient (i.e. less than world-class) competency of key players in local industries that have BPO market potential in Africa (e.g. airlines, airport, shipping, logistics, banking, insurance etc.).

Similarly, the **governmental** constraints include: insufficient understanding on the part of ministries and civil servants of various industries' capabilities, needs and strategies; a lack of trust and confidence between public and private sectors when it comes to each other's motives, practices and tendencies; and confusion about the values that Mauritius must have to be successful as a global centre for BPO – i.e. a more obvious 'hard-work' rather than 'work-to-rule' or 'work-to-hours' ethic, combined with honesty, efficiency, professionalism and integrity as personal attributes across the labour force.

There is no obvious ingrained sense of social responsibility in the Mauritian private corporate sector. Nor is there a lack of corruption, favouritism or perceived adherence to ethnic affiliations and loyalty, in the public sector. On all these individual attributes – critical where BPO value-addition is concerned – Mauritius needs to examine how short it falls.[21]

Structural constraints include the lack of quality/quantity of HR output compatible with meeting the needs of a labour market, which has to compete on equal terms with the rest of the world, and a public sector ethos/culture that is **not** attuned to quality, competency, efficiency, innovation or competition, but is geared to outmoded protectionist postures that emphasise what cannot be done, rather than focusing on what can be done and how. Additional structural constraints are: a private corporate sector that has traditionally been inward-looking, managerially weak and concerned more about protecting domestic market space, rather than having the vision and developing the ability to compete globally; a national attitude that is lacking in confidence, and that is wedded to political and social practices that rely on ethnic linkages, patronage and political connections rather than meritocracy in promoting talent; and a relative lack of emphasis – at the country, industry, company and individual levels – on investing in knowledge, innovation, competitiveness, and R&D.

Finally, the island's **socio-political** constraints concern the high, seemingly inherent instability of Africa, where democratic roots have not yet taken hold, and the risk of ethnically- and tribally-driven social unrest remains high. Security for people remains a major concern, with weak governments incapable of providing law and order. Africa is also plagued by uncertainty about policy and administrative consistency and continuity: will decisions taken by today's government be implemented under a new government tomorrow? While Mauritius remains a stable safe haven compared to its counterparts on the continent, will that situation always remain, in a polity that still places so much emphasis on ethnic loyalties rather than merit? These large and difficult questions remain to be answered.

Notes

1. Figures derived from National Information & Communications Technologies Strategic Plan (NICTSP).
2. The *National Information & Communication Technologies Strategic Plan* (NICTSP): Ministry of Information Technology & Telecommunications, Government of Mauritius, Port Louis, 2007.
3. AT Kearney Global Services Location Index 2007. As presented by Mr Johan Gott at the Symposium on the Export of ICT-BPO-ITES Services.
4. Survey carried out by the American Institute of Architects and the Harvard Design School at Harvard University, 2004 (reported in a book published by the Harvard Design School in 2005 entitled *Understanding Architectural Services Outsourcing*. See http://harvarddesignbooks.stores.yahoo.net/unouarse.html [accessed 5 January 2009].
5. Ibid.
6. The NASSCOM/Booz Allen study Globalization of Engineering Services – The Next Frontier for India is the first to take a systematic and comprehensive view of the role of emerging markets in engineering services, assessing the evolution of the engineering market from 2005–2020. The study examined product and component design, plant design, process engineering and plant maintenance operations, for industries including automotive, aerospace, high tech, utilities, construction and industrial machinery. See: http://www.boozallen.com/news/8471428 [accessed 5 January 2009].
7. See above two footnotes for sources.
8. See presentation by Ms Josie Lapierre, Symposium on the Export of ICT-BPO-ITES Services.

9. Source: Hildebrandt International. See http://www.hildebrandt.com/ [accessed 5 January 2009].

10. Source: Value Notes. See http://www.valuenotes.biz/ [accessed 5 January 2009]. Business research and competitive intelligence firm Value Notes is the number two market analysis and research vendor per survey results published in the 2007 edition of *The Black Book of Outsourcing*.

11. The Mauritian legal profession comprises some 500 practising lawyers and another 500 paralegals, with an annual output of 50 new law graduates. This compares to over a million lawyers in India, with an annual output of 80,000 new law graduates, and over 400,000 in the Philippines, with an annual output of 25,000 new graduates.

12. For more details, see presentation by Mr Pankaj Parnami, Symposium on the Export of ICT-BPO-ITES Services.

13. Note: Outsourcing HTT customer-service jobs, mainly to in-country phone agents, is still only a $3-billion-a-year business, according to PRC Inc.

14. For more details see presentations by Mr Vidia Mooneegan and Mr Rajeev Grover, Symposium on the Export of ICT-BPO-ITES Services.

15. HR Analyzer (2007). Hewitt Associates, LLC, New York, USA. The online HR Analyzer provides the factual insight you need to verify that HR resources are aligned with your organisation's business strategy, taking the guesswork out of assessing where and on what HR is spending its time and money.

16. Mr Vidia Mooneegan, Managing Director, Ceridian, Mauritius.

17. See http://www.everestresearchinstitute.com/ [accessed 5 January 2009].

18. Mr Rajeev Grover, HR Outsourcing, Asia/Pacific Leader, Hewitt.

19. Mr Vidia Mooneegan, Managing Director, Ceridian, Mauritius.

20. See: http://www.nasscom.in/Nasscom/templates/NormalPage____28721.aspx [accessed 5 January 2009].

21. Note: While these attributes are seen as critical for BPO success, if Mauritius is compared with India on these criteria, it comes out ahead on most.

5

Exporting Healthcare Services

Healthcare and life science services: emerging issues and conflicts

'Healthcare services outsourcing', 'healthcare exports' and 'medical tourism' are widely recognised terms used interchangeably. They embrace different activities, varying from simple medical transcription, to healthcare-related BPO (such as payroll, billing and patient records functions of hospitals) and the provision of a full range of complex surgery and medical services.

Sophisticated healthcare and life science services (HLSS) have been exported for over 150 years by OECD countries such as the US,[1] UK, France, Germany and Switzerland. However, until recently, these services were not recognised/quantified as 'healthcare service exports' explicitly. It was regarded as being in 'the natural order of things' for major metropolitan centres and imperial capitals to provide such services. Yet now, driven by the economics of globalisation and huge cost disparities, such services are being provided by emerging specialised corporate hospital groups – with a growing record of experience in healthcare services outsourcing – from **developing** countries.

These groups are establishing a global presence with recognised world-quality brands. Operating from developing countries like India, Malaysia, Thailand and South Africa, such groups are also based in the Gulf States and in newly developed economies (such as Singapore). Extending concepts of outsourcing/offshoring that have become established in sectors other than healthcare, their aim is to capture market share in global HLSS exports, especially in high-value medical activities such as: cardiovascular, neuro-, orthopaedic, obstetric, ophthalmic, urinary and paediatric surgery; long-term patient rehabilitation and psychiatric care; and increasingly in geriatric and terminal care. They are succeeding in doing so, despite facing many obstacles and barriers – ranging from the lack of portability of national healthcare insurance (especially when public) to accreditation and certification being used as protectionist barriers.

The healthcare/wellbeing sphere embraces more than allopathic (occidental) healthcare, including **alternative medicine** (homoeopathy, Ayurveda, acupuncture and acupressure) with oriental and natural origins, as well as cosmetic (e.g. plastic surgery, hair transplants, dermatology etc.) and **wellbeing therapies** (such as yoga, weight-loss, addiction treatment and meditation etc.) conducted in specialised spas or centres.

Often, 'export of healthcare services' includes implicitly **training** non-national medical personnel (doctors, nurses and paraprofessionals). This is because such training is highly specialised and invariably linked to, or dependent upon, a strong connection with healthcare delivery facilities such as teaching hospitals.

To explore opportunities for Mauritius in this burgeoning new global market, a symposium on the export of healthcare and life science services (HLSS) was held in April 2008. At that event, the case was outlined for Mauritius becoming: (i) a regional centre of excellence for medical tourism, medical and nurse training, and the outsourcing/export of a wide range of healthcare, life science and wellbeing services; as well as (ii) a regional centre for preclinical and clinical trials, and for particular phases of pharmaceutical and cosmetic-product research.

The symposium emphasised the willingness of the Government of Mauritius in general, and the Ministry of Health and Quality of Life in particular, to enact requisite legal, regulatory and policy changes to facilitate achieving this goal, in particular by encouraging public and private investment in the development of essential HLSS-related infrastructure. The importance of carefully structured public-private partnerships (PPPs) in facilities like hospitals and specialised clinics was underlined, as was the creation of dedicated zones and facilities to attract pharmaceutical firms to undertake preclinical/clinical trials in Mauritius. The government was committed to developing HLSS as a key area of new service export activity and was prepared to do whatever was necessary to achieve that goal.

Unlike the export of **financial** and **ICT/BPO services** discussed in previous chapters, **healthcare exports** are only incipient in Mauritius. For that reason, considerations concerning the **export** of HLSS – and the culture, policies and public, as well as private, institutional structures needed for that purpose – are invariably confused with **domestic** considerations and policies. Mauritian healthcare professionals (as well as political leaders, policy-makers, ministry officials and regulators) find it difficult to disentangle in their minds the distinct requirements of export markets from those of the domestic market for these services. Invariably, the implications of policy and practice aimed at encouraging HLSS **exports** spill over into concerns about what that would imply for the **domestic** healthcare domain.

In attempting to develop export capability for such services from Mauritius, this core confusion cannot be dismissed or overridden as a fearful protectionist response. It has to be anticipated and adroitly managed through a transitional phase. Given the diminutive size of the domestic Mauritian healthcare system and market – i.e. relative to the potential global market share (of 1–2 per cent) that Mauritius could capture for HLSS exports – it will, of course, be difficult to keep these two markets separate/distinct for all time. Indeed, it might be unwise and inefficient to do so. The domestic HLSS market was founded and has been run on UK/French-inspired lines – with 'free at the point of use' universal access to healthcare in government-financed clinics and hospitals. The HLSS export market is likely to be dominated almost entirely by private players charging full payment for services rendered on a 'total cost recovery plus a profit margin' basis.

The presence of such private players in Mauritius will not be ignored by the domestic population, especially if they provide better facilities (hospitals, clinics) and better (global) standards of service delivery and care. Politically and practically, it will be impossible to keep the two markets separate. The local population cannot artificially be denied access to better HLSS services enjoyed by a transient foreign population.

Eventually, the domestic HLSS sector will be absorbed into a unified HLSS-delivery structure operating on global lines. Paradoxically, that opens up the possibility that the Government of Mauritius will be able to provide universal free healthcare by **financing local demand**, but **not necessarily providing local supply**, through the public-health system. It can rely instead on private HLSS infrastructure created for the global HLSS market. The government may save fiscal resources (capital and recurrent) by 'piggybacking' on a much larger and more diverse **private** HLSS industry, one that is created and evolves to service (and is driven largely by) the global export market.

This policy challenge is not imminent, and the dilemma it poses does not have to be resolved immediately. Indeed, it is unlikely to be addressed until the export-orientated HLSS industry grows to be of sufficient size to exceed the domestic HLSS-delivery system. That may not happen for a decade at least. Yet it is an issue for which political groundwork and administrative preparation needs to start now. Dealing with the issue honestly and openly may be an effective strategy for overcoming domestic (professional, union and civil society) resistance to change (based on fear of change and the unknown) and to opening up the HLSS sector for private entry, even if it is limited only to HLSS exports.

The global market for HLSS exports

Global healthcare expenditure was estimated at US$4.5 trillion in 2006. This figure accounts for about 8 per cent of global GDP, with **per capita healthcare expenditure** averaging US$800 worldwide. However, that average can be misleading. When disaggregated, the US$4.5 trillion figure shows up the following pattern:

- A spend of US$2.2 trillion in the US, with healthcare expenditure of US$7,200 per capita
- US$2.0 trillion in non-US OECD nations, with expenditure of about US$2,600 per capita
- A spend of US$300 billion elsewhere around the world: i.e. outside the US and the rest of the OECD, healthcare expenditures account for less than US$50 per capita

- The top (income) decile of the population accounts for about 80 per cent of healthcare spending in the developing world; this means five billion people account for an average healthcare spend of less than $15 per capita per year!
- Thus an average American spends 480 times more annually on healthcare than the average person in the developing world, while the rest of OECD spends 180 times more
- Paradoxically, these large disparities in global healthcare spending are resulting in OECD populations and societies facing more challenging demographic trends than non-OECD societies and populations, which are growing more rapidly; they are also driving cross-border HLSS.[2]

Cost differences in healthcare delivery between developed and developing countries is driving outsourcing and offshoring, while disparities in per capita health spending between poor and rich countries are driving the rapid growth of the overall global healthcare market.

Healthcare costs continue to rise rapidly in the US and the developed OECD world, with annual increases averaging about 7 per cent. Those costs are now unaffordable. Stresses and strains caused by public expenditure constraints are appearing in every OECD country's health system. There is increasing pressure to reduce costs, as demand for healthcare continues to grow with aging populations, the application of expensive new technologies and therapies, and higher expectations for quality care as a fundamental 'human right' on the part of OECD populations.

Developed OECD countries have less than 20 per cent of the world's population, but account for over 93 per cent of global healthcare expenditure.[3] This asymmetry reflects exploding healthcare costs in the developed world, which are leading to a rapid increase in HLSS exports. Such service exports (including outsourcing and offshoring healthcare services [BPO], as well direct medical services) are a relatively new – but rapidly growing – phenomenon. Continuing advances in ICT are making HLSS exports increasingly possible, attractive and competitive. They are being driven further by continuous advances in medical technology, globalisation, the entrenchment of service exports as a feature of world trade and large differences in the cost of healthcare delivery, as well as in the amount being spent on healthcare around the world.

At present, HLSS exports account for less than 0.5 per cent of global healthcare expenditures. By 2015, it is likely that they will account for 2 per cent of global health expenditure. That would mean HLSS exports accounting for about US$145 billion by 2015, compared to the US$25 billion they are estimated at today (in 1995 HLSS exports amounted to barely US$1 billion). There are few global industries with such rapid compounded annual growth.[4]

Given the multitude of activities involved in the HLSS domain, and accounting for the obvious duplication of what is counted as BPO revenue when it is related to healthcare, the global HLSS export market was estimated in 2007 to be over US$25 billion.[5] Medical tourism alone accounted for about 80 per cent of that total. Some illustrative stylised facts about the potential for HLSS exports are recorded below:

- Medical tourists logged an estimated 19 million trips and spent over US$20 billion in 2008.
- In 2006, more than 50,000 people from the UK travelled abroad for some medical treatment.
- The UK figure is projected to increase to 200,000 by 2010, creating a UK-healthcare offshoring market of between £900–1,000 million (US$1.8–2 billion).
- Extrapolating for the EU, a conservative estimate would be US$6–8 billion in 2010, involving about 650,000 Europeans travelling abroad for treatment.
- In 2007, 150,000 Americans went abroad for treatment, driven by medical costs in the US, with healthcare expenditure abroad amounting to US$ 2.5 billion.
- The medical tourism industry from the US is growing by 15–20 per cent annually.
- Malaysia had over 85,000 medical tourists in 2006, spending about US$0.6 billion.
- India catered for 175,000 health tourists in 2007 and expected 200,000 in 2008, with health-tourism revenues expected to be US$2.4 billion in 2010.
- Thailand has a rapidly growing medical tourism industry. In 2005, one hospital in Bangkok catered for 150,000 tourists. The market was estimated to be worth about US$1.8 billion in that year.
- Singapore Medicine is a multi-agency government initiative. Some 374,000 health tourists visited Singapore in 2005. That figure increased to nearly 500,000 in 2007 and the country is targeting one million medical tourists in 2012 for export earnings of about US$5 billion.
- South Africa hosted 30,000 medical tourists in 2006.

Healthcare offshoring is being driven by demand, supply and cost factors. To illustrate, HLSS offshoring can result in lowering treatment costs by 50–70 per cent. For example, a breast implant in the US costs US$25,000 for the operation alone, with additional costs for hospitalisation etc. In India, the same implant costs US$8,000 **including** flights, two weeks in a 4-star hotel, surgery, hospital recovery, local transport and post-op consultation. Waiting lists for various treatments can vary from 5–12 months in the UK, Canada, Europe and Australia. Offshoring can reduce these times to less than two months, if not eliminate them altogether.

Table 5.1 Comparative costs of major surgery in different countries (US$)

Procedure	US cost	India cost	Thailand cost	Singapore cost	Malaysia cost
Heart bypass	>130,000	10,000	11,000	18,500	9,000
Heart valve replacement	160,000	9,000	10,000	12,500	9,000
Angioplasty	57,000	11,000	13,000	13,000	11,000
Hip replacement	43,000	9,000	12,000	12,000	10,000
Hysterectomy	20,000	3,000	4,500	6,000	3,000
Knee replacement	40,000	8,500	10,000	13,000	8,000
Spinal fusion	62,000	5,500	7,000	9,000	6,000

The main drivers of demand in the sector are: (i) **demographic differences** across the globe; (ii) a heightened degree of **'healthcare consumerism'**; (iii) changing **epidemiology**; (iv) **technological advances** in ICT and medical technologies; and (v) a **global shortage of workers** at all levels in the healthcare industry, resulting in a massive flow of such workers from the developing to the developed world. In an important sense, it is the last of these factors that is playing an important role in driving HLSS exports from developing countries, rather than continuing with the export of their people. The shortage is best portrayed in table 5.2, below.

In OECD countries, **demographic trends** are being determined by, and reflected in: (i) an ageing population; (ii) a substantial change in the role, structure and size of the family; (iii) extended families giving way to nuclear families; and (iv) a change in the role of women, a greater proportion of whom are working. All these factors are affecting healthcare trends and approaches to healthcare delivery. These trends are being felt more slowly in the developing world, with different ramifications for healthcare systems and for HLSS exports. In OECD countries, demographic trends are driving a shift in patient care from acute illness to chronic disease management

Table 5.2 Clinicians per 1000 population

	Physicians	Nurses	Dentists
Africa region	0.21	0.93	0.03
Americas	1.94	4.88	1.05
South Asia	0.52	0.81	0.06
Europe	3.2	7.43	0.52
Eastern Mediterranean	0.74	1.1	0.17
Western Pacific	1.1	1.7	0.17

Source: WHO Statistical Information System (2002). See http://www.who.int/research/en/ [accessed 6 January 2009]

and toward multidisciplinary care. There is an accompanying shift in care in hospitals, to care in the ambulatory and home setting with an emphasis on protocol-driven care.

Healthcare trends are also being driven by **heightened consumerism**. This is partly due to the larger role being played by instant global communications and the electronic/print media in influencing consumer information, expectations and demand. The result is a growing gap between rapidly rising expectations of 'healthcare consumers' and the ability of over-stretched healthcare systems in developed countries to meet those expectations at affordable cost. That gap is in turn creating large dichotomous 'divides' between rich and poor consumers and between urban and rural consumers.

Healthcare consumerism is encouraged by: the increased availability of medical information to patients; increased ability to receive care at home; increased desire to be informed and be part of decision making; increased costs driving consumer behaviour (i.e. 'shopping for value'), which includes medical tourism increasing on a global scale and patient resort to treatment outside of traditional medicine; and finally, there is increased consumer demand for 'transparency of outcomes' data. As more information about the outcomes of medical tourism and healthcare offshoring becomes available, the more this feeds back into increasing demand.

The inability of health systems in developed countries to meet consumer expectations, in real time at an affordable cost, is driving the growth of a **global** healthcare industry. Similarly, consumer dissatisfaction with allopathic medicine as practiced in the West is leading to challenges to conventional medicine and resulting in another significant divide: between Western (i.e. scientific or conventional) medicine on the one hand, and complementary or alternative therapies on the other. This divide will also influence HLSS exports.

Healthcare services demand (and therefore HLSS export potential) is also being influenced by changing **epidemiology**. This is reflected in a shift toward the management of: chronic diseases; smoking-related diseases, with an anti-smoking culture spreading around the world; growing **obesity**, which has become as much of a problem in the developed world as **malnutrition** is in the developing world; a growing incidence of stress-induced health problems, such as heart disease and diabetes; addiction management (smoking, drugs, alcohol etc.) around the world; and increasingly the global risk and impact of serious infections (including the risk of bioterrorism), which has been manifested in the HIV/AIDS pandemic, concerns about infections like SARS and bird-flu, and the return of diseases like drug-resistant tuberculosis (TB).

The fourth factor influencing global healthcare demand and HLSS export trends is **technology**. Rapid advances in ICT are resulting in new electronic devices emerging with capabilities that were unimagined before. Dramatic advances are also being seen in medical technologies such as: remote telemetry; minimally invasive procedures (keyhole surgery) and robotics; biotechnology, resulting in new, more potent and targeted pharmaceuticals and pharmacogenetics; intelligent devices for all types of monitoring, as well as slow-release drug application; and the potential of nanotechnology for changing healthcare practices even more dramatically.

Apart from the influence of these different variables creating growing demand pressures, the supply side of the equation for value in healthcare offshoring has also changed rapidly. For instance, quality medical services are now available (on a limited and specialised basis to the affluent) outside OECD countries that are on a par with those available in OECD countries. There is also a growing resource pool of highly trained medical personnel in the developing world that has obtained the same qualifications as personnel in the developed world. The services of this resource pool are available at a much lower cost, owing to lower costs of living, and as a result, complex surgery can be made possible at a fraction of the OECD cost. There has also been a dramatic increase in computerised hospital information systems, while software technology is making remote treatment and distance monitoring possible. Private hospital groups (like Parkway, Apollo, Wockhardt, Saudi-German etc.) are now becoming – and operating on the same basis as – global corporations. They are creating state-of-the-art medical facilities (better than those available in the OECD) of great repute and globally recognised branding.

Yet, despite the obvious positive demand-supply-cost factors impelling greater outsourcing/offshoring of HLSS, there are many barriers that need to be overcome before it emerges as a global industry (as manufacturing and commercial services have). These barriers mainly include perceptions in source countries concerning the **quality** of care and service. Potential patients from developed countries seeking treatment abroad are concerned about:

- The quality of treatment, surgery, facilities and credentials of surgeons and medical personnel;
- Hygiene and modernity of healthcare infrastructure facilities (hospitals, clinics, laboratories);
- Recourse in the event that things go wrong and access to proper aftercare;
- Post-operative complications in the recovery/rehab phase at home, which may incur massive costs;
- The problem of emergency-repatriation costs, which are seldom built into overall cost calculations in 'packages' available for treatment abroad and for which insurance is not easily available;
- Implicit protectionism by national public health services (e.g. in the EU), which are often in two minds about healthcare offshoring: they want to reduce costs, but do not want to see a large service market (accounting for 10–15 per cent of GDP) migrating offshore at public expense;

- Protectionism manifested through accreditation difficulties (of medical facilities and staff);
- Home physicians refusing to become involved in post-op care for treatment received abroad, due to vicarious liability and insurance implications; and
- The lack of portability of private and public health insurance and exposure to legal liability risk.

These non-tariff barriers are gradually being reduced (through concerted action in source and receiving countries, as well as by the professional bodies involved) to develop globally recognised standards for accreditation, certification and qualification of facilities and people. Gradually, private insurance systems will evolve that provide for portability of treatment, although public insurance systems (*de facto* provided by national health services, as in the UK) will take longer to catch up. Nevertheless, the overall picture is one of HLSS service export potential that is likely to grow at a compound annual growth rate (CAGR) of about 60 per cent over the next decade.

Quality control issues

For growth in HLSS exports to be sustained through the next decade, the healthcare industry will need to resort to global 'standardisation' of products, services and quality, as has been done in other globalised service industries. For that to happen, global standards will be needed for accreditation of personnel and facilities, and certification by qualified regulatory authorities operating at global, regional and national levels. Such authorities will need to have adequate powers for outcome/performance monitoring and the enforcement of global standards wherever healthcare services are being provided to a global clientele.

Such quality control is likely to be easier in theory than it is in practice, especially with the globalisation of the labour market in healthcare services that has already occurred. **There is probably no healthcare system in the developed world that is not dependent on personnel from developing countries.** Without such personnel, most OECD healthcare systems would face breakdown or become uneconomic to sustain. However, the economics of compensation have globalised the labour market in an asymmetric manner, with the flow of professionals almost entirely one-way – i.e. from developing to developed countries. That direction of flow has several ramifications, especially for healthcare in labour-source (developing) countries.

HLSS exports can stem or reverse that flow. Instead of personnel moving from developing to developed countries, the creation of world-class facilities for HLSS exports in developing countries could result in patients moving in the reverse direction instead. After all:

- 37 per cent of physicians practicing in the UK are **international medical graduates** (IMGs)

- 40 per cent of the new annual intake of nurses in the UK is from other (usually developing) countries
- 25 per cent of physicians practicing in the US are IMGs
- 11 per cent of nurses practicing in the US are IMGs, while 35 per cent of nurses in the EU are from another country
- More than 60,000 non-resident Indian (NRI) physicians are practicing in the UK, Australia and North America, with 38,000 in the US alone (5 per cent of the US physician workforce)
- Of the 5,000 IMGs entering the US physician workforce annually, more than 20 per cent are non-resident Indians[6]

With developing countries providing 56 per cent of all migrating physicians (almost all to OECD countries), this of course raises a host of accreditation and regulation (A&R) issues, including *inter alia* issues of:

- Licensing
- Accreditation
- Recognition of foreign national qualifications
- Nationality and residency requirements
- State and provincial requirements
- Immigration regulations
- Access to examinations for completion of qualifications
- Foreign exchange controls etc.

Yet the broader question this phenomenon raises is: If nationals of so many countries can operate at high standards of qualification and certification in OECD countries, why can't such standards apply globally – for healthcare facilities, as well as the people working in them?

Two common features need to be counteracted to achieve this. First is the use of accreditation and certification by many countries (and by the professions practising in them) as **protectionist** devices to block foreign competition in the domestic healthcare services market, rather than applying A&R simply for quality assurance/control. Second is the reluctance on the part of developing countries to embrace global standards on the grounds that they are too high and too costly (for their economic circumstances) to adopt/implement. The issue of quality control, and the roles that A&R play in different parts of healthcare systems (especially those geared to cross-border HLSS exports), can be understood through the following four diagrams.

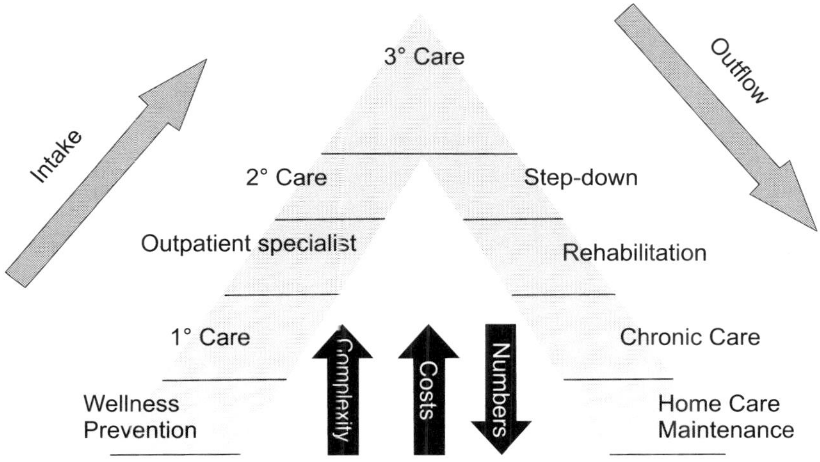

Figure 5.1 Level of care in healthcare system

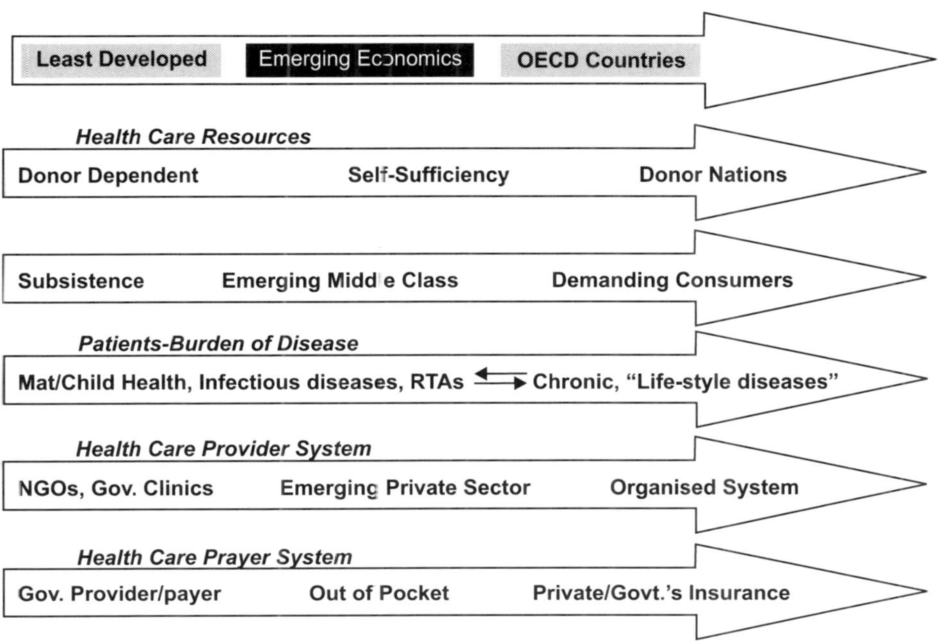

Figure 5.2 Economic development and health

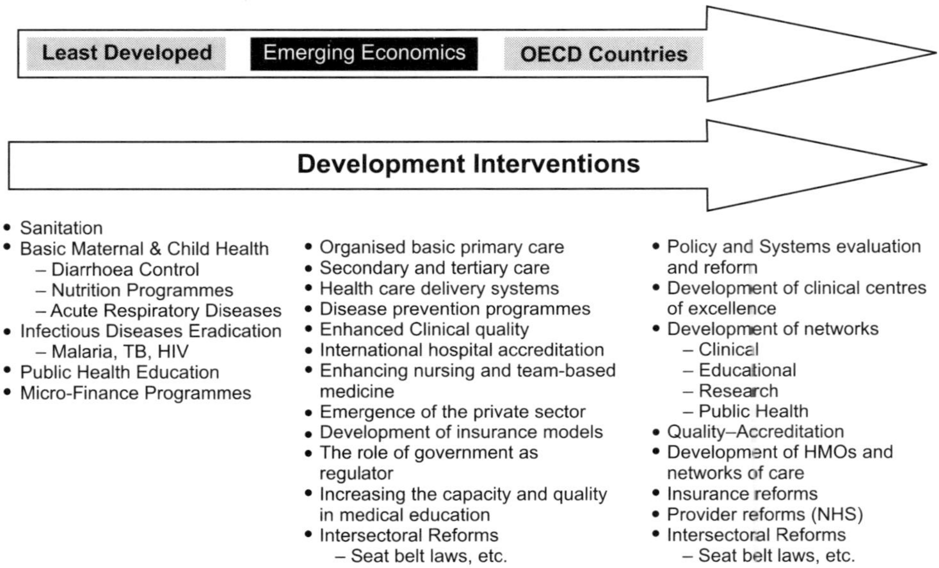

Figure 5.3 Economic development and health interventions

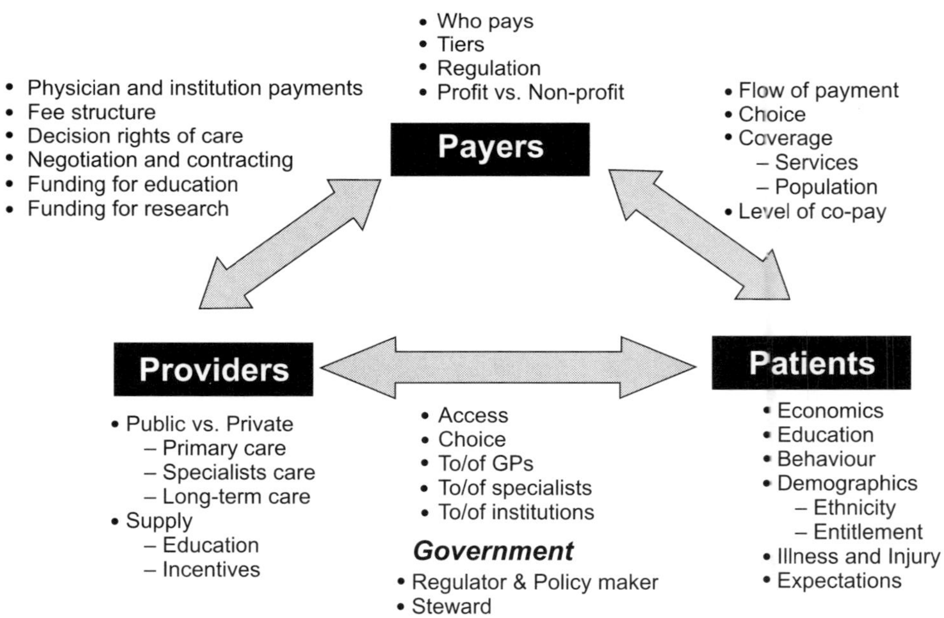

Figure 5.4 Health care system components

Every aspect of healthcare delivery requires A&R to be exercised in order to assure quality of service, protection of consumer rights and the protection of professional service providers from wrongful accusations of misconduct or malpractice liability. Consumers of healthcare need assurance that they are being treated by qualified professionals in certified facilities. By the same token, healthcare professionals need assurance that their qualifications are not subject to question, that they are widely recognised (across borders and around the world), and that they have protection from liability in the facilities they operate from. Facility managers as well as officials, regulators and policy-makers (not to mention insurers) need to be assured of quality control at every level for what they are managing, regulating, insuring and funding.

Effectively, A&R must influence (and be part of) overall healthcare system design, whether for the domestic or export markets. Usually, it is best not to have dual markets with dual standards (as, unfortunately, is the case in most developing countries). It is better to have single markets (for domestic and exported services) that are uniformly regulated, so as to avoid A&R arbitrage. The A&R regime must embrace performance assessment across providers, payers and purchasers of healthcare. It also has to incorporate priority setting from the top level, i.e. as part of the democratic political process whereby governments determine healthcare priorities and achieve them through their line ministry. However, A&R has to accommodate inter-sector priorities and advocacy (insofar as there are specific policies to assure equality of access and opportunity, equality of gender, race, caste, ethnicity or creed in access to healthcare services, policies to protect the rights of women and children and those of the aged).

The **regulatory** part of A&R has to assure: hygiene and sanitary regulation on the part of healthcare providers, and has to enforce standards that assure consumer protection, as well as maintaining a level playing field between consumers, providers and payers. To do this, it has to cover:

- Health institutions and their performance
- Development and management of health infrastructure
- Application and use of health technologies
- Private operators as natural persons, companies or legal entities
- Health business operations, including competition rules
- Prudential measures to protect the integrity of public health and malpractice[7]

In so far as gearing healthcare systems to exporting HLSS is concerned, the main barriers affecting A&R in the 'exporting' country are:

- Perceived quality of healthcare professionals
- Standards of quality assurance in healthcare facilities
- Mutual recognition of professional credentials

- Non-portability of insurance coverage
- Lack of standards for electronic medical records (EMR)
- Concerns over patient privacy and confidentiality in distance healthcare delivery
- Difficulties in cross-jurisdictional malpractice liability
- Potential negative effects of what is commonly recognised as 'brain-drain'

The **accreditation** part of A&R involves different considerations. It underlines the need for the continuous upgrading of healthcare facilities (hospitals, clinics etc.) **through accreditation** in order to: 'encourage those which are doing the best work, and to stimulate those of inferior standard to do better'.[8] Usually accreditation is a **voluntary** process by which a government or non-government agency grants **recognition** to healthcare institutions that meet certain **standards** that require **continuous improvement** in structures, processes and outcomes.

Improving accreditation has become a global trend. The picture around the world is as follows:

- The US, Canada and Australia have the oldest accreditation systems (the Joint Commission [JC] being the accrediting body since 1951)
- In Europe, Germany, France, Ireland and Spain have new accreditation systems
- In the Middle East, Egypt, Jordan, Saudi Arabia use the JCI for accreditation
- In India, the National Accreditation Board for Hospitals (NABH) is the principal accrediting body
- In South America, the *Instituto Técnico para la Acreditación de los Establecimientos de Salud* (ITAES) and the Consortium for Brazilian Accreditation (CBA) have been leaders
- The WHO, World Bank and development banks recognise and endorse the accreditation model

A common core of healthcare practice around the world ensures that accreditation is carried out by a recognised body which:

- Establishes and publishes standards
- Conducts objective, on-site evaluations
- Publishes accreditation decisions
- Requires across-the-board professional involvement of all professional categories
- Achieves consensus on standards of quality and safety
- Uses professionals to serve as external evaluators
- Focuses on continuous improvement of personnel and facilities

- Undertakes external, objective evaluations with qualified foreign peer evaluators
- Uses consensus standards
- Involves the health professions
- Is proactive, not reactive
- Applies benchmarks and standards on an organisation-wide basis
- Focuses on systems, institutions, structures, processes and procedures, not individuals
- Stimulates quality culture throughout healthcare organisations
- Undertakes periodic re-evaluation against standards, and reviews the standards as well
- Applies an appropriate 'risk reduction strategy': doing the right things well

Credible accreditation for countries planning to undertake HLSS exports

If each HLSS exporting country decided to adopt its own national A&R regime, while trying to make it compatible with similar regimes in other countries, major co-ordination problems and problems of reciprocity with mutual bilateral recognition would arise. To avoid that difficulty, an attempt has been made to facilitate the globalisation of the highest standards across the healthcare services industry in all countries. The Joint Commission responsible for accreditation in North America (i.e. US and Canada) decided unilaterally in 1997 to provide international accreditation through an affiliated body, the **Joint Commission International** (JCI).

That decision was based on work in over 50 countries and requests from healthcare organisations to be evaluated against JC standards, viewed as global 'benchmarks'. JCI has subsequently established a regime for achieving (through its accreditation) maximum quality standards that are: (i) patient centred; (ii) culturally adaptable around the world and in any country environment, yet which respect sufficient standardisation; and (iii) amenable to an accreditation process that incentivises and stimulates continuous improvement.

To achieve its goals, the JCI has developed a full range of international programmes, and established a number of international offices, with its standards and procedures being translated in 14 international languages (for the third edition of *Hospital Standards*). In addition JCI has appointed:

- An International Board of Directors (of JCI)
- International members on its Accreditation Committee
- An International Standards Subcommittee

- Regional Advisory Councils for Europe, the Middle East and Asia-Pacific regions
- A South American Regional Advisory Council in 2008

At the time of writing, the JCI had accredited over 140 hospitals in:

- The Gulf and Middle East: the United Arab Emirates (UAE), Saudi Arabia, Egypt, Jordan, Lebanon and Qatar
- East and South Asia: Thailand, China, Hong Kong, Taiwan, Philippines, Rep. of Korea, Singapore, Malaysia, India, Indonesia and Pakistan
- Europe: Italy, Spain, Ireland, Germany, Denmark, Austria, Czech Republic and Turkey
- Latin America and the Caribbean: Brazil, Chile, Costa Rica, Mexico and Barbados
- Several hospitals are preparing for JCI accreditation in Kuwait, Oman, Bahrain, Sudan, Nigeria, Bangladesh, Nepal, Iran, Israel, Colombia, Lithuania, Poland, Portugal and Switzerland

With the cross-country experience it has gained over the last decade, the JCI's accreditation standards now have a system-wide framework. They address all the important clinical and managerial functions of a healthcare organisation. They also:

- Focus on patients in context of their families;
- Have a balance of structure, process and outcomes;
- Are designed to be interpreted/surveyed within the culture and legal framework of a country;
- Are felt to be optimal, with achievable and measurable expectations;
- Contain many of the quality-control and quality-leadership International Organization for Standardization (ISO) 9000 criteria, as well as criteria of the European (the European Federation for Quality Management) and US (Baldrige) quality awards; and
- Are capable of evolving over time (third edition of *Hospital Standards*) as changing country and global circumstances demand.

Focus on patient safety

JCI's accreditation approach is focused primarily on assuring and protecting patient safety. To that end, it has adopted proactive strategies to reduce the risk of medical error and reflect good practices proposed by leading patient safety experts. It has taken a significant step toward incorporating these new tools into its accreditation requirements. The fact that its client organisations have voluntarily assumed responsibility for using JCI's **international patient safety goals** (IPSGs) to foster continuous improvement is even more important. IPSGs involve: identifying patients correctly; improving communications between professionals and patients; improving the safety of high-alert medications; ensuring correct site, correct patient, correct procedure surgery; reducing the risk of infections; and reducing the risk of patient harm from falls. The critical steps to improvements in patient safety involve: the identification of all significant errors; analysis of each major error to determine root causes; compilation of data about error frequencies and root causes; dissemination of derived information to permit redesign of systems and processes; and periodic assessment of effectiveness of risk-reduction efforts.

Nonetheless, having described what is involved with JCI accreditation to achieve global standards in establishing a suitable healthcare system for HLSS exports, what has actual experience with such accreditation been? Is it worth the high cost involved? Does it make much of a difference? To answer these questions, the JCI has conducted research across a sample of accredited hospitals abroad to determine the value of accreditation. In doing so, it found that accredited hospitals reported significant improvements accruing from the accreditation process in: improving the quality of management and team leadership; medical records management; infection control; reduction in medication errors; staff training and professional credentialing; and quality monitoring.

The overall finding was that all stakeholder groups involved reported improvement in every dimension measured, with an overall improvement 49 per cent over the baseline. This raises an important policy question for Mauritius. **When it comes to A&R, should the government and the Ministry of Health & Quality of Life attempt to adapt its own extant A&R regime for the domestic healthcare system to comply with higher global standards, or should it simply adopt and apply JCI accreditation to establish its credentials firmly and unquestionably in the HLSS export space?** This is an important issue, upon which some time needs to be spent to consider the pros, cons and costs involved.

Medical tourism

Medical tourism is growing rapidly and turning out to be an immense business opportunity for nations that are positioning themselves correctly. Examples of countries promoting medical tourism include India, South Africa, Malaysia, Thailand, Israel, Hungary, Turkey, Jordan, Lebanon, Lithuania, Cuba and Costa Rica. With medical travel spends growing at 20 per cent plus year-on-year,[9] what potential does Mauritius have to become another destination for **medical tourism** on a significant scale? Can Mauritius capture 1–2 per cent of the global market for medical tourism and make healthcare and life science services exports as significant as exports in other service industries?

Oddly unrecognised, Mauritius has already become a destination for 'medical' tourism on a highly specialised and limited scale: it has established a global reputation for hair transplants. However, it is unclear what amount of total revenues, export revenues and value-addition Mauritius derives from these services. This is an area in which official statistics need to be greatly improved. Yet Mauritius does have the potential to become a destination for medical tourism in both the regional and global contexts. The arguments favouring this view are outlined below.

'Medical tourism', as the term is commonly understood, involves travel from a place of residence to a destination at which medical or surgical treatment is provided, and involves more than one night away from the country of residence. Generally the term applies to patients from developed countries going to less-developed countries for medical treatment (usually surgery), although there is probably an equal flow of medical tourists in the opposite direction. Some advertising is involved in attracting medical tourists, as it is for attracting tourists in general.

Medical tourists are usually able to obtain treatment of the same or higher quality at home, unless they are from a developing country. They are not referred by a physician, and do not receive any medical follow-up at home. By and large, medical tourism is cost-driven. It affords privacy along with a holiday. The fees charged in the destination where treatment is received are usually lower than in the home country. Within this broad field, there are a growing number of specialised sectors of medical tourism, including: surgery, cosmetic treatment, wellness/spa treatment, dental treatment and infertility and reproductive treatment.

Countries that have succeeded in exporting HLSS usually organise around a narrow set of services; they provide specific high-value services for niche local/regional markets. They compete on the basis of strength in specific clinical service lines adopting a Centre of Excellence (CoE) approach. Only with a critical mass of patients for individual services are they able to achieve competitive quality at reasonable cost. Inviting private companies to provide specific services for the public health system can create a springboard for these services to be provided to foreign patients. The countries listed above are actively promoting medical tourism as a service export activity. A number of other countries are also involved, including Argentina, Bangladesh, Bulgaria, France, Switzerland, Russia, Australia, the UK and the United States.

The areas that suggest themselves for medical tourism in Mauritius include, among others: (i) e-medicine and Telemedicine for the African region; (ii) specialisation in stem cell transplants for patients with sickle sell anaemia (prevalent in Africa) and thalassaemia (prevalent in South and South East Asia, the Middle East, Mediterranean and North Africa) and (iii) for intensive diabetes care. In addition, Mauritius might build on its successful experience with hair transplantations by promoting a wider range of cosmetic surgery (including plastic surgery and dermatological clinics), dental surgery (with new prosthodontic facilities and laboratories), infertility treatment, diagnostic imaging and medical spa treatment.

Possible further areas for exploration include the creation of purpose-built facilities for long-term addiction treatment, long-term psychiatric care and terminal care. Mauritius could choose to add to the facilities that Switzerland and the Netherlands are providing to EU citizens suffering from incurable illnesses and facing a lifetime of fatigue, stress and pain, to seek voluntary euthanasia at a time and in a manner of their own choosing in special facilities that provide supervised care and treatment in the final stages.

Relying on these specific activities, the Government of Mauritius (through the Board of Investment and the Ministries of Tourism and Health working together) might consider developing **integrated health tourism packages** that emphasise the cultural and ethnic strengths of the island by marketing in specific geographies (right column, below) to play to particular language skills and ethnic connections (left column):

- French – Europe
- English – UK, Singapore, Australia, South Africa
- Indian – India and South Asia
- Chinese – ASEAN and East/North East Asia
- Muslim – North Africa, the Middle East, the Gulf Emirates, Saudi Arabia

However, for Mauritius (along with South Africa, which has made rapid strides to establish itself) to become a medical tourism CoE for Africa, the Indian Ocean Rim and proximate Asia, it needs to combine three core elements and become a CoE simultaneously for: medical education, life sciences services and a selective range of healthcare services. Success in these three elements will create a self-reinforcing virtuous circle.

As in other service industries, Mauritius cannot aspire to be 'everything to everybody' in the way that larger countries like India can. It has to focus on niche specialisations that play to its strengths. Mauritius does not have – in the case of any of these three core elements – a sufficiently wide or deep domestic healthcare system, medical educational or research base, or a sufficiently large economy, population or environment. It does not have a large enough base of healthcare professionals, although it has exported a number of these and continues to do so. For that reason it cannot export HLSS from its extant resource base in the healthcare system. It can only do so by creating a convenient 'plug and play platform' for operators from elsewhere to establish themselves in Mauritius to export the services that are needed from that location and to provide labour market entry/exit conditions that permit total openness and flexibility.

To take advantage of global medical tourism export opportunities, Mauritius may need to create a specific medical tourism programme (MTP) driven by a dedicated taskforce involving all stakeholding organisations embracing: a **medical** cluster, a

tourism cluster and a business services-cum-retirement cluster. Such a taskforce would aim to bring all stakeholders together to solve problems, create new protocols, and adapt continuously to changes in the global healthcare industry that may affect Mauritius's competitive position.

The base (policy, institutional and infrastructural) for engaging in medical tourism does not appear to be particularly strong at present. However, it has much potential that can be developed relatively swiftly through appropriately structured partnerships with foreign players:

- A few globally recognised facilities (e.g. Darne, Apollo) already exist and can super-specialise even further
- New specialist services can be built up rapidly in the areas of orthopaedic, cardiac and general surgery
- The medical tourism market should be developed in outward concentric circles, beginning with local areas and spreading to wider regional neighbourhoods, then to the EU and rest of the world. The initial focus would be on:
    - o Indian Ocean Rim Islands
    - o Africa (around South Africa) – all SADC
    - o India and South Asia
    - o The Gulf countries (with which complementary partnerships can be developed)
- Reliance needs to be placed on corporate partnerships with globally recognised and branded hospital groups in South Africa, India, Malaysia and Singapore to capture a 1–2 per cent share of the medical tourism market worldwide.

Alternative medicine and drug research

Mauritian resorts are already investing in wellness and spa treatments, and they are attracting a broad clientele from their traditional tourist client base. Yet Mauritius has unexploited potential for offering alternative therapeutic treatments in Indian Ayurveda as well as Chinese acupuncture and acupressure. Both are becoming increasingly popular worldwide. The Indian Kairali Clinics group (which has established a global reputation for Ayurvedic treatments and has invested in spa franchises in the UAE and Japan) has indicated its interest in investing in a facility in Mauritius.

Mauritius as a centre for natural drug research

Apart from these obvious opportunities for offering alternative medicine treatments, Mauritius may be able to exploit opportunities for research and development into the role of traditional/alternative medicine in pharmaceutical drug development and healthcare. The potential in this niche is considerable. To illustrate: **Bionovo**, an unconventional drug company specialising in this area of natural drugs research and development, observed that eight out of 29 small molecule drugs launched in 2000 were derived from natural products (NPs). Large drug companies did not have a significant role in deriving these drugs. For cancer, the percentage of small molecule, new chemical entities that are non-synthetic has remained at 62 per cent averaged from 1981–2002. In the antihypertensive area, of the 74 formally synthetic drugs, 48 can be traced to natural product structures/mimics. To date there is no *de novo* combinatorial compound approved as a drug. In infectious diseases, over 75 per cent of the drugs were shown to be of natural origin.[10]

Moreover, resort to some form of alternative medicine is growing rapidly in the EU and US, in fact at a faster growth rate than is seen in the use of conventional allopathic treatment. Again, to illustrate with some stylised facts regarding the US market:

- About 34 per cent of Americans used some form of alternative medicine (Eisenberg, 1997)
- In 1994, the Dietary Supplement Health and Education Act (DSHEA) 1994 created the Office of Dietary Supplements within the National Institute of Health (NIH)
- Post-DSHEA supplements grew from 4,000 to 30,000
- In 1998, National Center for Complementary and Alternative Medicine (NCCAM) was formed
- In 2003, the NCCAM budget was US$113 million
- In June 2004, the Food and Drug Administration (FDA) published 'Guidance for Industry: Botanical Drug Products'
- The botanical/dietary supplement industry in the US is estimated to be worth US$50 billion
- About the same amount is true for the EU; the total US+EU industry is worth more than US$100 billion
- At the time of writing there were 50 active commercial investigational new drug applications for botanical drugs granted by the FDA
- Chinese pharmacopeia contains 14,000 substances
- There may be problems translating the traditional tenets into modern biomedicine

In this particular area of drug development, what is needed in a country environment is:

- Sophisticated intellectual infrastructure

- A collaborative/integrative scientific environment
- 'Bricks and mortar' scientific space, preferably connected to a university research cluster
- A favourable and proper regulatory environment for drug development and healthcare
- Strong IPR protection by global standards
- Access to hospitals and patients with target indications

Developing such an environment has a high pay-off, but it involves a considerable amount of upfront investment in hard and soft infrastructure. For Mauritius to become a Centre of Excellence for this purpose, it will need to:

- Support the build-up of the necessary intellectual infrastructure (a long-term task)
- Legislate strong IPR protection/enforcement (there is already a good regime, which can be strengthened)
- Build bricks and mortar scientific space (this can be done through PPPs)
- Provide access to hospitals and patients with target indications (this is limited at present)
- Attract collaborations with pharma/biotech companies (the BoI needs to work on this)
- Provide pharma/biotech services by creating contract research organisations (CROs) and contract management organisations (CMOs)
- Collaborate with academic/industry affiliates to guarantee long-term interests
- Serve as international hub as well as a regional centre

The overall conclusion at the symposium was that for Mauritius to engage in this space it would need to take a number of actions on the policy, investment and educational/research frontiers. None of these could be accomplished in the short term. However, the long-term objective had to be kept in view as being desirable to reach given the considerable pay-off and spin-offs that could result.

Clinical trials

What is involved with clinical research and what would Mauritius need to do to establish more contract research organisations (CROs)? In answering these questions, it has to be recognised that there are presently a number of barriers between clinical and basic research in pharmaceutical drug development. There are also increasing complexities involved in conducting clinical research and it has become more difficult to translate new knowledge to the clinic and back again to the bench.

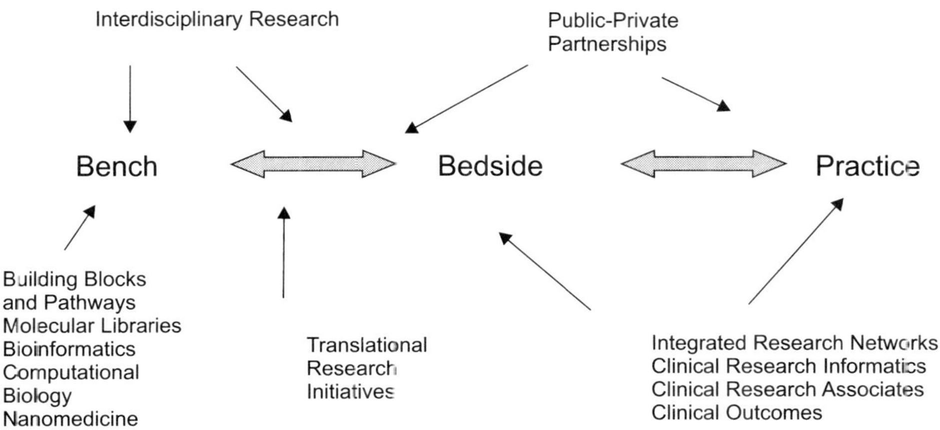

Clinical Research covers all studies of diseases and trials of treatments that take place in human subjects. Translational Research is broadly defined as research that will provide a scientific link between laboratory research and human trials.

Figure 5.5 Re-engineering clinical research

Source: Presentation by Dr Kok Wei Yap at the Symposium on the Export of Healthcare and Life Science Services

The research and development functions of the pharmaceutical industry have become phenomenally expensive in relation to new drug approvals.[11] There is also a fundamental shift occurring in the geography for CRO from OECD to developing countries, which is being driven by regulatory requirements.[12]

Mauritius has a history of limited clinical research from 1971 through 2006. The most recent research was done on the chikungunya virus epidemic. Up to the late 1980s, health research was carried out mainly by the Ministry of Health (MoH) to provide the necessary knowledge and background to facilitate the design of public health programmes. The lack of such knowledge often imposed constraints on improving the way in which these programmes were formulated. Research was scanty and geared particularly towards communicable diseases and fertility control. The financial input for research was mainly from overseas (usually through aid-funding).

Currently, Mauritius is undertaking biomedical research in: genetic factors intervening in breast cancer and diabetes, infectious diseases (AIDS and chikungunya) and sexual and reproductive health. However, the research being carried out is characterised by non-invasive investigations, no administration of drugs and no experimentation with new surgical techniques. The research is also limited to studies of strictly national (not international) relevance, and is based on observation, carried out on small samples of the population and driven by academic requirements. The principal institutions undertaking such research in Mauritius include:

- The Mauritius Institute of Health
- The University of Mauritius
- SSR Medical College
- Central Health Laboratory (MHQL)
- Mauritius Research Council
- Mauritius Family Planning
- Cardiac Centre Pamplemousses
- The Cambridge Infectious Diseases Consortium (CIDC) specialising in trials on cosmetics

Whether Mauritius can become a Centre of Excellence for clinical research depends on the following factors influencing drug research in general and Mauritius's attributes in particular:

- The ability to bring new drugs to the market faster (simultaneous development)
- Faster growth in pharmaceutical global markets
- Genetic ethnic and racial diversity of the population yielding better results at lower costs
- A relatively large, treatment-naïve patient pool (especially if Africa is included as Mauritius's hinterland)
- A high prevalence of certain diseases in Mauritius and its Africa and Indian Ocean Rim (IOR) hinterlands
- Relatively good quality of extant medical infrastructure
- Implementation of International Clinical Health-General Council of Practitioners (ICH-GCP) guidelines
- Relatively lower cost per patient trial cost
- An environment that allows that 'one-dose-for-all' may not suitable (i.e. the island does not insist on a uniform rigid approach to clinical trial design)
- Trained clinical research investigators can easily be imported from South Africa and Asia
- A multilingual population
- Limited time difference with Europe (+2h in summer and +3h in winter)
- Availability of trained persons in biological sciences and informatics

- The high literacy rate of the population
- A good number of doctors per 1000 population
- Good training facilities in the paramedical field
- A well-regulated domestic pharmaceutical market
- Existence of high-quality health services in the private and public sectors
- Updated law on protection of intellectual property rights for confidentiality of data (2002)
- Lower turnover rates of skilled staff than, for example, in India and other CRO countries
- Availability of good epidemiological data
- Cancer register established since 1989
- Excellent data on diabetes and cardio-vascular disease arising from non-communicable disease (NCD) surveys 1987, 1992, 1998 and 2004
- A morbidity pattern that is similar to developed countries
- Diseases with urgent demands for better therapies in the EU/US are also prevalent in Mauritius
- A naïve population with respect to experimentation (i.e. the island has a varied and mixed native population that represents much of the world at large in terms of race and ethnicity)
- Lower drop-out rates than elsewhere
- Managing the supply chain and transport are easier given the island's geography
- Excellent scope to set up a solid chain of custody
- No problems with the customs department
- Corruption of officials is not an issue (although in fairness some foreign investors feel it is)
- The possibility of having purpose-built sites for clinical trials
- Excellent communications with foreign countries
- Existence of a high-calibre courier service
- Good facilities for commissioning of specialised clinical research sites
- All biomedical studies are submitted to the Ministry of Health and Quality of Life (MHQL) for approval (including soft trials on cosmetics)
- Scientific validity is vetted by the sponsor and the Biomedical Research Committee of the MHQL

- Ethical aspects are cleared by the Ethics Committee, set up under the MHQL
- Essential clinical research aspects are properly catered for, such as informed consent, confidentiality of data, protection of minors and vulnerable groups and ownership of samples

During the symposium, Mauritius's potential for contract research organisations (CROs) was explored further via the illustrative example of South Africa (RSA), which has a larger economic, educational and established research base. In South Africa, clinical research capability was established in the past because of a clear strategy by government and industry to make South Africa a Centre of Excellence for CRO, leveraging of some core advantages and its intellectual capital, human capital and infrastructure. There was also a competitive rand to US$ exchange rate, the country formerly had a well-regulated environment for the industry and medical innovation capacity is highly regarded worldwide. However, the dynamics influencing South Africa's supposed advantage in CRO have changed and there is now a major problem with 'brain drain' of high-level human capital. Meanwhile, tertiary care budgets and the attention of academia are shifting to primary care, there has been a shift from institutional teaching and research priority into service provision, the South African rand has appreciated too much against the US$ and regulatory agencies have become less capable.

Given the reversal in the South Africa environment for retaining CROs, and looking at the potential that Mauritius had, it was suggested at the symposium that there might be some benefit to be derived from a strategic South Africa-Mauritius partnership focused on CRO. Such a partnership would enable stakeholder congruence, especially between both governments and their private sectors and sustainable, long-term strategic partnerships between relevant pharma CRO groups and Centres of Excellence – i.e. academic institutions and private organisations. It would also be of benefit in terms of clustering of similar minded countries (regionalisation), access to new patient populations (niching) and sharing of best practice (hubbing). An EU mutual recognition process could be facilitated, while the partnership would also encourage more informal communication e.g. with Kenya, Uganda, Tanzania and Zimbabwe and best practice sharing (hubbing) of regulatory activities.

The advantages of such a co-operative arrangement for Mauritius would be:

- Access to capacity building and hubbing
- Access to larger pool of intellectual property
- Access to regulatory best practice knowledge, procedures and functions
- Expanded export of health services
- Import of research and investment capital from the global pharma industry
- Significant upward leveraging of health tourism potential
- Critical mass development in institutions, people and infrastructure

Conversely the advantages for South Africa would be:

- Access to a pool of new 'niche' patients
- Broader opportunities for health tourism
- Opportunities for exchange of knowledge and information
- Opportunities for new strategic alliances
- Centres of Excellence
- Better risk management for retaining CRO capabilities

However, there are also constraints and concerns in developing Mauritius's role as a CRO centre. These include difficulties with recruitment/training of staff at regulatory and operational levels, commitment to ensuring that legislative timelines are met and limitations of existing physical infrastructure and the administrative set-up. Further constraints include complications in setting up adequate clinical trial sites, harmonisation of procedures and guidelines with SADC countries, keeping the Mauritian public fully informed (it is a small place and bad news travels quickly) and competition for highly skilled staff between government and the private sector. There also exists the risk of the island being flooded with demands for soft trials of limited interest or for dubious studies or that trials driven by sponsors' needs may be unconnected to the health interests of the country. Finally there may be concerns about: continuity of treatment at the end of the trial and equity issues, limited transfer of technology, the time needed to meet international standards and shortage of staff experienced in toxicology, pharmacovigilance and clinical pharmacy.

These constraints notwithstanding, there has been an increase in the number and complexity of tests being conducted in Mauritius on both cosmetics and dermatological preparations. At the time of writing, applications were in the pipeline (for approval) for studies in pharmacogenetics, especially for NCD and anticancer drugs and on drugs causing photosensibilisation. Studies have been commissioned by the WHO on anti-retro-virals (ARVs) and an important CRO in Montpellier is focusing on Hepatitis B research.

If clinical trials are to have a sustainable future in Mauritius, the government and the private sector will need viable partnerships, with established institutions, experienced in the field. Compromising on standards to meet timelines or to attract investors is not a solution. The principle of precaution has to prevail in case of doubt. For Mauritius to become a CRO, a considerable amount of specialised training will be necessary in clinical pharmacy, pharmacovigilance and toxicology. What is needed even more is 'joined-up government', in which a clear vision and strategy for the future, coupled with inter-ministerial co-operation rather than conflict, drives the pace of progress in this domain.

Finally, in considering the potential for Mauritius as a CoE for clinical research, what might be learnt from the example of Singapore's extraordinary ambitions and achievements so far in becoming a global CRO and creating a new Biopolis for healthcare services, research and intellectual capital? That example illustrates clearly what can be achieved with the right commitment on the part of government and industry, and the right strategy being put in place with the right people to execute it.[13] Singapore had set up the Institute of Molecular and Cell Biology before 2000. The Genome Institute of Singapore was established in 2000, followed in 2001 by the Bioinformatics Institute, and the Institute of Chemical Engineering Sciences in 2002. Other institutions, such as the Singapore Institute for Clinical Sciences and the Institute of Medical Biology have followed more recently. Singapore has developed research and development human capital using both a pro-global and a pro-local approach: pro-global through international talent recruitment, creating a diverse multinational R&D hub; and pro-local through its scholarships and fellowships programme, building a pipeline of well-trained local scientists. This has led to exceptional biomedical manufacturing growth.

Pre-clinical research

What is the difference between **preclinical** and **clinical** trials in R&D for drugs for the pharma industry? Before a new drug can be put into use for human consumption it undergoes several phases of preclinical and clinical testing (after discovery) in the development and market approval stages. These stages of research are heavily proscribed and tightly regulated (in OECD countries, but increasingly in developing countries as well) to assure patient safety and avoid malpractice and legal liability claims from arising over time with extensive use and experience.

Pre-clinical trials are carried out on a variety of animals and (in later stages) on primates whose anatomies resemble that of humans. Clinical trials then follow on human subjects. Pre-clinical trials involve both breeding and supplying animals and primates, and conducting drug tests on animals and primates. These activities must be conducted along lines that use appropriate standards and are subject to various stages of regulation.[14]

The different phases of trials result in tested compounds numbering in the tens of thousands in the early stages, but boiling down to one or two at the end of the process. That adds enormously to R&D cost, which can amount to US$1.5 billion or more per new drug brought to market. Given the draconian regulatory approval standards that are now in force in OECD countries, it can take 10–15 years to bring a new drug to the approval stage and up to 20 years to obtain an international patent right (IPR). Such economics have now become prohibitive for global pharmaceutical companies, who are now actively seeking other options to reduce the time and cost involved in the process from discovery to use approval.

A direct consequence of the industry's quest for greater efficiency and economy in the R&D phase is resulting in a shift in the geography of CROs where preclinical and clinical trials are conducted before drugs are approved for human use. The

1950s
Kidney transplants
Polio vaccine
Replacement heart valves
Hip replacement surgery
Drugs for high blood pressure

1960s
Heart bypass operations
Drugs to treat mental illness
Rubella vaccine

1970s
Chemotherapy for leukemia
Drugs to treat stomach ulcers
Inhaled asthma medication

1980s
Drugs to control transplant rejection
Life support systems for premature babies
Hepatitis vaccines
Treatment for river blindness

1990s
Meningitis vaccine
Combined drug therapies for AIDS
Drugs for breast and prostate cancer

Figure 5.6 The importance of animals in biomedical research
Source: Presentation by Mrs Mary-Ann Griffiths at the Symposium on the Export of Healthcare and Life Science Services

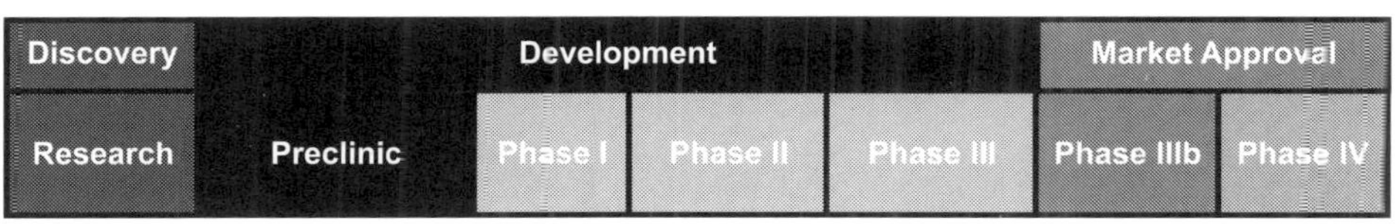

"Preclinic" = "prior clinic" = before human studies

⇨ Animal testing = regulatory required safety assessment

Clinic = " with humans in the hospital"

Phase I	Healthy, mostly male volunteers
Phase II and III	patients
Phase IIIb and IV	patients / case reports

Figure 5.7 The development pathway
Source (Figures 5.7, 5.8, 5.9): Presentation by Dr Rainhard Korte at the Symposium on the Export of Healthcare and Life Science Services

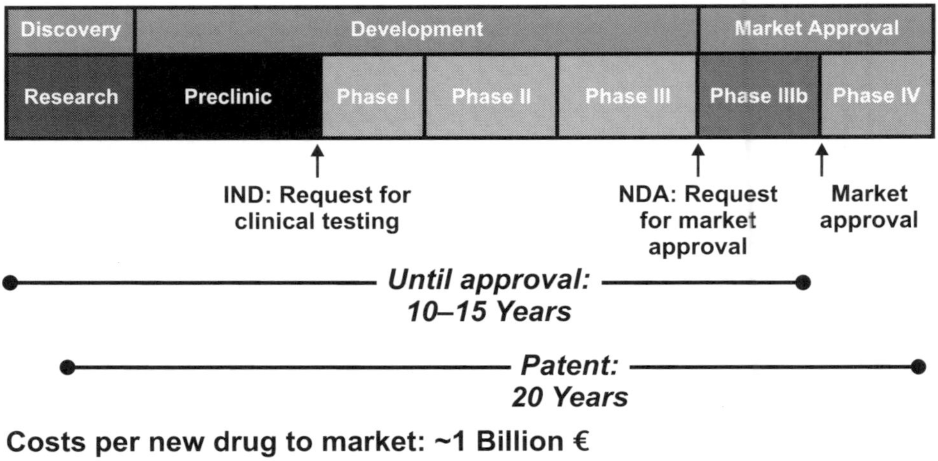

Figure 5.8 The way to market approval

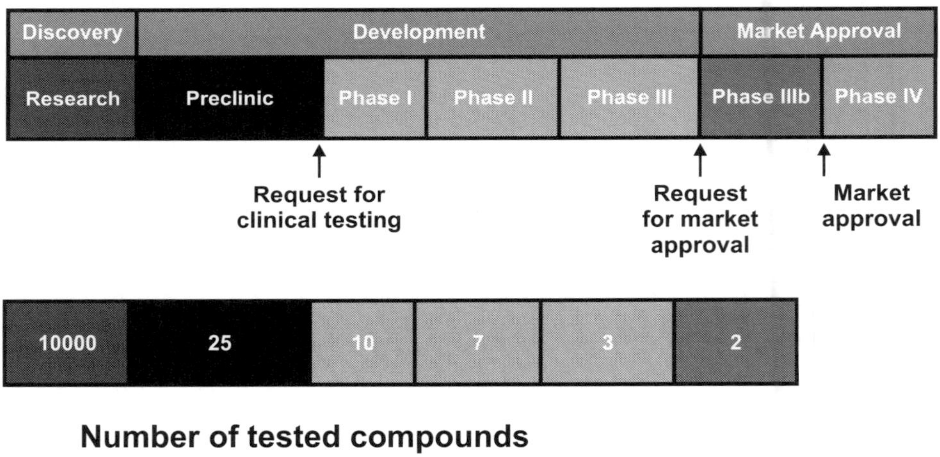

Figure 5.9 Success rate for new drug substances

locations of CROs is shifting from the USA, Europe and Japan to India, China, Taiwan, Vietnam and possibly Mauritius. East and Central European countries are barred from competing in this area by their quest for entry into the EU, which is governed by common regional standards and regulation.

While there may be possible competition for CRO status in a number of emerging markets, there are still minimum requirements that the pharmaceutical industry needs to be met for regulatory purposes. For example, the non-clinical safety requirements for market approval of a drug involve: single and repeated dose toxicity studies, reproduction toxicity studies, genotoxicity studies, assessment of carcinogenic potential, safety pharmacology studies, local tolerance studies, pharmacokinetic and toxicokinetic studies, absorption, distribution, metabolism and excretion (ADME), immunotoxicity and phototoxicity, with provisions for special populations, e.g. children and juveniles.

These demanding requirements notwithstanding, preclinical studies, especially toxicity studies in primates, can be a valuable addition to the healthcare portfolio of the Government of Mauritius. However, the success of a venture in this area will be depends on the market situation, competitive investments, quality and time. At present, the dominant view among global pharma firms is that the highest potential for CRO industry lies in China and India: together they account for 38 per cent of the world's population and their rising incomes and rapid development make these two countries the most interesting growth areas for the pharmaceutical industry. For that reason, it should come as no surprise that the pharma industry is focusing on these markets when it comes to conducting R&D.

Yet Mauritius is closely connected with both countries. It has a sizeable, representative sample of the Indian and Chinese ethnic populations with the same genetic traits. For that reason, and given other attributes, Mauritius could be a useful microcosmic practical laboratory for pharma firms to carry out applied research. Even so, the investment required for the requisite facilities and qualified staff is high. The relocation of specialised staff from Europe and the US may be difficult, but perhaps less so in the case of Mauritius. A ten-year period from start to international acceptance (by governments and pharmaceutical industry) may be needed before a conclusion can be made about the quality and profitability of a preclinical facility in Mauritius.

More than 20 million animals of various species are used for preclinical testing by the cosmetics and pharma industries every year. Of these, about 60,000 (0.3 per cent) are primates. Despite that small percentage, trials on primates have resulted in fundamental medical breakthroughs, such as the eradication of small pox, polio and viral diseases (measles, rubella, whooping cough) through the use of vaccines developed as a result of such testing. Ongoing studies on primates hold the promise of vaccines or cures being developed for HIV, Parkinson's disease and Leukaemia.

Mauritius already breeds primates for preclinical research and exports them around the world. The Mauritian primate breeding industry has steadily expanded over the last 25 years. It includes five suppliers exporting 10,000 primates annually. They have come to be recognised (in the EU and Japan) as among the best for preclinical testing. The conduct of preclinical trials in Mauritius would be a step toward vertical integration of an industry that is ready to, and capable of, blossoming – probably more quickly than clinical testing. With greater volumes of preclinical packages being outsourced to CROs by the global pharma industry, and a supportive government ostensibly encouraging development of the HLSS sector, a shift to preclinical contract research would appear to be an opportunity that Mauritius could grasp and develop. It should be relatively simple to tailor the development of legislation and industry capabilities to meet current and future needs of the pharmaceutical and biotechnology industry. With the Mauritian primate breeding and export industry having established a worldwide reputation, it would be a natural next step to locate preclinical trials in Mauritius and tap into an existing resource.

For that aspiration to be translated into reality, the Government of Mauritius needs to create an environment that enables the island to become a centre of excellence in certain areas of preclinical research. Its limited resources require a sharp and narrow focus that plays on its existing strengths. Its strategy for locating preclinical trials on the island through domestic and foreign CROs must combine clinical research with clinical services. It must address regional needs, and explore/exploit all available sources of funding, whether financed by not-for-profit NGOs, private pharma corporations or multilateral organisations and governments.

The strategy must seek to develop suitable infrastructure based on models such as Cape Town in South Africa, with over 25 biotech firms established in a research park, the Biopolis in Singapore, Scripps in Florida and European biotech clusters such as Cambridge, Munich, Paris, Medicon Valley (Denmark & Sweden), Biovalley (around Basel in Switzerland) and Oxford. Obviously dedicated infrastructure in Mauritius will need to be adapted to reflect its own circumstances and realities, and should be financed in partnership with the private sector with the government's role being limited to partnering through land contributions on appropriate terms.

An effective strategy would incorporate the following features and aim at:

- Forming alliances with overseas institutions such as Scripps, Harvard, NIH, Cleveland Clinics, Mayo Clinics and Institut Pasteur
- Forming corporate alliances with large pharma firms, technology companies, service companies and financial sponsors
- Providing land on appropriate terms for the initiative to take off e.g. Biopolis Singapore
- Providing good general infrastructure e.g. University of Mauritius for Biotechnology and Healthcare Campus
- Ensuring quality of service, quality of care, General Council of Practitioners, good laboratory practices (GLP) standards etc.
- Providing and attracting the necessary funding: Government of Mauritius, World Bank, Bill and Melinda Gates Foundation, private equity, sovereign wealth funds and banks
- Forming an international advisory board

- Starting discussions (in parallel) with leading institutions with respect to alliances, with corporations, not-for-profit organisations, financial sponsors, sovereign wealth funds, banks and international organisations.

However, such a strategy is more widely applicable to developing HLSS exports as a whole and not just one confined exclusively to developing preclinical research capabilities in Mauritius. Ideas were exchanged between the Board of Investment (BoI) and a European corporate finance group that offered to assist with articulating such a strategy and directly assisting the government/BoI to implement it. It will take experienced people to make these ideas a practical reality. The government/BoI should not hesitate to find and work with such people. The Ministry of Finance and Economic Development (MoFED) must make available the necessary budget resources. These ideas should be followed up and put into practice sooner rather than later.

Next steps (roadmap) for HLSS exports

In considering a roadmap and next steps for developing the HLSS sector in Mauritius and gearing it to maximise service export potential perhaps something can be learnt from the example of South Africa, which undertook a similar exercise recently. This approach can (and should) be suitably adapted in formulating a more tailor-made roadmap for Mauritius. The foregoing is confirmed by the experience of many countries that have also attempted to develop an HLSS industry and encourage HLSS service exports. A detailed review of best practices in biotech clusters allows a pragmatic positioning of the Mauritian context[15] (Figure 5.12) Globally there are over

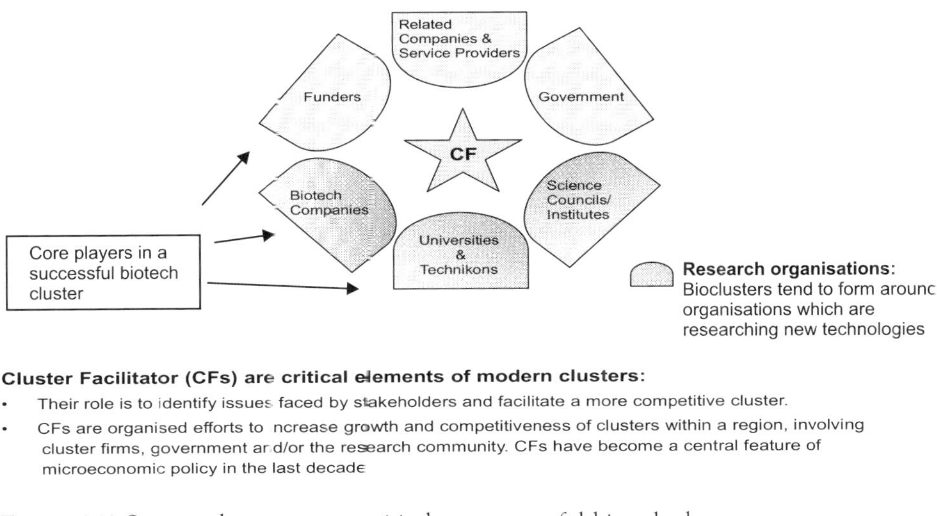

Figure 5.10 Structural components critical to a successful biotech cluster

Source: Presentation at the Symposium on the Export of Healthcare and Life Science Services, adapted from Cluster Initiative Greenbook

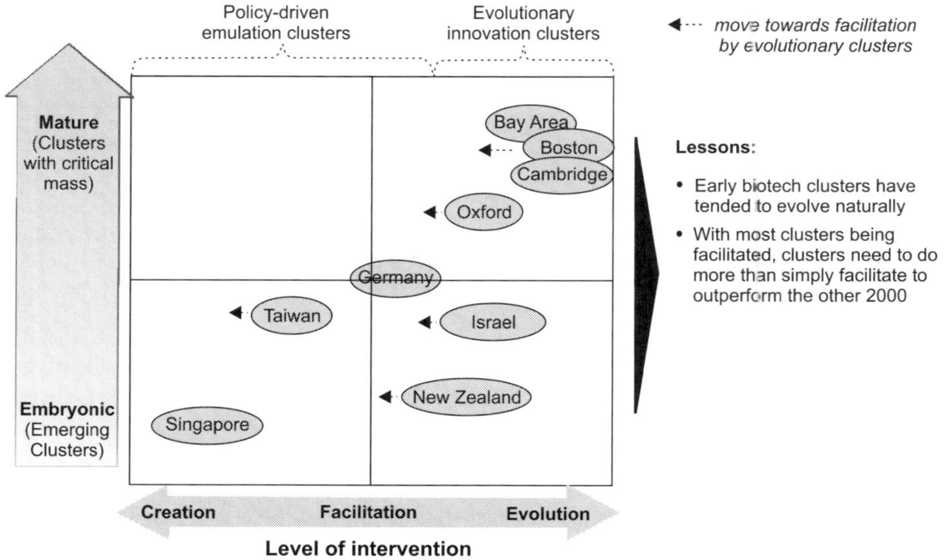

Figure 5.11 It is becoming accepted practice amongst regions and countries to actively promote the growth of their biotech clusters

Table 5.3 Key success factors for biotech clusters

Key success factor	Description
Strong science base	Leading research organisations, critical mass of researchers, world leading scientists
Skilled workforce	Skilled workforce, training courses at all levels
Ability to attract key staff	Critical mass of employment opportunities, image as biocluster, attractive place to live
Entrepreneurial culture	Culture of commercial awareness and entrepreneurship, role models, second generation entrepreneurs
Effective networking	Shared aspiration to be a cluster, trust, frequent collaborations, trade associations, shared infrastructure
Availability of finance	Venture capitalists, business angels, government seed funding
Premises and infrastructure	Incubators, premises with wet labs and flexible leasing arrangements Good transport links: motorways, rail, international airport Business support services and large companies Specialist business, legal, patent, recruitment and property advisers services Large companies in related sectors (healthcare, agriculture, agrifood)
Supportive policy environment	National and sectoral innovation support policies, and fiscal and regulatory framework Support from RDA and other development agencies, sympathetic planning authorities
Growing company base	Thriving spin-out and start up companies. More mature role model companies

Source: Dr Mark Fyvie, biotechnology consultant, presentation at the Symposium on the Export of Healthcare and Life Science Services

4,400 biotech companies, with those in North America and Europe earning over 97 per cent of global biotech revenues. More than one hundred cities and regions worldwide are now attempting to establish biotech clusters, to join the existing 150–200 clusters, most of which are only five to ten years old.

The HLSS market holds considerable promise for Mauritius in diversifying and enhancing its service exports. Mauritius is already involved in limited service exports such as hair transplants, primate breeding and cosmetic contract research being undertaken by CIDC in Ebene. However, there is more that the Government of Mauritius can do in increasing HLSS value-addition and exports. It can realign its policies and enter into appropriate partnerships with a number of domestic and external players and stakeholders. Areas in which Mauritius could benefit from exploiting a small but significant share of the rapidly growing global market for medical tourism have been highlighted above. This is also the case for medical education, alternative medicine and a larger presence in the preclinical and clinical trials domain for contract research.

In view of the potential that HLSS holds, the government and Ministry of Health have been focusing more clearly and defining a timeline for much needed (and much delayed) action on the legislative and policy fronts. Hopefully, the new timelines established and conveyed to the world at large will be met by appropriate and timely actions taken by parliament and the government. Some potential investments have been lined up in the expectation that such action will be taken (e.g. Saudi-German Hospital Group and the Kairali Clinics). Clearly more needs to be done in attracting a wider range of investments in all these areas. The way forward was pointed to by corporate finance and investment banking experts who participated in the symposium. Their active involvement and inward investment will need to be secured to make things happen.

Peer group clusters	→	**Reasons for comparison**
• Australia • Cuba • Ireland • Israel • New Zealand • Singapore • South Korea	→	• Small/developing economies with limited resources • Far from large markets • Proactive biotech strategy • Similar size economy • Similar definitions of success
Best practice clusters		**Reasons for comparison**
• UK (Cambridge) • US (Bay area, Boston)	→	• Most successful bioclusters (allowing evolution to critical mass to be studied) • Important lessons to be learnt as the Mauritian industry needs to compete globally

Figure 5.12 A detailed review of best practices in biotech

Notes

1. For example, US healthcare firms and hospitals (e.g. the Mayo Clinic or the Cleveland Clinic) export services by treating foreign patients in American healthcare facilities. The 2006 revenue for the Mayo Clinic was US$6.3 billion and that of the Cleveland Clinic was US$4.4 billion. American companies and hospitals also maintain 'on-ground' operations abroad. The most common is the operation and management of hospitals and clinics in other countries, followed by managed care and emergency evacuation ventures. US providers are also active in home healthcare, dental care, health insurance, strategic planning and pharmaceutical retailing activities abroad. US firms annually collect international licensing fees and royalties for healthcare expertise and information technology provided.
2. See, for example, http://ucatlas.ucsc.edu/spend.php [accessed 6 January 2009] and other sources such as OECD and UN/WHO/World Bank databases on country healthcare indicators and expenditures which are continuously updated.
3. Dr Derick Pasternak, Managing Director, Middle East International Office, Joint Commission International. Figures presented at Symposium on the Export of Healthcare and Life Science Services, April 2008.
4. Projections made by author based on trends emerging from the source data referred to in the previous footnote.
5. Some estimates are as high as US$40 billion, but those double-count revenues already being counted as health service related ICT-BPO revenue.
6. See, for example,

   http://www.lse.ac.uk/collections/pressAndInformationOffice/newsAndEvents/archives/2007/EurohealthJuly.htm or

   http://www.hse.gov.uk/migrantworkers/healthcare.htm [both accessed 6 January 2009].
7. For more details on the complexity of a sophisticated regulatory system such as that of the UK, see presentation by Mr Harry Cayton, Chief Executive, Council for Healthcare Regulatory Excellence (CHRE), at the Symposium on the Export of Healthcare and Life science Services, April 2008.
8. Quote from the American College of Surgeons, 1918.
9. Sobhi Batterjee, Symposium on the Export of Healthcare and Life Science Services.
10. Dr Isaac Cohen, Chairman and Chief Executive Officer, Bionovo, USA, at the Symposium on the Export of Healthcare and Life Science Services.
11. See presentation by Dr Mark Fyvie, Symposium on the Export of Healthcare and Life Science Services.
12. See presentation by Dr Kok Wei Yap, Symposium on the Export of Healthcare and Life Science Services.
13. For more details on this see presentation by Dr Kok Wei Yap at the Symposium on the Export of Healthcare and Life Science Services.
14. For more details see presentation by Dr Rainhard Korte at the Symposium on the Export of Healthcare and Life Science Services.
15. Full details can be found in the presentation by Dr Mark Fyvie at the Symposium on the Export of Healthcare and Life Science Services.

6

Exporting Human Resource Development Services

Growing market for global human resource development service exports

In an increasingly knowledge-intensive, knowledge-dependent world, global human resource development (HRD) exports in vocational and tertiary education (VTE) and professional training are pervasive and large. At present, such exports are dominated by OECD countries, which have a sophisticated and well-developed institutional infrastructure for the provision of VTE. They have much larger, more diversified faculties and facilities with a head start in knowledge accumulation. However, that reality is changing with two significant trends: (i) the size of the global and export market for tertiary education is increasing rapidly; and (ii) a larger share of the export market is being captured by developing countries, driven largely by cost economics.[1]

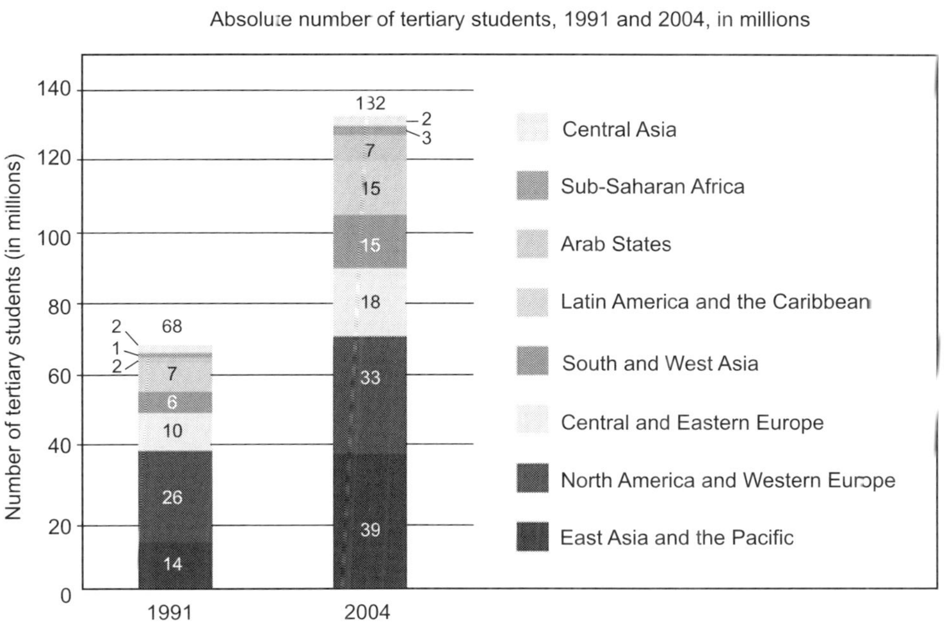

Figure 6.1 Growth in the number of tertiary students worldwide since 1991
Source: UNESCO Institute for Statistics database

Worldwide VTE enrolment in 2005 was more than 40 per cent higher than in 1999, and double that of 1991. There were 138 million students enrolled for VTE in 2005 compared to 68 million in 1991 and 93 million in 1999. In all likelihood, at current rates of growth there will be 250 million students in VTE by 2020. According to the United Nations Education, Science and Culture Organization (UNESCO), 2.5 million students were studying abroad in 2004, with that number rising to over 4 million in 2008. About 3 per cent of students enrolled in VTE worldwide are now studying abroad. That proportion is likely to rise to 5 per cent by 2015.[2]

The all-inclusive **annual** costs (between 2005 and 2008) of an overseas education varied from US$100,000 (in the best US universities) to US$15,000 in lower-cost countries, with a median of about US$25,000 per foreign student. That implies an annual global HRD export market of about US$100 billion in size. **It is a market that Mauritius could quite easily capture a 1–2 per cent share of**.

Students seeking **international** higher education will exceed seven million by 2015 and 15 million by 2025 – i.e. about eight times global demand in 2000. In 2025, the size of the global HRD export market will be between US$400 and 500 billion, with a 1 per cent share accounting for $4–5 billion or about 75 per cent of Mauritius's existing gross national income (GNI), but probably less than 20 per cent of the GNI projected for 2025.

The basic drivers for VTE emerging as a major *global* service industry include: (i) a shift in the world's economic centre of gravity from OECD countries to the large emerging economies (mainly of Asia), especially China, India and members of ASEAN; (ii) a larger number of students from developing countries (especially from Asia) enrolling for VTE due to demographics and rising living standards; and (iii) cost escalation in OECD countries, with annual tuition plus living costs of tertiary education now rising to US$70–100,000 annually for a postgraduate degree, whereas costs in developing countries are still between US$5–15,000. That size of this differential is bound to drive global VTE provision toward lower-cost economies.

In the 20th century it was normal for individuals to remain in one profession, vocation or occupation for most of their working lives of between 40 and 45 years. By contrast, the 21st century will see individuals change their professions or occupations three to five times in the course of their (longer) working lives, which will stretch between 50–55 years. The challenge will be to maintain:

- a high quality of VTE (and using established brand equity through partnership arrangements with reputable institutions) wherever it is provided from – i.e. with increasing adoption of global standards in course curricula, accreditation, certification of students, institutions and qualifications; and
- ensuring the relevance of VTE (through continuously evolving curricula) for a world in which new technologies are shortening the shelf life of acquired skills and creating hitherto unprecedented demands for continuous training and retraining.

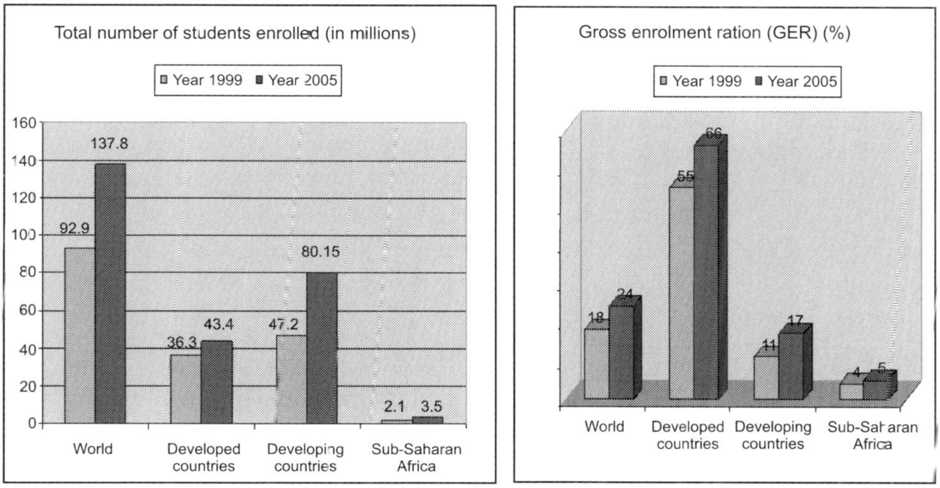

Figure 6.2: Progress made in tertiary education
Source: Presentation by Dr Qian Tang at the Symposium on the Export of Human Resource Services

Asia heads the list of regions sending students abroad for higher education at the present time, accounting for 42 per cent of the global total. Europe is second, accounting for 35 per cent, although EU students mainly go to other EU and OECD countries. Africa accounts for 12 per cent of the global total of students abroad, mainly in OECD countries. North America accounts for less than 7 per cent, South America for 3 per cent and Oceania for 1 per cent.

Over the next two decades, Asia offers the highest potential as a market for HRD service exports. It is expected to account for 70 per cent of global demand for foreign procured HRD services in 2025. India and China together will account for 50 per cent of global demand, while ASEAN will account for another 15–20 per cent. Thus, while Africa remains a captive regional market for Mauritius to exploit in exporting for HRD services, it cannot ignore the potential of the Asian market to which it is equally well connected and attractive from the viewpoint of Asian students wanting to study abroad.

The highest proportion of VTE students studying abroad is from sub-Saharan Africa, Central Asia and the Middle East – where VTE capacity and infrastructure are least developed. The lowest percentage is from North America – where VTE is advanced. A large proportion of EU students go to another country, but usually to another **European** country (just as US students go to another state to study); however, an increasing number are now studying in North America and Asia.[3]

Asia accounts for a smaller **proportion** of students studying abroad than three other continents. However, it accounts for the largest number of them in absolute terms.[4]

Where do most of the globally mobile VTE students go? As might be expected they go to countries with an established reputation for providing high-quality VTE, offering qualifications that are internationally recognised, and have a well-developed and diversified VTE infrastructure offering courses in a wide range of disciplines. Countries that attract the most foreign students are the **US** (mainly from Asia and Latin America), the **UK** (from former colonies with a similar educational system), **Germany** (which attracts students from Europe in disciplines like engineering), **France** (which is the epicentre for VTE from francophone countries) as well as **Australia** and **Japan**. Together these six countries accounted for over 67 per cent of all foreign students in the world.[5]

Nonetheless, many other countries are establishing a larger presence in competing for foreign students in the growing global VTE market. They include **Malaysia, Singapore** and **China,** which together account for about 250,000 students in all with a combined share of 12 per cent of the global market. Malaysia enrolled 44,390 foreign students from over 110 countries in 2006 – i.e. 2.5 per cent of the global market. In 2005, about 66,000 foreign students enrolled in Singapore, an increase of 32 per cent over 2004, with Singapore positioning itself as a regional centre of excellence offering the best of 'East' and 'West' and hoping to attract 150,000 by 2015 (although it suffered a setback when the University of New South Wales decided to close its Singapore campus (UNSW Asia). That leaves about 140,000 foreign students studying in China as at 2006.

India is another country with a large number of foreign students, mainly from South Asia and the Indian Ocean Rim. India's handful of world-class VTE institutions (i.e. the Indian Institutes of Management and Technology [IIMs and IITs]), are overcrowded. Domestic competition for entry into them is so intense that they do not have room to accommodate foreign students. With exceptions like the Delhi School of Economics and the Manipal Complex, the quality of the rest of India's VTE is so poor that it does not attract many foreign students. Were India's VTE system to be privatised, with greater openness to the entry of foreign institutions, India would emerge as one of the largest host countries for a foreign student population, particularly from Asia, the Middle East and Africa.

South Africa also has a large number of foreign students from the rest of Africa. These five countries (i.e. India, China, Singapore, Malaysia and South Africa) provide reference points for, and pose competition to, Mauritius as a potential HRD exporter. However, many more countries are now entering the HRD export market as service providers. For that reason it is essential if not urgent for Mauritius to: (i) develop its capabilities in this sector at a much faster rate than at present, so as not to suffer **'last mover disadvantage'**; (ii) pinpoint the areas and disciplines in which capabilities should be developed in order of priority; (iii) identify the partnerships it needs (with countries and established institutions from around the world) to make a success of its initiatives; and (iv) ensure that the quality standards it adopts and the degrees, diplomas and certificates it awards to students are accepted and recognised around the world.

The **markets** that Mauritius should focus on are: **Africa** – eastern, southern and francophone; **Indian Ocean Rim** islands; the **Gulf** States; **India**, in partnership with Indian institutions; the rest of **South Asia**, especially **Bangladesh, Nepal** and **Sri Lanka**; ASEAN, especially **Burma, Cambodia, Laos** and **Vietnam**; **China** and **Taiwan; Australia, New Zealand** and **Oceania**; and **Europe**, particularly **new Europe** as well as **Britain** and **France**.

To penetrate those markets systematically and credibly, Mauritius will need to consider partnerships with governments, educational establishments and private players in South Africa, India, Malaysia, Singapore, China and Australia as well as with the UK and France.

Background, evolution, challenges and obstacles

It was to explore the possibilities and challenges of expanding HRD service exports that a symposium was held in April 2008. At that event, the Government of Mauritius's intent to make the island a **regional** centre for HRD service exports was underlined. However, it was noted that a national strategy had been announced **five years ago** to:

- Position the island as a knowledge hub for the region;
- Attain world-class status in vocational and tertiary education;
- Attract an international student community – with special focus on IOR and Africa;
- Attract high-quality institutions of higher learning from around the world; and to
- Attract a highly qualified international teaching staff.

Accordingly, procedures were streamlined by the Ministry of Finance and Economic Development (MFED) for rapid approval of applications by institutions providing VTE (private and public, foreign and domestic). The Ministry of Education and Human Resources (MFED) went even further and prepared a National Policy Framework for the Board of Investment to attract FDI in VTE. However, after five years it was reasonable to ask what exactly had been achieved? Had regionally focused objectives been met? Had HRD service exports been increased to any significant degree?

Since 2000, Mauritian VTE has expanded and diversified, but only to meet its growing *domestic* needs. It now has two public universities – the **University of Mauritius (UoM)** and the **University of Technology in Mauritius (UTM)** – providing undergraduate and postgraduate education in a number of disciplines. In addition, there are four specialised institutions.[6] These six **public** entities are regulated by the Tertiary Education Commission (TEC). Three public polytechnics – managed by the Technical School Management Trust Fund – along with the **Industrial & Vocational Training Board**, offer diploma and certificate programmes for vocational training. The **Mauritius Institute of Health** provides specialised tertiary education in the medical field. Augmenting this **public** VTE infrastructure (and regulated by an unduly complex regulatory regime given the size of the country) are four **'regional'** institutions viz. the **University of the Indian Ocean (UIO), the Institut de la Francophonie pour l'Entrepreneuriat (IFE)', the SSR Medical College (SSRMC) and the Mauras College of Dentistry (MCD).**

In addition to these 15 public institutions, there are over 40 **private** institutions licensed to deliver tertiary education/training in specific areas. They cover subject areas such as: IT, law, management, business studies, accountancy and finance. Most such entities are local counterparts, agencies or franchisees of overseas institutions; however, they are not all of a high enough standard to establish the right brand image for Mauritius in this competitive domain. They offer courses ranging from sub-degree diplomas and certificates to postgraduate degrees through a mixed-mode system involving distance learning, as well as face-to-face tutorials in classroom settings. Enrolment in **private** institutions has been outpacing that in **public** institutions by a significant multiple. The steady expansion of private institutions has also enabled Mauritius to attract a higher calibre of fee-paying student and permitting it to offer multi-cultural exchange programmes and offshore campuses. In addition, the rapid growth of the ICT, BPO and ITES service industries has been encouraging applications for distance and e-learning.

Yet, taken together or separately, does this panoply of more than 55 public and private institutions provide appropriate or adequate foundations upon which to build the institutional structure needed for HRD exports? What do these institutions contribute to HRD service exports at the present time? The reality is that almost all these institutions cater to the local market, although there are some foreign students in Mauritius. They do not constitute an important enough market for export earnings from HRD services to register as a significant source of revenue. Statistics from the Tertiary Education Commission revealed that in December 2007, the total number of foreign students in Mauritius was 570.[7] The gap between this figure and the more than 66,000 overseas students in Singapore, suggests illustratively the potential for HRD exports from Mauritius. The island's foreign students originate from the Seychelles, Comoros, South Africa, Uganda, Kenya and India, among others.

So far, Mauritian stakeholders have been more concerned by the gap between **local human resources demand** (i.e. the needs of the evolving labour market in Mauritius) and **local supply**, i.e. the output of the VTE system. The mismatch has resulted in the paradox of a high and growing unemployment rate (more than 10 per cent) in the face of acute labour shortages (for high-level personnel) in all sectors of the economy, particularly in financial services and ICT industries where expansion has been constrained by the unavailability of qualified personnel. Studies will have to be carried out on the same demand-supply gap for the surrounding **region** (IOR and Africa) or the **rest of the world** to establish the context for Mauritius's plans to expand HRD services. The focus of these studies should be on: (i) which markets –

other than Africa – present opportunities for exporting HRD services and which of these Mauritius should be focusing on; (ii) which areas of VTE it should specialise in; (iii) how VTE should evolve from where it is now (serving the domestic market) to where it aspires to be (catering to regional and global markets); and (iv) what needs to be done by a variety of players (government, regulators, domestic and foreign stakeholders) to move the island to its intended destination as a significant HRD services exporter.

The pertinent question should be how a successful HRD **export** capacity might be developed. Given where Mauritius is now, what is the optimal path? With too much emphasis on the domestic scene, there tends to be insufficient focus on the policies, mindset and infrastructure (hard and soft) needed for **exporting** such services: i.e. by attracting the requisite FDI from educational institutions abroad. An export-orientated focus would result in establishing a VTE infrastructure that was far larger than required or justified by domestic needs, but commensurate in the context of wider regional and global needs for such services.

Discussions at the symposium in 2008 reflected the difficulty experienced by domestic policy-makers/regulators (the Ministry of Education and Human Resources and related commissions) in visualising what needs to be done to develop **HRD service *export* capabilities**, regardless of implications for domestic VTE. These discussions suggested an implicitly closed mindset, reluctant to open VTE space to foreign competition or to depart from a **public** to a **private provision** model in education. This fundamental attitudinal difficulty has to be overcome before progress toward exporting HRD services can be made.

It is also questionable whether the TEC is qualified (in terms of constitution and capacity) to apply **global** standards for regulating **private** VTE institutions that exported HRD services. There is a clear risk that if the TEC's **domestic** regulatory function was extended to the export domain, it could compromise exports by adopting a protectionist stance, for example, using its accreditation and certification powers to restrict or delay entry, competition and innovation. This seems to be happening now, with a queue of private entrants complaining about being blocked from investing for no good reason. What was said in chapter 5 on this issue, insofar as it concerns the healthcare domain, applies with equal validity and force to the education domain. The underlying difficulties and fears are the same and should be dealt with in the same way.

In terms of the disciplines that Mauritius needed to focus on for HRD/VTE exports, the ones identified at the symposium included (not necessarily in order of priority): areas in which the island has established and demonstrated strengths; areas in which it is developing a capacity for future growth; and other areas of global market interest and special African interest.

Areas in which Mauritius has established and demonstrated strengths include sugar technology and plantation management (for students from Africa – particularly

Mozambique, Zimbabwe, Madagascar and Tanzania – and India/Asia) as well as undergraduate and postgraduate education, along with vocational training, for all levels of personnel in the hospitality and tourism industry. In the latter area, Mauritius needs to establish strong partnerships with established hospitality industry schools in Switzerland and India. Finally, given Mauritius's ambitions to move up the value chain in textiles, garments and haute couture, it was thought that VTE in the fashion and design industry would be useful as well.

Areas in which Mauritius is developing a capacity for future growth include financial services with a wide range of VTE offerings, ranging from basic bookkeeping and accountancy to more sophisticated financial analysis for corporate finance and quantitative finance, with MBA and MSc. course offerings (with a finance major) as well as VTE in banking, insurance, corporate and trust management services, private banking and asset management. Other areas are the full gamut of training for the rapidly growing ICT/BPO/KPO/RPO industry; medical education for doctors, nurses and paraprofessionals, as well as for hospital and health system administration; specialised teacher training for an growing education sector intent on expanding its export capability; and VTE in civil and mechanical engineering, as well as architecture, design and urban planning for the growing construction industry.

The foregoing areas play to Mauritius's own needs and strengths while serving the needs of export markets. In addition, other areas of global market interest and special African interest might include possibilities such as business administration and management sciences; public administration and parastatal organisation management; central banking; and regulation and regulatory agency management in areas such as regulation for financial services, utilities and for ensuring fair competition in the economy. With its plurality and multilinguality, Mauritius has the potential to become a major regional centre for language training for students from the Asian, Antipodean, Middle-Eastern and African markets.

Some of these specific areas are discussed further in the following sections, beginning with the critically important issue of the approach that should be taken to accreditation and regulation of VTE institutions, especially those in the private sector.

Accreditation and regulation of VTE institutions

As with healthcare and life science services (see previous chapter) accreditation and regulation (A&R) assumes a critical significance in exports for vocational and tertiary education. While it is not 'a matter of life and death' as in healthcare, educational A&R influences 'reputation' in a way that could result in the difference between success and failure in global market acceptance of the human resource development (HRD) services that Mauritius would wish to export. With the Treaty of Bologna (1999), the globalisation of HRD services requires globally recognised/accepted standards to be applied and maintained. At the same time, increased access to export opportunities on the part of more countries/players is increasing global competition and innovation in course curricula, teaching methods/modes and materials. Such competition now occurs mainly among *private* institutions. The pervasive influence of the Internet and world wide web offers hitherto unimagined opportunities for increasing access to global markets by making the world effectively borderless. However, it also encourages fraud and malpractice on a significant scale.

Given these circumstances, successful export of HRD services depends on quality institutions awarding recognised qualifications. For consumer confidence to be inspired and maintained, both of these need to be assured and continuously upgraded through credible accreditation, regulation and reporting, undertaken by qualified bodies (whether public or private, international or national).

The most meaningful regulation is imposed by the marketplace when similar services are exported competitively around the world. Providers of good services flourish from the market's favour and patronage, while poor service providers fail through lack of patronage by the marketplace. Consumers would not use poor services in VTE and this is even less the case in HLSS. However, such market outcomes do not materialise overnight. It takes time for reputation to be built and established, but less time for it to be lost.

In the burgeoning HRD export domain, new private institutions compete with, among others, Harvard, Stanford, Oxford, Cambridge, the Sorbonne etc. These institutions have reputations built up over centuries. Some of them are private, strengthened through endowments. Many (especially in the EU) are publicly funded. They pose 'unfair subsidised competition' to new private institutions competing in the global HRD service export market: it is not a level playing field as far as endowments and attributes are concerned. Players in HRD exports are also competing with newer institutions such as the Open University of the UK and UNISA in South Africa (both of which are also publicly funded), which have now built up global reputations in distance and e-learning even more rapidly than the ancient universities.

Over the last few decades, a loose network of global A&R in HRD services has emerged in Mauritius, more through default and coincidence than through design. It embraces: **national** accreditation systems in every country, **regional** systems such as the European Higher Education Area, Bologna beyond Europe, the National Academic Recognition Information Centre and the European Network of National Information Centres and, at the **global** level, UNESCO and the International Network of Quality Assurance Agencies in Higher Education (INQAAHE), which include regional branches.

Accreditation is important for an educational institution exporting HRD services because of the: credibility it engenders in the minds of potential students; recognition it creates of an institution's quality and reputation; linkage that it provides in joining the world's academic and professional communities; spur it provides to continuous self-improvement; potential it creates for introduction to more desirable suitors (i.e. if a particular institution has internationally recognised accreditation, it becomes more attractive as a merger or takeover target); and the 'risk insurance' it gives in protecting against uncertainty.

At present most A&R in the VTE domain is national. However, its credibility is enhanced if the national A&R system is tied to a globally recognised body such as the INQAAHE. The credibility that membership of such a body provides can be strengthened by enabling national laws that protect higher and further education and punish fraud. It can be enhanced by the adoption and use of benchmark standards and criteria. Having the right standards is necessary, but not sufficient. Conformance of day-to-day practice with such standards has to be monitored and enforced, and that can only be done by having inspection teams that are beyond reproach. Such teams are usually drawn from a range of disciplines, but they need to be trained as 'integrated teams' rather than as a loose collection of disparate individuals and specialisations. A sound A&R system for VTE needs to define progression and pathways. It has to have decision-making independence on the part of the apex A&R body, yet needs to involve all stakeholders in the decisions it makes. It has to be transparent, but not in a way that embarrasses the well-intentioned.

A model from which Mauritius might learn, or use directly to meet its own A&R requirements for HRD exports, is that of the British Accreditation Council. BAC is a body recognised by governments and other stakeholders in education all over the world. It is the leading UK provider of accreditation for independent higher education. At the same time, the UK is the world's second largest exporter of HRD services. BAC was set up in 1984 as a 'charity' (i.e. not-for-profit NGO) limited by guarantee and governed by a council of stakeholders. It operates through an executive committee and an accreditation committee. It has developed common global standards by working with accreditation bodies around the world, through INQAAHE and its regional groups and also with the Australian Quality Assurance Association (AQAAN).

BAC is dedicated to establishing and raising standards in education through teams of skilled inspectors (mainly Her Majesty's Schools Inspectors from the Quality Assurance Association [QAA], the Office for Standards in Education [OFSTED] etc). It works with private and public educational institutions and government ministries. BAC is an accrediting agency registered with OFSTED in the UK to accredit institutions under the new Home Office points-based system for managed migration. It maintains good relations with all government departments with a vested interest in improving education at all levels, including VTE: i.e. the Department of Children, Schools and Families (DCSF), Department for Innovation, Universities and Skills (DIUS), Home Office/Border and Immigration Agency, British Council, Open and Distance Learning Quality Council (ODLQC), QAA and NARIC-UK.

Though British in nationality and location, BAC's remit is not limited to the UK. It has accredited over 260 educational institutions in 12 countries including the UK,

Bulgaria, the Czech Republic, France, Germany, Greece, India, **Mauritius**, Pakistan, Spain, Switzerland and the UAE. It employs a three-stage inspection procedure (see below), coupled with ongoing spot checks and frequent visits, to substantiate accreditation.

Stage 1 comprises **vetting of application documentation** through comprehensive checking of the subject institution's legal status, audited accounts, references and company records; employers' liability insurance; health and safety compliance and record; comprehensive risk assessment; its publicity (i.e. prospectus and website); staff and student handbooks; and faculty CVs. Prior to stage 1 and during it, BAC ensures conformity with statutory requirements such as: requirements for fire, health and safety standards; rules on visa students and employment; copyright regulations; checks of residential accommodation, if offered as part of the course; background checks of all staff, if students are under 18 years of age; and responses to disability or other anti-discrimination legislation.

Stage 2 comprises **compliance with statutory requirements and minimum standards** which involves inspecting: (i) the institution's premises and the efforts made to respect health/safety regulations, to ensure that premises are secure, properly equipped and offer suitable accommodation; (ii) arrangements in place for student background checks and ensuring student welfare, e.g. support for local and overseas students and meeting special needs (in terms of diet, disability or language for example), accommodation and other statutory requirements e.g. criminal record bureau checking; and (iii) the institution's management and staffing, i.e. to ensure effective management, the right quantity of qualified staff, staff and student attendance monitoring and ability to meet all statutory requirements in conforming with applicable employment legislation, PAYE, clear entry requirements etc.

Stage 3 is **management of quality, teaching and learning**, which involves: (i) examining detailed course requirements, student progress, standards review and monitoring, student feedback and complaints handling, monitoring accredited qualifications, internal awards and degree programmes and the quality control system; and (ii) reviewing/monitoring on a regular basis the planning and delivery of courses, staff knowledge and skills, EFL support, study resources and learning materials, and advice provided to students on further study and employment

Following this three-stage inspection process, accreditation is awarded by BAC's accreditation committee for up to four years. In terms of **post-accreditation**, BAC expects to see continuous improvement over this period i.e. a commitment from the accredited institution to keep upgrading itself, its staff, its courses and its facilities. It monitors performance of accredited institutions through spot-checks, interim visits and a complaints procedure, with no advance notice of spot-checks being given.

BAC is an example at the high end of the A&R continuum. India offers another, different kind of example for A&R in the HRD/VTE domain. Its regulatory structure and architecture is more complex than UK's, because its size and federal constitution require different levels of statutory control. Unfortunately, the education and VTE sectors in India are dominated by **public** institutions of a low quality. Emphasis on public education has retarded delivery of proper education to the country's large population.

India's regulatory structure and practices reflect weaknesses that a country like Mauritius must avoid. A complex, multi-layered Indian regulatory structure for VTE has failed to ensure quality education and the effective use of public resources, a large proportion of which are diverted from the purposes they are intended for. This situation has created much regulatory conflict and failure.[8] It has impaired India's ability to be an effective competitor in the global market for HRD service exports, despite endowments that give it a natural advantage in this domain. Prolonged and counterproductive government intervention in, and domination of, education have prevented India from being as competitive an HRD service exporter as it otherwise would be if such exports were left to the private sector and to its world-class institutions.

Under a model proposed by the *Conservatoire National des Arts et Métiers* (CNAM) for the development of HRD services in Mauritius, the suggestion is that the authorities (i.e. the government and the Ministry of Education and Human Resources) draw up a strategy for the future with the participation of all stakeholders, including regulators. That would involve: (i) setting up Centres of Excellence in specific disciplines; (ii) encouraging foreign and local specialists to share experience and practical know-how; (iii) encouraging collaborative partnerships between local companies and established foreign VTE-multinational corporations; (iv) supporting distance and lifelong learning; (v) establishing a benchmark for Africa; and (vi) creating a climate conducive to setting up foreign HRD institutions.

Figure 6.3 HRD services model proposed

What is unclear under this model is what the regulatory structure and protocol would be for new private institutions (many of them foreign or local–foreign partnerships) set up to cater to the HRD export market? Would TEC regulate them? What would that imply? What risks would it entail? Alternatively, should an A&R solution be sought that would bypass TEC, relying instead on existing international bodies to assure quality and reputation (e.g. BAC)? That would have the advantage of eliminating any possibility of A&R being used as a protectionist rather than quality control device, and would avert any hint of bias where existing **domestic** private VTE institutions are concerned, especially when connected to politically vested interests.

During the symposium, the Mauritius Employers Federation (MEF) – which provides a significant amount of VTE – had a firm view on the over-complexity of A&R in Mauritius. For what is a small, self-contained sector, the governance of VTE seems to MEF to be too elaborate and fragmented. Disparate legislation has created too many governing bodies. Legislation governing VTE includes: the Education Act, the TEC Act, the Mauritius Qualifications Authority (MQA) Act, the Human Resource Development Council (HRDC) Act and the IVTB Act. These multiple acts had created multiple institutions charged with governance and oversight responsibilities including IVTB, TEC, MQA and HRDC.

In MEF's view, to attract investment by the private sector in VTE exports, the government has to act as facilitator. It has to delegate to private institutions the role of investors, promoters and operators. Regulatory institutions have to catalyse inward investment in VTE rather than block it. Broadly, MEF agrees on government policies, but it has reservations about the way in which these are being implemented. Instead of promoting and facilitating HRD service exports, existing regulatory institutions focus on control, blockage and the exercise of statutory power in the name of 'regulation' for quality control.

TEC and MQA operate in ways that are not conducive to expanding HRD service exports from Mauritius. For that reason, MEF feels that their powers to accredit and regulate **in the export market** have to be removed. It is also debatable whether they have the competence or knowledge needed to regulate the export market for HRD services with its large, challenging and continually evolving needs. Moreover, with the international market acting as a regulator in its own right, there is no need for TEC and MQA involvement in that market. It would be better to get established international A&R institutions involved instead.

These concerns of the MEF are not trivial. They are supported by anecdotal evidence from a variety of sources, which suggest that the present A&R infrastructure in Mauritius for VTE, and particularly for **exports** of VTE, needs to be overhauled. If concerns expressed at the symposium about the manner in which these regulatory bodies operate are even partly valid, it is unarguable that they would pose bottlenecks to the expansion of HRD service exports.

The following sections provide brief accounts concerning particular fields of VTE provision in which Mauritius might choose to specialise.

Vocational and tertiary education in the ICT and business process outsourcing industry[9]

Of all the disciplines in which there is a global, regional and national shortage of qualified people, the ICT/BPO industry is top of the list and requires urgent expansion of VTE capacity. In Mauritius there remains a clear need for a diversified, results-oriented, localised IT education platform. It is needed at all levels of IT skill development, moderate as well as high, and in a number of niche sectors (as discussed in chapter 4). Mauritius has attracted a number of Indian training institutes that specialise in this domain, but their output barely meets the needs of the island's domestic IT labour market. These and other institutions need to expand and ramp up scale to create sufficient capacity for IT/BPO/KPO training to meet *regional* needs as well, through triangulation with India, South Africa, Malaysia and Singapore to diversify the partnership base.

For VTE in the ICT/BPO industries, particular attention needs to be paid to enhancing skills in **IT engineering and R&D services**, which are likely to form a significant part of many service providers' revenues and contribute to expansion of the outsourcing market; **systems integration and IT infrastructure management; and enterprise resource planning (ERP), product development and testing**. In these three areas, vocational training based on a modular higher education approach is crucial. A specialised area related to the second of these skills areas is 'network development' – i.e. construction of corporate IT networks for email, voicemail, customer support and supply chain management – from the bottom up. With even

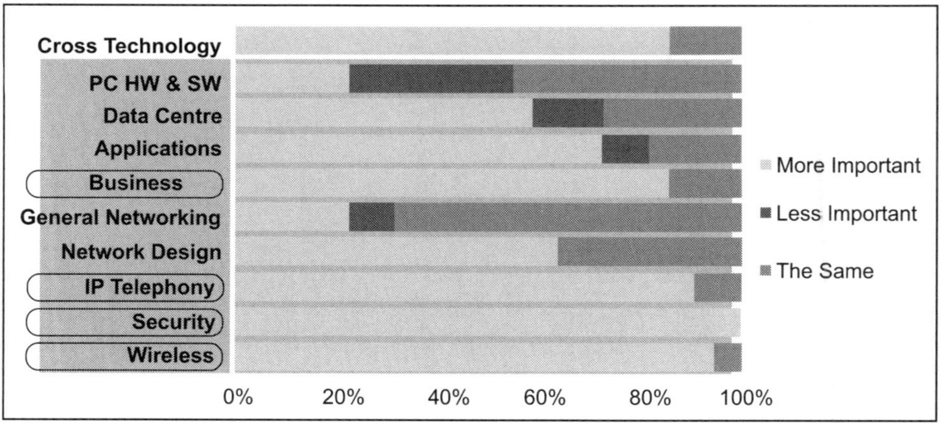

Figure 6.4 Future importance of skills by technology/skills area

small and medium-sized enterprises (SMEs) now having dedicated internal networks (intranets), the demand for skilled network specialists has exploded.

For example, a survey carried out in South Africa recently involving a number of companies, suggested that 36 per cent of them had hired network engineers in the last 12 months. Of these, 62 per cent found it difficult to find network engineers with the right skills, while 50 per cent struggled to find any IT people with the right skills and 40 per cent felt that the right skills were too expensive. The findings of that survey were typical and would probably be the same in any country.[10]

Specific ICT skill sets that Mauritius needs to develop the VTE capacity to provide for the domestic and export markets include (in order of importance): security, wireless, IP telephony, business, applications, network design, data centre, general networking and PC hardware/software.[11]

Vocational and tertiary education in financial services

Exporting VTE for financial services requires building on sound education foundations in basic and advanced mathematics and computing skills. Such VTE is best provided in/from environments where there is a science and mathematics culture in high schools, complemented by the teaching of micro/macro economics at 'A' and undergraduate levels. VTE in finance has to focus on financial markets, institutions and analytical financial economics. The ideal postgraduate Master of Science (MSc.) degree in finance is invariably built on a high-school mathematics background, with an undergraduate economics education heavy on quantitative skills. It is only on such foundations that postgraduate work can be structured to include quantitative financial and statistical analysis, econometrics, corporate finance analysis, derivative structures and contracts, options pricing, portfolio and stock analysis and value analysis.

Postgraduate qualifications apart, the financial services industry requires continuing education for the professionals involved through tailored vocational training geared to specific job functions. Such training has to be made mandatory by regulators, and must be certification-linked. Generally, for entry-level professionals, this requires certificate courses of the kind provided in India by the National Stock Exchange (NSE) and NSE Certification in Financial Markets (NCFM). Other courses that emphasise quantitative finance need to be designed for frontline supervisors and middle managers. Such training helps finance professionals with weak quantitative maths foundations to operate successfully. It enables people with the right foundations to deal with real-world applications and stay abreast of current developments. For senior finance managers finance, continuous exposure to high-end strategic thinking and to knowledge about new market developments, derivative contracts and risk management, is essential if not critical. This is usually achieved through conferences with a strong substantive training/learning component aimed at senior management (for example, of the kind provided by the Invest India Economic Foundation).

As far as Mauritius is concerned, particular features worth emphasising if the island is to provide properly designed VTE in finance probably include:

- **Multinational exposure**: As far as financial VTE is concerned, Mauritius has to project itself as a blend of Africa, the Middle East, India and East Asia. That regional geography adds a dimension of region-specific expertise that aspiring graduates would wish to acquire.
- **Hugging the frontiers of financial knowledge**: Finance VTE in Mauritius has to emphasise the global shift away from bank-dominated finance to market-dominated finance, emphasising the roles of derivatives for risk management and speculative price discovery.
- **Emphasis on quantitative finance training**: Highly sophisticated mathematics and statistics are required as foundation pre-requisites for training in financial economics and derivatives trading. The highest value VTE for finance is in those two sub-specialisations, where there is an acute global skills shortage.
- **Dealing with computational complexity**: All the new ideas in quantitative finance work only when they are turned into operational algorithmic IT systems that can trade automatically.
- **Development of strong financial real-time databases**: No sophisticated analytical training in finance can be provided without strong operational databases. This may require buying databases on (say) India or South Africa. However, there is an opportunity to create unique databases on Africa and Mauritius so as to get an IPR and region-specific training edge.

An ecosystem for providing/exporting VTE in finance

Providing VTE in finance successfully to a global population of students requires a complex supporting ecosystem. If Mauritius (or any country) were to offer recognised VTE in finance, it would need a globally respected financial services industry, rooted in the domestic economy but with global reach. A financial services industry focused only on the Mauritius market would be inadequate as an 'applied research laboratory' for finance students, who are likely to operate on a regional if not global basis. In addition to a credible international financial services industry, such an ecosystem also needs a critical mass of senior finance and economics academics and intellectuals working at universities and think tanks. They need to be tightly linked in a systematic, programmed way to knowledgeable senior managers/professionals in the financial services industry and other industries that provide it with crucial support (for instance, the consulting industry and the IT industry).

Private firms can provide short-term training and conferencing in finance successfully. For example, in India the Invest India Economic Foundation (IIEF), Dun & Bradstreet, the Institute of Management Accountants (IMA), the Economist Intelligence Unit and a number of similar entities (domestic and foreign) have established a global reputation in this domain. However, they draw on extant intellectual and practitioner resources in the local (and global) financial world to deliver such training, as do other Indian institutions like IIMs, IITs and leading business schools.

Building multiple academic–industry linkages in economics and finance is crucial if Mauritius is to capture a market share of high-value added VTE in finance. The only way of establishing such linkages quickly is to attract foreign talent. That is, the country should contract globally known financial academics (from South Africa, India, Singapore, Hong Kong and China) to commit to spending a certain number of weeks/months each year in Mauritius. In part, they could organise key conferences and seminars for regional/global attendance with a strong training feature attached. More importantly, a core group of such people spending part of their time in Mauritius on a regular basis would help to incubate and grow similar local capabilities.

Building such an ecosystem would result in VTE **supply** capacity and **demand** for Mauritius-based financial education reinforcing one another. On the supply side, Mauritius needs to attract (with private rather than public financing) about 50 top-quality finance scholars from around the world to its two universities, and to two or three more financial and economic policy research institutes that need to be created. These scholars would do research and teach on a part-time basis for one or two terms each year under contracts stretching over five years. This 'critical core' need comprise no more than 20 'senior fellows' resident in Mauritius at any given time, with the remaining 30 being on call abroad. In terms of infrastructure to support such a 'faculty', Mauritius would need four or five finance 'departments' or institutions with 10–15 senior fellows each.

The body of available 'tutors' attracted to Mauritius on a part-time basis would meet three specific demands: (i) consulting and research, which local and regional financial services industries require and are willing to pay for; (ii) engagement in local/regional policy debates and policy-making processes; and (iii) delivering the fully array of VTE in finance. The Government of Mauritius's role would be critical for kick-starting the building of such an ecosystem. It would need to make a large intervention at the outset, which would taper off to roughly half its start-up intensity over a ten-year period and down to virtually no public input after 15 years.

It was proposed at the symposium that Mauritius could be used as a base for training professionals in **Islamic banking and finance (IBF).** At the time of writing, there were over 300 Islamic banking financial institutions operating out of 75 countries worldwide, with total assets managed under IBF exceeding US$1 trillion. The growth rate of the global Islamic financial industry is 15–20 per cent annually. Private wealth in the Arabian Gulf is estimated to be more than US$1.5 trillion. Switzerland is home to an estimated US$200 billion or more in Muslim-owned private accounts. Kuala Lumpur, Jakarta, Singapore and Dubai are now developing dedicated systems and expertise to manage Muslim wealth. Since the September 11 attacks in 2001, this wealth was looking for safer havens outside the western world, which is seen as increasingly hostile to Islam and to predominantly Muslim countries.

Of the 1.6 billion Muslims in the world, over 22 per cent (or 442 million) reside in Africa, making the continent an enormous potential market for IBF. Sudan, Egypt, Gambia and South Africa are among the African countries that have IBF operations. Mauritius is in a unique position to be an IBF hub for the continent given its location, infrastructure and government support. The island has a strong independent judiciary, which is essential for the resolution of disputes arising out of contracts upon which IBF is based, and has a legal system that is easily adaptable to accommodating Islamic financial services. The present tax regime allows IBF products to compete on a level playing field with conventional financial products.

Several types of training programmes need to be put in place for the implementation and development of IBF in Mauritius and Africa. Specialised IBF courses need to be designed for accountants, auditors, regulators, risk-management specialists, lawyers, bankers, insurance operators and other professional groups. Such programmes would cover Islamic accounting; Islamic jurisprudence and Islamic law; IBF products and services; Islamic insurance; and permissible risk management under Islamic law. Training for regulators in IBF is also needed through special arrangements with:

- **The Islamic Development Bank** (IsDB): through its technical co-operation programme.
- **The Accounting and Auditing Organization for Islamic Financial Institutions**, which is the main standard-setting organisation for Islamic finance. It has issued 56 standards on accounting, auditing, governance, ethical and Shariah standards, including a statement on capital adequacy. At the time of writing, its membership stood at around 140 financial institutions from 30 countries.
- **The Islamic Financial Services Board (IFSB)**: an international standard-setting organisation that promotes and enhances the soundness and stability of the IBF industry by issuing global prudential standards and guiding principles, broadly defined to include banking, capital markets and insurance. The IFSB also conducts research and co-ordinated initiatives on industry-related issues. It had 20 full members, 15 associate members and 90 observer members, including central banks, international organisations and financial institutions.

Vocational and tertiary education in business and management studies

Business and management education influences the growth of companies and economies at the local, regional and global levels through: (i) **training** and specialised skills development in marketing, operations management, HRD, finance and accounting; (ii) **innovation**, which requires management teams capable of prioritising investment, allocating resources and aligning human capital to achieve key objectives; and (iii) **research** conducted by business school faculty that contributes to expanding knowledge and helps companies to acquire a better understanding of their strategies for competition and innovation.

The classic Master of Business Administration (MBA) is now a well-accepted, globally recognised degree replicated in almost every country as a university course. MBAs from different universities vary considerably in terms of the recognition they attract, depending on the school they have been awarded by and the majors or minors that students have specialised in. MBAs have also developed various regional and lingual flavours. European schools specialise in offering multilingual and multidisciplinary degrees that equip students to operate better across borders in an increasingly globalised business environment.

Business and management schools have three main missions: (i) **knowledge creation**, which requires original research to be done and made accessible to a broad constituency, with research contributing to improving continually the practice of management and helping managers/firms to improve performance; (ii) **knowledge dissemination**, which necessitates that research is translated into applied know-how through skills that can be taught to students; and (iii) **knowledge certification**, which requires the qualifications awarded through degrees to be widely recognised and relevant in today's business world.

However, the content and nature of business education and the qualifications sought by students around the world keeps evolving and changing. What seems apparent from the London School of Economics' experience is that in the UK there has been a strong increase in applications for all postgraduate programmes, with a growing interest in **part-time** programmes (MSc. and MBA). There has also been an increase in foreign and female applicants, confirming the trends toward globalisation and gender equalisation of management education at the top level. North American MBA programmes are admitting younger candidates (i.e., graduating students or very recent graduates with little or no work experience) and encouraging the introduction of more pre-experience Masters (MSc.) programmes, including the London School of Economics MSc. in management in 2008. The London Business School (LBS) and Massachusetts Institute of Technology have announced plans for their own MSc. degrees in management in 2009 or later.

The new two-year MSc. in management course being introduced by the LSE combines the best aspects of the MSc. and the MBA. It offers an integrated management course that requires both academic rigour *and* practical work experience over a 21-month period, with the degree offering customised career programmes and internships. The course has been designed for recent graduates from any discipline with demonstrated quantitative abilities and superior communications skills. Students tap into 'the LSE experience' to gain a global political understanding in addition to the business studies knowledge they acquire.

This is a feature that Mauritius could emulate in a different way by offering a unique MSc. course that immerses students in specialised knowledge about the business environments, economies and financial systems of Asia and Africa (as well as IBF). The LSE Master's course has an optional international exchange via the Community of European Management Schools (CEMs). This is another feature Mauritius could emulate, by offering similar exchanges with top universities in South Africa, India and Singapore/Hong Kong/China.

A useful outcome of the symposium was the interest expressed by the SP Jain School of Management & Finance in India to set up a satellite school and campus in Mauritius. With some effort by the Board of Investment (BoI), interest could be attracted on the part of a number of other Indian institutions (such as the Manipal Group), which have established campuses abroad and acquired a regional reputation. Yet Mauritius's attempts to attract private investment in this domain should not be restricted to Indian institutions. The BoI should attract qualified institutions from the UK, France, South Africa, Singapore and Australia to set up in Mauritius and enhance their capacity to serve the African, Middle-Eastern and Asian student markets by doing so.

Vocational and tertiary education in the hospitality industry

Mauritius has established a global reputation in the hospitality and tourism industry. Its training facilities in that industry are world class for lower and mid-level personnel, but not yet of that standard for top personnel. There is no reason why in this industry Mauritius cannot aspire to offer the best VTE available in the world, through partnerships with hotel and hospitality management schools in Switzerland, Australia, France and India.

A pertinent case study presented at the symposium was that of the *Ecole Hôtelière de Lausanne (EHL)*, which seems to be the type of partner Mauritius should attract to set up a campus in the country for Asian and African student populations. EHL has been in existence for over a century, developing talent and encouraging innovation in the hospitality industry. EHL undertakes research in the hospitality industry (Lausanne Hospitality Research) and carries out hospitality consulting and executive education. It also undertakes a technology and entrepreneurship (EHLITE) programme. Each term it attracts more than 1,700 students representing 82 nationalities and runs three accredited university-level degree programmes:

- **Masters degree in hospitality administration** – 40 students (taken by 2 per cent of students). This postgraduate programme is designed for professionals aiming to develop their capacity to anticipate changes, seize opportunities at the right time and analyse complex problems facing the hospitality industry.

- International hospitality management programme (Bachelor of Science) – 1,520 students (i.e. taken by 90 per cent of EHL's students). This BSc. course stretches over four years including two practical internships (of 16 and 20 weeks). After a grounding in hospitality operations and theoretical knowledge, students acquire transferable knowledge to broaden their career prospects in other fields (such as banking, the healthcare sector etc.).
- Hotel and restaurant management programme (Associate of Science) – 140 students (or 8 per cent of the intake). This programme stretches over four semesters, including two spent on in-company experience for six months each. The course is designed for working professionals aiming for top careers, while encouraging entrepreneurship.

VTE provided in Mauritius for this industry needs to emulate EHL's approach, which aims to: (i) develop managerial competencies while emphasising the strategic dimension of hospitality business management; (ii) expose students to a culture of service (*'savoir-être et savoir-vivre'*); (iii) test management and service theories through practical application; (iv) develop the personality needed to be successful in the industry, i.e. open-minded, energetic diplomatic, innovative, at ease in different social situations, a leader, but also part of a team; (e) develop students' instincts for coping with a mix of cultures/languages, an appreciation of quality, an eye for detail, a strong sense of making sure that everything is 'just right'.

When one considers these attributes, it becomes obvious that Mauritius is a 'natural' for specialising in this particular field. It has all the ingredients, the recipe, the environment and a plethora of resorts and hotels for providing practical training – not just for its own nationals, but for regional students as well from Africa, the Indian Ocean Rim, South Asia, East Asia and the Antipodes.

Vocational and tertiary education in public administration

The idea of establishing a regional Centre of Excellence in Mauritius for vocational and tertiary education/mid-career training in public administration and professional parastatal management has been mooted on several occasions, the first dating back to the late 1970s. However, this aspiration has not yet taken shape, despite oft-declared intent (but no follow-up) on the part of the Mauritian authorities to proceed with such a CoE; and equally frequently declared intent on the part of multilateral and bilateral donors to provide capital and recurrent funding for such centre if it were ever established.

The African Capacity Building Initiative aimed at improving governance on the continent was launched in the 1980s, but located in Harare rather than Mauritius. Subsequent events in Zimbabwe have shown how misguided that decision was, although foresight is always foggier than hindsight. The consensus at the symposium was that this idea should be revived again and followed up on this occasion by the BoI and MFED to translate Government of Mauritius intent into reality.

Mauritius has one of the better performing public administrations in the developing world, indeed it is probably the best model of public administration in Africa. It is often regarded as **non-African**, discounting its ethnicity. For that reason, if no other, it would make the most sense to locate a regional CoE for Africa's public administration in Mauritius. There are a number of other reasons for this location, including: the island's remoteness, which insulates it from the conflicts that plague every other part of Africa; political stability under a plural democratic regime for over 40 years; reasonably good rule of law; the continuity of professional civil administration, regardless of the political hue of the government in power; and, not least, the ability to attract partners from the EU, Asia and the Antipodes, as well as multilateral partners (such as the AfDB, the World Bank, IMF and the European Development Fund) to provide and fund programmes designed to rectify, over the medium and long term, the serious public administration deficits that Africa confronts.

VTE in public administration cannot be confined to the **national** civil service. It must include **provincial** (sub-sovereign) and **local** governments (rural or urban), as well as supra-national **regional** institutions, of which Africa has a plethora. Such institutions employ large numbers of people engaged in activities whose purpose is unclear and whose outcomes are often unintended. Public administration VTE would also embrace parliaments and parliamentarians, parastatals (state-owned corporations), the police force (which usually has its own specialised academy) and the judiciary, for which legal training and knowledge alone is grossly insufficient. As in private firms, it is the human dimension that is **the** crucial factor in determining the quality of public administration.

Africa faces enormous challenges in improving the quality and knowledge base of its public administration across the board. Resort to advanced technology could help to re-shape public administration and facilitate communications at the government–citizen interface, ensuring efficiency, effectiveness and transparency. E-governance can transform traditional modes of operating by providing access to public services that cut across ministries, departments or public agencies through electronic networks. It can enable better real-time monitoring of government performance. E-governance can re-engineer archaic procedures and eliminate civil service dysfunctionality. It can make officialdom more citizen-friendly than traditional government-to-citizen interfaces, adding value to improved governance by greater exercise of the public's right to information, by encouraging transparency and accountability to prevail.

Nonetheless, 'public administration VTE' poses more complex challenges than meets the eye. Such training is much more complicated and difficult to provide/deliver effectively than business education or education in the hospitality, financial services or ICT industries.

First, basic VTE in public administration at the entry level (reinforced through mid-career and senior executive ranks) has to inculcate a culture/ethos of commitment to national interest and public service. It has to develop strong personality traits among civil servants of loyalty, honesty, integrity, immunity to corruption, and a commitment to ensuring fairness and impartiality in the treatment of – and extension of public services to – all citizens regardless of their tribe, colour, caste, creed, race, religion or ethnic affiliation. It has to inculcate a culture of responsibility in the deployment and use of scarce public resources, funded by taxpayers and society at large. It has to assure equality of access to all public services/goods and create a culture of transparency, accountability and acknowledgement of responsibility in policy-making, decision-taking and for administrative action. It also has to create in the civil service the essential capability of dealing with **supranationalism** at regional and global (multilateral) levels, especially given the increasing importance of multilateral collaboration for tackling problems/issues that can only be dealt with sensibly at the global level. It has to cope with the reality of globalisation in the corporate and private worlds, while coping with the asymmetry of political governance proving ineffectual beyond the national level.

Second, the substantive content of public administration VTE courses and training of various types (conferences, symposia, seminars, study tours, government-to-government exchanges etc.) must embrace a wide range of line ministerial disciplines. These range from foreign diplomacy (with specialised knowledge in such areas a global finance, trade, global commons, environmental issues and economics, conflict situations, peacekeeping etc.) to internal security, immigration, emigration and defence, as well as sectoral disciplines such as agriculture, marine resources, manufacturing industry, commerce, health, education, welfare, energy, communications, transport, new technologies, social services, sports, culture, media, arts and so on. VTE in public administration must therefore embrace and engage other educational institutions in the public and private sectors (at home and abroad) in enhancing the quality, knowledge and capability of the civil service at all levels. It must strive to bring together those with the necessary knowledge and experience (again from home or abroad) to with those that need to acquire it.

Third, public administration in the 21st century must enable governments at all levels to adapt and redesign public services and administrative coping capabilities continuously, to meet evolving requirements in rapidly changing socio-economic circumstances that engender higher expectations on the part of citizens and the electorate. It has to facilitate modernisation of anachronistic administrative structures inherited from colonial times, by deploying modern ICT and learning from BPO models in the outsourcing and offshoring worlds. It has to create enabling policies and structures, as well as an overall economic-social-political environment, to encourage rapid growth of investment, employment, output, trade and exports by the private sector. At the same time, it has to strengthen social development, deal with poverty alleviation and provide access to basic services, as well as minimum incomes for the poor to ensure that the fruits of growth are equitably shared to assure its sustainability.

Increasingly, public administration has to be sensitive to regional and global commons, such as checking the cross-border spread of endemic diseases (such as HIV-AIDS or tuberculosis, cholera, bird-flu, SARS etc.) as well dealing with the effects of climate change, global warming, global crime and large-scale cross-border movements of people (legal and illegal) for economic or security reasons. It has to be able to create the capacity to cope with natural disasters (floods, famines, tsunamis, earthquakes, chemical explosions, building collapses etc.), wars, riots and civil disturbances of all kinds.

In short, it is critical to create VTE in public administration (PA-VTE) structures for Africa in Mauritius capable of producing civil servants and administrators who have the knowledge, skills and understanding required to perform the crucial responsibilities of government and adapt governance to constantly evolving requirements in an effective and efficient manner. For that reason, it is essential that the PA-VTE capacity can discern clearly which of the many transitions occurring in the contemporary world will impact most significantly upon the African public sector, and understand what the implications of these changes are likely to be for the training of effective public managers.

That PA-VTE capacity must take into account, for example: (i) the steady weakening of state capacity and disintegration of the state (in the face of global economic forces) alongside growing demand for increased standards of governance; (ii) the implications and consequences of new technologies and media power in instant mass communication, which makes information far more freely available and impossible to filter or control; (iii) the increasing necessity for negotiating with international organisations on matters that affect everyday lives; and (iv) new approaches to political and administrative leadership in a rapidly changing national, regional and global environment.

The PA-VTE structures and institutions built in Mauritius for Africa will need to develop effective public administrators/managers of the future, who will require:

- **New technical competencies** in areas such as strategic planning capability, collaborative capability, substantive policy expertise in the emerging areas, performance measurement skills, presentation skills and regulation in specific areas such as finance, utilities, competition etc.
- **Managerial skills** in areas like understanding of individual and organisational psychology, professional and personal development, capacity to build and nurture a multicultural, multiethnic environment, analytic capability etc.
- **Leadership skills** that understand the demands globalisation will place on future leaders of public ministries and organisations for more creative and effective leadership. This includes the ability to adapt rapidly to change, ethical awareness, sensitivity and commitment, encouraging entrepreneurial and risk-taking ability etc.

- Accordingly, the themes on which PA-VTE should focus are:
    - o Developing future leaders
    - o Fostering public service excellence
    - o Fostering people-centric governance and public service
    - o Strengthening the political and public service interface, as well as fostering public-private partnerships
    - o Fostering integrity and honesty in public service
    - o Developing new ways of working and regulating the economy

Taking the foregoing into consideration, what should the PA-VTE in Mauritius focus on? It should consider formulating courses for African public-sector managers, with participation from other developing countries for experience sharing. In doing so, it should rely on examples of other countries with similar environments, such as Indian institutions, and international exposure of its 'students' through country visits, industry visits etc. The design of courses should combine sector and management issues, emphasising technical knowledge and management principles. The island should make its training as practical as possible, by focusing on governance and policy along with management in specific areas such as trade, investment etc. Financial constraints impinging on African governments should not lead to curtailment of training. Quite the opposite: capacity building should be enhanced with a modified three-pronged approach that incorporates technical and policy aspects, managerial aspects and leadership issues in training programmes. Inviting participation from civil servants in other countries should be encouraged as far as possible.

One of the most valuable outcomes of the Symposium on the Export of Human Resources Services was a gesture by the Administrative Staff College of India (ASCI), which was represented at a senior level. Weeks after the symposium ended, ASCI indicated to the Government of Mauritius and the Commonwealth Secretariat that it would be willing to consider a partnership arrangement with a counterpart in Mauritius to establish joint capacity for PA-VTE on the island, aimed at serving the African regional market for public service training and education. It indicated that, if officially invited to do so by the government via MFED, it would formally undertake to visit Mauritius and work out a basis for taking such a partnership forward to create permanent institutional capacity for providing PA-VTE, with supporting donor funding. As ASCI has considerable cross-border experience in providing PA-VTE and is a respected institution in India and Asia, it would be worthwhile for the government to follow up on this initiative immediately, and create the kind of capacity in Mauritius for establishing a regional Centre of Excellence for PA-VTE that has eluded it for too long.

Vocational and tertiary education in central banking

Training for central bankers and financial system regulators (like the Financial Services Commission) is a specialised extension of VTE for public administration. Equally, it might be considered an extension of VTE in finance. Both perspectives are correct, but only partly. Vocational and tertiary education in central banking (CB-VTE) involves both disciplines, but it involves more than that. For example it also requires specialised knowledge of monetary economics, the formulation of monetary policy, the interplay between fiscal and monetary policy, central bank accounting, and payment settlement and clearing systems.

CB-VTE requires an understanding of relationships between financial and real economies: the impact of liquidity and interest rates on the real economy through public, corporate and household investment, savings and consumption behaviour. It also requires knowledge of inflationary processes and drivers, exchange rate policy/management, open-market operations and intervention, sovereign debt markets and structures, reserves management, liquidity emission and broad as well as narrow money and currency control, along with an understanding of the shifting tectonics in global economics and key commodity prices. It requires knowledge of quantitative economics and quantitative finance, along with knowledge of regulation and supervision of financial systems, markets, institutions and complex financial instruments. In that context, CB-VTE needs to offer training on anti-money laundering and countering the financing of terrorism (AML-CFT) and fraud detection. Finally, it necessitates understanding of international monetary economics and, increasingly, the need for internationally co-ordinated central bank intervention and action, especially in times of financial crises when the impact is almost always globally transmitted.

The above paragraphs make clear why a proper grounding and continuous training (delivered on a regular as well as exigent basis) is so important for central bankers, and they convey an impression of the sort of training needed. Before asserting that an institute for CB-VTE should be set up in Mauritius, it is important to ask which institutes currently train central bankers around the world and in Africa? Can Mauritius serve as a base for training Africa's central bankers? What facilities should be offered? And what are the problems likely to be encountered?

Given the highly specialised nature of central banking, and the reality that there is only one central bank in each country (although there may be a separate regulatory authority, as in Mauritius), it is usual for each central bank to have its own training institute. The better known ones include, for example: the Federal Reserve Training Center in the US; the Centre for Central Banking Studies at the Bank of England in the UK, which provides training to central bankers of former British colonies; the Studienzentrum Gerzensee of the Swiss National Bank, and its national counterparts in almost all continental European countries; and the Bankers Training College, the National Institute of Bank Management and the Indira Gandhi Institute for Development Research, all of which are financed by the Reserve Bank of India (RBI) to deliver different programmes for training central bankers in banking, central banking, monetary economics, econometrics and quantitative finance. More pertinent and proximate for Africa are the South African Reserve Bank College, the Kenya School of Monetary Studies and the Bank of Tanzania Training Institute, to mention but a few.

In smaller countries (such as many in Africa) the cost of a training institute for each central is unaffordable. For that reason, some are created by several central banks pooling their resources. These include, for example, the Southeast Asian Central Bank (SEACEN) Research and Training Institute in Malaysia, which is a joint effort of the central banks of Brunei, Cambodia, Fiji, Indonesia, Korea, Malaysia, Mongolia, Myanmar, Nepal, Papua New Guinea, Singapore, Sri Lanka, Taiwan, Thailand and Vietnam; the West African Training Centre for Banking Studies in Dakar, Senegal; the Institute of Banks of Central African States in Yaoundé, Cameroon; and the West African Institute for Financial and Economic Management (WAIFEM), established by the central banks of The Gambia, Ghana, Liberia, Nigeria and Sierra Leone. More to the point for Mauritius, there is the Macroeconomic and Financial Management Institute of Eastern and Southern Africa (MEFMI), owned by 13 countries, namely Angola, Botswana, Kenya, Lesotho, Malawi, Mozambique, Namibia, Rwanda, Swaziland, Tanzania, Uganda, Zambia and Zimbabwe.

Regional multilateral banks and some regional monetary authorities and central banks (such as the European Central Bank (ECB) and the West African Central Bank for the Central African franc [CFA] zone) also sponsor programmes, conferences and seminars for training central bankers in their respective regions. This is done through either regular or episodic pooled arrangements to provide exigent training when a special situation arises, or to address common urgent concerns (for example, AML-CFT, co-ordinated intervention in a currency crisis, co-ordinated liquidity provision in a systemic crisis etc.)

Then there is the IMF Training Institute and the VTE function in the Bank of International Settlements (BIS), to support central bank training at an apex global level. There is also the more recently established Financial Stability Institute, a joint effort of the IMF, World Bank and the BIS. Apart from providing training at its headquarters in Washington DC, the IMF Institute has set up a number of **regional** training arrangements:

- The Joint Regional Training Centre for Latin America in Brazil, established by the Government of Brazil and the IMF. Courses are generally offered in Spanish, with interpretation into Portuguese, for officials mainly from Latin America and the Caribbean.
- The Joint China–IMF Training Program (CTP), which organises courses in China for Chinese Officials in collaboration with the People's Bank of China.

- The Joint India–IMF Training Programme in Pune, India, is a co-operative venture of the Reserve Bank of India and the IMF, with support from the Government of Australia.
- The Joint Africa Institute (JAI) was established by the African Development Bank, the IMF and the World Bank. It is located in Tunis, with courses offered in English and French.
- The IMF and Arab Monetary Fund, located in Abu Dhabi, United Arab Emirates. It established the Regional Training Programme (RTP) to increase and co-ordinate the training offered to member countries in the Middle East and North Africa region
- In collaboration with the Government of Singapore, the IMF organises courses for officials from countries in the Asia/Pacific region at the IMF–Singapore Regional Training Institute
- The Joint Vienna Institute in Austria, which is supported by two primary members (IMF and the Austrian authorities) and four contributory members (the European Bank for Reconstruction and Development, the International Bank for Reconstruction and Development, the Organisation for Economic Co-operation and Development and the World Trade Organisation) and other bilateral donors.

Any initiative to set up a CB-VTE institute in Mauritius would necessarily require Bank of Mauritius (BoM) to be involved. It could be: an initiative of the BoM alone; undertaken jointly with other banks in Mauritius; in collaboration with other central banks, such as the Bank of England or Reserve Bank of India; with the IMF and/or BIS; or it could be any combination of the above. There would clearly be a financial cost involved. The institute would need to attract high-quality lecturers, resource persons and top academicians from the region and around the world to focus on topical, complex central banking and monetary management issues.

Given the specificities of central banking and the particularly challenging problems that the African continent faces (including the unique peculiarity of monetary management being complicated by proportionally excessive aid flows), it is important that the training provided is relevant to Africa. It must combine Africa's special situation with what pertinent lessons might be learnt from other countries and regions in which similar problems have been encountered and successfully dealt with (e.g. India in the 1970s and 1980s). One of the projects the Bank of Mauritius could undertake is to develop, with the collaboration of other African central banks, the IMF, the World Bank and the BIS, an accurate and comprehensive unified statistical monetary and economic database that could be used by local, national and international researchers. At present, monetary data on Africa – compiled by different sources, using different methodologies and hardware as well as software systems – is fragmented, contradictory and confusing.

However, to add real value, a CB-VTE institute in Mauritius would need to avoid duplication with what is already being done by institutions such as MEFMI, as well as by other national and regional CB-VTE arrangements in SADC, in other regions of Africa, and by the IMF or BIS independently or jointly with these institutions. Given the number of institutions currently providing training to central bankers in the region, duplication would result in a waste of scarce resources and would make it difficult to convince partners to participate. If a CBT-VTE institution in Mauritius was to be established, it would need to be located somewhere with a serene, isolated atmosphere for learning on land donated either by the government or BoM. It would need to have the latest multilingual translation facilities, as well as a well-equipped up-to-date library with the latest books, periodicals and e-resources in central banking. It would also need to have boarding and lodging facilities of a high standard (whose operation might be outsourced to one of the local hotel management groups), with adequate recreation, sports and medical facilities.

Short of setting up a CB-VTE institute in Mauritius, the BoM could on its own, or with others, take a lead in organising training courses, seminars, workshops and conferences on a regular/scheduled as well as *ad hoc* basis. The cost of this less-ambitious option would be much lower. However, it would not have the same impact in the medium and long term as a CB-VTE institute in making Mauritius an regional Centre of Excellence. Clearly some preliminary work has to be done in analysing what other institutions established in the region are doing, and what type of training/research they are **not** undertaking that is needed in Mauritius, in the immediate SADC/COMESA region and more widely in Africa. Only after such an analysis can clear ideas be developed on what a CB-VTE institution in Mauritius could do to add value.

If the case for value-addition can be made clearly and unambiguously, the next step would be to explore options on how such an institution could be set up, funded and what role would be played in the process by the Government of Mauritius, the BoM and external players (e.g. MEFMI, the IMF, BIS, RBI, Bank of England, Banque du France, ECB and Monetary Authority of Singapore) in making available the necessary financial and human resources that would be needed, along with the necessary know-how inputs, to ensure the long-term success and value of such an institution.

Distance learning and e-learning

Distance education and e-learning (DEEL) was institutionalised in Mauritius with the Mauritius College of the Air (MCAIR) being established in 1985 to promote education, arts, science and culture through mass media and distance education. Interest in media and distance education was reinforced with World Bank interest in funding the development of the education sector in Mauritius in the 1980s. Emphasis on the potential of distance education was highlighted in two reports published in 1989: i.e. *Open Learning and its Potential in Mauritius* by Lord Young of Dartington, and *Distance Education for HRD in Mauritius* by John Daniel.

Following those reports, MCAIR collaborated with Napier University in 1993 to develop a Higher Certificate in librarianship and information science, which enabled over 100 people to enhance their professional competence. In 1994, the AfDB helped to fund the Department for Distance Education (DDE). In 1995, MCAIR was asked to help with upgrading the skills of 500 secondary school teachers through course material developed collaboratively with the National Extension College and Oxford Open Learning (OOL) in the UK with special funding provisions to offer a Master's degree in education and human resources (MEd. and HR).

Over the last decade, MCAIR has established a number of international partnerships to expand its repertoire for open distance learning (ODL) with: the National Extension College/OOL in the UK; Napier University in Canada; Stevenson College, UK; the Chartered Institute of Logistics & Transport (UK) through its counterpart in Mauritius; the Indira Gandhi National Open University (IGNOU) of India; UNICEF/MIE; the Chartered Institute of Marketing (UK); the Tele Universite of Canada for capacity building; and IGNOU/COL through the Rajiv Gandhi Foundation Science Centre in Mauritius (RGFS).

MCAIR has also developed **local** partnerships with: the University of Mauritius (UoM) for an MSc. course in risk management; the University of Technology, Mauritius (UTM) for a diploma as well as undergraduate (BSc. Honours) degree courses in management; the Mauritius Institute of Education for a course offering a Certificate of Proficiency in early childhood education (CPECE) as well as a Teachers' Certificate for pre-primary schooling; (d) the Ministry of Civil Service and Administrative Reforms for distance education courses in customer care and quality management; and the Ministry of Co-operatives for an Advanced Diploma in co-operative studies.

The advantages of these international and local partnerships have been to: (i) lower the costs of courseware engineering for MCAIR that the college could not afford on its own; (ii) make MCAIR more cost-effective and able to offer quality education on a flexible basis at an affordable cost to mid-career working professionals; (iii) enable economies of scale; (iv) provide wider access to sources of course material, as well as to a wider potential market; (v) permit MCAIR to share/pool limited public resources with other educational institutions and ministries; (vi) facilitate adaptation of course material; (vii) provide IPR negotiating rights for material developed with MCAIR inputs; and (viii) enable MCAIR to cope with changes in the environment and opportunities/challenges thrown up by the globalisation of education.

Over the 16 years from 1993 to 2008, MCAIR has offered 42 programmes/courses through ODL to over 11,400 distance learners. Its students comprise the public at large (for 'A' levels, undergraduate/postgraduate degrees and diplomas in management). It has also tapped into more specialised adult student pools through specially designed programmes. These pools include police officers, teachers, professionals in the ICT industry, fire officers, trade union officials and workers, personnel from various ministries and National Transport Authority (NTA) officers.

However, as the above list indicates, MCAIR has focused exclusively on the domestic market in a limited set of specialised study domains. The question is whether providing VTE for an average of about 700 students a year justifies public expenditure on a separate institution, when DEEL could be provided by a dedicated department of the UoM, UTM or both? For MCAIR to be economically viable, its capabilities need to extend to DEEL exports over a regional geography and beyond, by offering a wider range of general educational and specialised career-specific courses. To do so, it must compete with the University of South Africa (UNISA) in the same regional space.

It can compete in this manner effectively by engaging in a partnership with the Open University of the UK, which has an established global brand and an internationally respected repertoire of courses and tutors, an Indian DEEL institute or by triangulating with both to reach the Asian-African-Antipodean markets. It could also bring in a partner from France, like the *Conservatoire National des Arts et Métiers* (CNAM) operating out of Reunion for DEEL exports to francophone African and Asian markets.

Entering into such partnerships would enable MCAIR to focus on the world, rather than the domestic market, which is trivial in size and less demanding in nature. MCAIR could also be transformed by being privatised and freed from existing domestic regulatory constraints to evolve in a market-determined manner and develop state-of-the-art capabilities in DEEL for the general public, as well as the more specialised corporate markets (especially for e-learning).

MCAIR specialises in **distance learning**, which is not the same as **e-learning**, although the two terms are often used synonymously. E-learning refers specifically to use of the power of the Internet (and the corporate intranet) to deliver a broad array of VTE solutions that contribute to the enhancement of knowledge and performance. While all e-learning is distance learning, the opposite is not the case: not all distance learning involves e-learning – in fact, much of it is still conducted via hard copy correspondence courses. Both distance and E-learning enable tutoring/learning (i.e. VTE delivery) costs to be reduced. They also enable larger economies of scale to be achieved than through traditional teaching modes. E-learning is superior to distance learning in enhancing responsiveness; it can be customised and updated more quickly than any other form of teaching/learning in real time, with learning being made possible on a 24/7 basis. E-learning encourages universality and community building, it is rapidly scalable, permits easy cross-platform accessibility to course materials and it saves on travel and time costs for students and tutors.

Yet not all the aspects/attributes of e-learning are necessarily positive. It has some drawbacks. For instance, it has bandwidth limitations. Disparate computers replace human contact and instantaneous face-to-face interaction, which can be an indispensable feature of effective learning. With e-learning, unless there is a human at the other end, the level of interactivity is limited. The capital expenditure (capex) cost involved in establishing the requisite technological infrastructure and maintaining the relevance of course material is large and continuous. It requires constant updating to keep pace with rapidly evolving technology (in order to remain competitive) and frequent changes in course content to retain relevance. Not all courses are amenable to being delivered well by computers (e.g. courses for artisans).

An effective strategy for exporting e-learning services needs the right kind of learning architecture, a good technological and faculty/resource infrastructure and a champion to promote it. Such a strategy also requires a sound business case. In addition, for Mauritius to expand its e-learning capacity and gear it for exports there must be a clear national strategy to support such an initiative, unwavering political support for it and requisite investment in the necessary infrastructure and 'info-structure', which Mauritius has with its rapidly developing ICT/BPO/KPO/RPO industry.

To move forward the idea of MCAIR developing wider regional and global capacity, requires fundamental re-thinking of the original ideas behind it and gearing its focus and activities to the offshore market, with the domestic market being treated as a residual rather than the other way around. If MCAIR can develop global reach and capability through appropriately structured partnerships with the right partners from India, France and the UK, it can compete more effectively with UNISA for the African market and can carve out a significant share of the Asian and Antipodean DEEL markets as well. Yet MCAIR is not the only player in town. The University of Mauritius also has its own centre for virtual learning.

The entry of Mauritius into the global market for e-learning is justified by the size and growth of that market. For example, the worldwide e-learning industry is estimated to be worth about US$60 billion, according to conservative estimates. By 2006, nearly 3.5 million students were learning online at institutions of higher education in the US alone. Students generally appear to be at least as satisfied with their online classes as they are with traditional ones. Online education is no longer a myth; it is a well-established pedagogical alternative in its own right in many leading universities worldwide (The Sloan Report).[12]

Mauritius would have some advantages (with its relatively advanced endowments) as a relatively low-cost e-learning 'content provider', with a number of resident 'subject experts' and bilingualism as its main advantages. It would have an advantage in areas such as instructional and pedagogical design, multi-media development, e-based consultancy services for e-learning initiatives and hosting solutions and providing technical support.

However, Mauritius would need to scale up from a compact self-contained shell catering to its domestic market, to a regionally 'distributed' institution. It would need to build on existing infrastructure, expertise, experience and assure quality of content, pedagogy, outcomes, delivery, service and certification standards. The questions that arise in the area of e-learning certification are whether certification should be carried out by only one university? Or should it be done through a joint/consortium approach involving UoM, UTM and MCAIR? That would imply adopting common qualifications with an open content philosophy.

The main obstacle to making faster progress in establishing Mauritius as a player in the global e-learning domain remains an absence of the right mindset at political and senior-academic levels in the educational establishment. This is reflected in resistance to change on the part of academics and educational policy-makers/managers steeped in the old school of thought, who remain sceptical of the efficacy of new technologies (in which they are untutored) and of new pedagogical alternatives and techniques (for fear that deploying these would displace them and make them redundant). There is also a shortage of e-learning and innovative pedagogical design experts in Mauritius, as well as a lack of research facilities and funding related to innovative pedagogies and technologies.

Yet it would be negligent for the Government of Mauritius to not capitalise on the opportunities that exist as a result of inertia and lack of sufficient initiative on the part of the educational establishment, which is too remote and inward looking, content to focus only on the domestic market cushioned by state policy. The world wide web (www) is the largest freely accessible knowledge resource platform ever created in history. It permits any individual anywhere in the world to **'learn anytime and anywhere, but most important of all to learn differently and just-in-time'**. It is estimated that there are already 1.3 million users of e-learning facilities in the entire African continent, of which 750,000 are in Southern Africa and 75 per cent of those in South Africa. However, the real number of African users may be five times that.[13] The main player in the field is UNISA and Mauritius does not even feature on the African e-learning map. It should be a priority government policy to rectify that shortcoming.

Developing human resource development export capacity in Mauritius: next steps

Human resource development (HRD) exports present an immediate opportunity for Mauritius to diversify its sources of external revenue and develop a fertile area of opportunity, without much domestic effort or investment. Institutions from around the world have queued up waiting to invest in Mauritius. It provides a naturally idyllic environment for global educational institutions to locate in order to tap new student populations in the Asian and African markets. What is holding up progress is an antediluvian, anachronistic mindset on the part of the extant educational establishment (i.e. Ministry of Education and Human Resources, the Tertiary Education Commission [TEC] and public institutions). That establishment is attempting to protect the domestic market by blocking foreign participation in the education sector (even for exports) in a way that is no longer tenable. The Government of Mauritius has come to accept over the three years since 2005 that the private sector's previous efforts to block foreign competition in the domestic commercial space have been, overall, detrimental to the longer-term economic interests of the country.

That is no less true of the public sector's efforts to protect domestic space in areas like healthcare and education. Efforts to protect the past in this manner can only result in seriously compromising the future. The present educational establishment appears either unable or unwilling to see the opportunity that exporting HRD services holds in terms of future growth. It seems more concerned with an imagined loss of privilege, budget, power and control if the VTE sector is opened up to foreign private entry to make tertiary education in Mauritius more competitive, innovative and world class. However, such resistance has to be overcome by the government at a higher political and policy (cabinet) level to get HRD exports moving. If not, then Mauritius will lose out on the opportunity to develop exports in a domain where they could amount to the equivalent of between 20-30 per cent of future GNI by 2020.

What do the next steps for expanding HRD exports entail? Essentially they call for a strategic focus, a new and better policy framework and milestones for measuring progress. They require the right kind of interplay between Mauritius's natural and HRD endowments, its educational infrastructure and its institutions. There are both explicit and implicit barriers blocking more rapid progress.

Explicit barriers include: (i) prohibitions and quotas of various kinds that are imposed on foreign providers, if not by the new supposedly open policy regime then by those implementing it in the VTE sector keeping it effectively closed; (ii) restrictive visa regimes, which although becoming more open are still not open enough; (iii) an investment regime in the education sector that is artificially restrictive and contrary to the openness to FDI underlined in the last two budgets; and (iv) an adherence to preferential procurement of educational services by the public sector from public institutions rather than from all institutions.

Implicit barriers include regulatory bodies using accreditation, regulation, qualification and licensing requirements, as well as other criteria and standards (for instance, those used for approving new institutions and courses) as protectionist barriers rather than as quality control measures. When it comes to accreditation, for example, it is important that the TEC sends an unambiguous message about what it is effectively looking for: is it the curriculum, the faculty, the investment in infrastructure facilities being proposed or the examinations? It is clear that the capacity and knowledge of the TEC will have to be enhanced for it to be able to deal with the new landscape. If this is not done quickly, this may have an adverse impact on the aspiration of Mauritius to become a knowledge hub. The example of New Zealand may be relevant. There, transnational providers of HRD services can operate with no restrictions other than those that relate to any type of foreign investment.

Foreign investor willingness to provide foreign direct investment for HRD-VTE and get things moving is clear and unambiguous. For example:

- There are a number of applications pending by UK universities to establish themselves in Mauritius
- The SP Jain School of Management has expressed an interest in investing in Mauritius

- A number of medical and nursing schools have applied to invest in the country
- Maya Entertainment has expressed interest in establishing an animation academy there
- The financial services industry is interested in starting finance programmes
- The ICT industry wants to ramp up industry-focused VTE on a substantial scale
- The Mauritius Employers Federation (MEF) wants to progress with VTE tailored for its membership
- The Administrative Staff College of India has expressed definite interest in collaborating with the Government of Mauritius to set up VTE for public administration

These are just a few examples of the interest being shown by potential foreign and domestic investors and VTE providers in this sector. In other areas, the Board of Investment may need to take the lead in attracting investors/partners to develop capacity and infrastructure in the right areas. It is clear what geographical export markets Mauritius needs to target with HRD services. The issue is how it should go about doing this.

To market effectively, Mauritius needs first to create sufficient minimum core capacity in each area of advantage. In some areas it already has a core that it needs to expand rapidly. These areas include **business and management studies** in which more than one institution has established credence, but many more are needed, and **VTE for the hospitality industry**, where core capacity exists for training lower- and middle-level professionals, but where Mauritius needs to establish significant partnerships (e.g. with EHL, La Rochelle in Switzerland, the Oberoi Training centre in India or the Cornell Hotel Management School in the US) to upgrade its ability to train the highest levels of professionals as well. Other areas are **the ICT industry,** where basic VTE capacity has been established but needs to be significantly upgraded through the right partnerships with Indian and other training institutions, **DEEL,** where a minimum core capacity already exists but needs to be expanded dramatically through appropriate partnerships, and **VTE for the healthcare sector** including medical education for doctors, nurses and a number of paraprofessional categories.

The Government of Mauritius needs to ensure that the accreditation and regulation (A&R) process as wielded by TEC, MQA and other concerned agencies in the tertiary education sector is not used as a device for delay, obfuscation and protectionism. The TEC needs to be relieved of any responsibility for regulating institutions set up to export HRD services. For that purpose and to acquire global credibility, Mauritius needs to adopt global VTE quality standards applied by an institution that is familiar with and properly qualified to apply such standards and monitor performance in terms of adherence to them.

Notes

1. See table: Growth in the number of tertiary students worldwide since 1991, UNESCO Institute for Statistics database.
2. Böhm, Anthony (2003). Also UNESCO Institute of Statistics, Table 18, International flows of mobile students at Tertiary Level, updated annually. See:
   http://stats.uis.unesco.org/unesco/TableViewer/tableView.aspx?ReportId=171 [accessed 6 January 2009]. And UNESCO, Global Education Digest, 2006, 2007.
3. UNESCO Institute of Statistics; reference year 2004: Statistical Tables 9 and 10; previous years: UIS Database.
4. UNESCO Institute of Statistics Database.
5. UNESCO Institute of Statistics; reference year 2004: Statistical Table 9; previous years: UIS Database.
6. These are: the Mauritius Institute of Education, set up for the training of teachers and educational research; the Mahatma Gandhi Institute, which provides training in languages, the performing arts, fine arts and ethnic studies; the Mauritius College of the Air, which encourages distance learning in collaboration with recognised overseas institutions; and, in 2002, the Rabindranath Tagore Institute, which was established for the study of Indian culture and traditions.
7. These were broken down as follows: University of Mauritius – 50; UTM – 10; Mauritius Institute of Health – 38; SSR Medical College – 277; College of Dentistry -121; and Institut Francophone de l'Entrepreneuriat – 71.
8. For example, there are a number of regulatory contradictions concerning the provision of distance learning within and outside individual states in India that create major complexities and hinder the spread of distance learning. Similarly there are a number of regulatory contradictions in the treatment of public vs. private VTE institutions resulting in a small proportion of private institutions not seeking accreditation or certification yet providing education to a large number of people in absolute terms because of the feedback that the market provides on their quality and the widespread acceptability in the labour market of the qualifications that they award.
9. For more details on this and other fields of VTE provision, see presentation by Mr Altaaf Hamid at the Symposium on the Export of Human Resources Services in April 2007.
10. Industrial Development Corporation (IDC), Johannesburg, Networking Skills in South Africa, May 2006.
11. IDC: Networking Skills in South Africa, May 2006.
12. See: http://www.sloan-c.org/publications/survey/index.asp [accessed 6 January 2008].
13. The number of PCs and laptops available in Africa with Internet access are unknown despite a plethora of initiatives by multilateral and bilateral donors and the private sector to expand e-learning. Access to PCs/laptops is growing, but the exact statistics are unknown. Access seems to be limited to the elite, employees of public/private corporations and institutions, and the middle class in big cities (i.e. civil servants, teachers, doctors, lawyers, engineers, consultants, bankers etc.). Fixed-line Internet access costs to individuals in African countries are still high, ranging from US$30-130 per month compared to US$15-50 per month in OECD countries. There are a limited number of Internet cafes that poor students can use in Africa. Communication bandwidth is still low for accessing streaming multimedia, for example.

7

Conclusions

Chapters 3 to 6 have highlighted the potential that exists for Mauritius to export **financial services, ICT services, healthcare services** and **education services**. The four symposia held in January and April 2008 covered these four sectors, which have the greatest immediate potential for realising enhanced service export earnings. However, opportunities in other important service sectors, in which Mauritius might also become globally competitive, remain unexplored and unaddressed.

These sectors include **construction** and construction-related engineering, consulting, architectural and urban planning services; **logistics,** involving regional supply chain management, storage, break-bulk and distribution; **transport** services and transport infrastructure, especially airborne and seaborne transport and ports; and **media, entertainment and leisure** service industries, including sporting events and gaming infrastructure for widening and deepening export revenues associated with tourism flows, as well as independently. Whether the Government of Mauritius will use the tried and proven symposium approach to developing a similar understanding of the potential that these other service domains hold, remains an open question. Nonetheless, some action in these areas needs to be taken.

Previous chapters clearly and unambiguously suggest what can be done and what needs to be done by the Mauritian government and the private sector (domestic and foreign) to convert potential into reality in each of the four service-export areas scrutinised in this book. The symposia held in each of these areas identified several issues for consideration and action by the government and the private sector. This chapter summarises those issues and outlines what the next steps might be for policy-making and action by the Government of Mauritius and the private sector.

Implications for policy and action

Several policy issues were identified. They are reiterated below in adumbrated form. The key issues of macro-policy – for government and the industries concerned in each case – thrown up by discussions in the four symposia are outlined below.

In the case of all four service areas (financial services, services for the ICT-BPO-ITES [IBI] industry, healthcare and life science services [HLSS] and human resource development services [HRDS]), **representation of the overall 'private industry' interest in Mauritius is fragmented and disjointed.** In financial services, two of the extant three sub-industry associations (**banking** and **insurance**) work well. The association of **management companies** was coming together under its new chair at the time of writing. However, a sense of 'every firm for itself' still prevails in that sub-industry, with larger management companies not being members. Financial services sub-associations are effective to varying degrees in lobbying with government for protecting or advancing the specific business interests of their members (whether banks, insurance or management companies). However, they are not effective in coalescing to represent the economic interests of the financial services industry **as a whole**, with policy-makers or in export markets.

If Mauritius is to succeed in exporting value-added **financial services** to a wider range of geographies, it is essential for this infirmity to be overcome. What is needed is a merger of the sub-industry associations into a **single financial services industry association** (FINSIA) that represents the views and advances the interests of the entire financial services industry coherently. FINSIA could play a more pro-active role as an active interlocutor with government (MFED) and regulatory agencies to work jointly in guiding the future development of the industry (not just of individual banks or firms) and to develop new service export areas such as private banking and wealth management and asset management in the face of fierce global competition from other international finance centres.

That observation is even more applicable to the ICT-BPO-ITES (IBI) industry, which has a very weak industry association. Barely 15 per cent of firms in the industry are members. What the industry needs is an association modelled on NASSCOM in India. Key suggestions emerging from the Symposium on the Export of Services for the IBI industry in Mauritius were that: the Mauritian IBI industry association should seek direct assistance from NASSCOM to develop its capabilities in a manner that could guide future IBI industry evolution and development; and that strengthened and more representative 'new' IBI industry association should facilitate the formation of international partnerships of a kind that the industry (and firms within it) needed to succeed.

In the case of HLSS and HRDS, these 'export industries' are too nascent and incipient for any sort of industry association to have built up, even in nebulous form. This has disabled effective interaction between the 'industry' and regulators in these domains. Ministries and regulators in healthcare and education have a myopic perspective that focuses exclusively on the domestic market for these services. They seem incapable of comprehending the different issues and dimensions that developing export capacity in these domains entails. Despite the growing presence of private-service providers in both areas, the 'governing establishment' in both is still operating on the old paradigm that considers them to be public goods rather than commercial goods that should be provided by private parties.

There is a visceral tendency therefore on the part of regulators to block rather than facilitate the growth of the private sector's role in these domains for fear that, even if initially restricted to providing only export-orientated services, these providers would eventually operate in the domestic domain as well. As a result, legitimate processes of accreditation, certification and regulation tend to act as protectionist barriers rather than exercising quality control.

Despite an unemployment rate of 9–10 per cent in Mauritius at the time of writing, the financial services, IBI, HLS and HRD sectors are all witnessing **an acute shortage of human resources,** i.e. trained, qualified staff at every level. There is a particular problem with English language knowledge in the labour force. There are also problems with functional literacy and numeracy of a kind that make secondary school leavers (and some university graduates) unemployable. The labour situation is being ameliorated through training-cum-employment schemes under the Empowerment Programme, which reduce training costs dramatically for employers. The Human Resource Development Council is looking into this complex but critical issue, and reformulating its approach to align the output of the schooling and vocational and tertiary education (VTE) system more in keeping with the rapidly and continuously changing/evolving demands of the labour market.

The paradox of an acute skills shortage co-existing with a high unemployment rate reflects the inefficacy of current education policy and extant curricula in turning out employable school leavers. It also reflects the absence of sufficient specialised pre-employment vocational training in financial or IBI services, and lacunae in immigration policy that prevent skilled workers from being imported freely and automatically through normal labour market functioning. All these shortcomings need to be remedied expeditiously, although a comprehensive and fundamental change in education policy would take a longer period of time. The HRD Symposium brought out clearly the dysfunctionality of existing education infrastructure and policy, which turns out too high a proportion of 'graduates' at school and tertiary levels who were unemployable without further VTE inputs provided by industry.

Financial services regulation is an integral, inseparable part of any financial product/service being provided or exported. For Mauritius to export value-added financial services successfully, its financial **regulation** (quality, quantity, probity, approach, reputation and cost) has to be world class. At the same time, the burdens and costs of regulation cannot be so high as to make Mauritius globally uncompetitive. Substandard regulation would damage Mauritius's reputation as an exporter of high-value financial services. However, MFED and the Financial Services Commission (FSC) need to recognise both the costs that excessive regulation impose and the fact that some regulatory standards imposed on Mauritius by external interlocutors – e.g. AML-CFT regulation – are more onerous than standards employed by those interlocutors in their own home countries.

That reality was acknowledged in 2006, with efforts to strike a balance between regulation that is world class and the cost burdens that such regulation imposes on operators. However, this balance is a moving target and needs to be watched closely. The financial services industry expressed the view that generating new rules and regulations has now become an FSC (or industry) objective in its own right, and that the industry is finding it difficult to cope with this deluge. It is not helping Mauritius to become more competitive.

A pause is needed in the drawing up of new regulations, with wider prior consultations with the industry on whether new rules are helpful or counterproductive, and what their impact on Mauritius's global competitiveness might be. This might be judged by periodically comparing Mauritian regulations with those of competing jurisdictions. A suggestion was also made to have periodic **regulatory impact assessments,** to remind regulators of the balance that needs to be struck between **appropriate** and **excessive** regulation.

A key policy issue for the financial services and IBI industries is the **cost of telecommunications.** While not explicated at the HLSS and HRD symposia, this issue affects both those sectors as well, especially for services that rely heavily on Internet broadband linkage such as telemetric patient monitoring or e-learning. Mauritius Telecom (MTL) argued at the IBI services symposium that it has reduced costs for a bulk communication line dramatically in the last year and is competitive with the rest of Africa. However, the IBI industry felt that costs were still about 30 per cent above the world average, with no provision for back-up redundancy. Communications costs accounted for 40 per cent of total cost for the average IBI firm at the time of writing. That put ICT/OCC (outsourcing connected companies) firms at a 12 per cent operating margin disadvantage to global competitors. With 5 per cent variations in margin making the difference between profit and loss in the IBI business, Mauritius can explore only limited niches where operating margins are generous enough to accommodate such a structural disadvantage. This situation constrains IBI service exports and may also affect financial services, HLS and HRD export margins and viability.

Secondary policy questions that arise are:

- Does MTL have the right strategic partner in France Telecom (FT) to ensure that: (i) internal transfer pricing is not always done in FT's favour; (ii) MTL's costs will be globally competitive soon; and (iii) investments that need to be made to achieve this objective will be made by FT and MTL in 2008–09?
- Does more competition need to be introduced into Mauritius in the telecom sector, both terrestrial and cellular and in providing competing services for wireless broadband on an island-wide basis?
- Should MTL now be privatised to achieve greater levels of efficiency and better quality of service?

It is critical that both the primary and secondary questions raised by this important issue are addressed and resolved as a matter of utmost urgency, as telecommunications costs compromise the prospects of not just the IBI industry, but those of every other service export industry (in particular financial services) as well.

Physical connectivity in Mauritius is as deficient and costly as teleconnectivity. Airline and shipping connections from Mauritius to Africa and the rest of the world are poor, compared with competing centres. The island's airport and seaport are also comparatively poor, while critical physical and social infrastructure needed by the service export industries to develop and grow rapidly is missing. At the same time, traffic infrastructure and public transport services are inadequate, resulting in excessive congestion: rush-hour traffic delays are comparable to those in much larger cities.

Coinciding with the symposia that took place in January 2008, the Government of Mauritius announced that two new PPP projects (the Port Louis harbour bridge and city ring road) would be launched. This is a first step. Public transport services are weak, with firms having to bear the costs of transporting their staff to/from their workplaces; this is especially the case out of normal daytime working hours. Water and power infrastructures are also reaching critical limits, and significant new investments need to be made in these areas urgently. Deficiencies in communications infrastructure have already been highlighted. Remedial policies are needed across the board.

These constraints may affect HLS and HRD exports particularly badly. The expansion of both will rely more than financial services and ICT on access to large amounts of suitable space for medical and hospital complexes, medical training facilities, life science research clusters and purpose-built campuses for foreign educational institutions locating in Mauritius to export HRD services. Addressing the infrastructure constraint is particularly important if export objectives in the latter two areas are to be realised. Such infrastructure could only be developed rapidly through public-private partnerships (see below).

Office space accounts for around 10 per cent of the total costs of financial services and IBI firms. The island's cyber-city has not developed sufficiently rapidly and much of its space is occupied by firms outside the IBI industry. Nor has the cyber-city got a dedicated communications infrastructure (of the kind Indian ICT firm-clusters have) to lower costs. At the time of writing, the Government of Mauritius was proceeding with plans to build an entirely new city in the Highlands on a PPP basis.

The general picture is one of years of under-investment and neglect in essential infrastructure, which now needs to be over-compensated for rapidly. It is clear that the investment needed is not affordable for the government/public sector to undertake on its own. Private investment, integrally associated with public-private partnerships (PPP) for service provision, will be essential. Much of the finance and PPP skills will need to be sourced from abroad.

Given the size and urgency of the island's infrastructure needs, the key policy questions are:

- Can the present policy framework sustain the kind of investment that is needed, or does it need radical overhaul on a 'big bang' basis?

- Will a series of small incremental steps suffice? Or are radical approaches needed to achieve urgent infrastructure transformation? For example, to achieve better air/sea connectivity with Africa and the rest of the world, should public airline and shipping companies be privatised and should these transport sectors be thrown open to global competition?
- Should Mauritius have an 'open skies' and 'open seas' policy?
- Should public companies in every key infrastructure sector be privatised and the sectors opened up to domestic and foreign private competition?

Answers to these questions will have direct feedback implications for service exports in all four areas discussed in this book. Large scale privatisations and PPPs will create opportunities for the development of new financial services areas, with skills development potential that could be applied competitively across Africa (first) and globally (thereafter). These policy changes would have implications for the entry of a larger number of investment banks into Mauritius, of which there is a present paucity. While Mauritius is overbanked commercially, it is under-banked as far as investment banking and corporate finance are concerned. These specialist firms cannot be viable if they operate only in the domestic market; rather, they need to operate across Africa and the Indian Ocean region. That is equally true for the sweeping opportunities in IBI exports that such policy transformations will trigger.

In all four services industries (financial services, IBI, HLSS and HRD), Mauritius has characteristics different to those in many other countries (especially India). In those countries, policy reform succeeded in triggering unprecedented growth, which has been sustained over long periods, simply by removing shackles on private entrepreneurship. In Mauritius, such reform does not appear to be enough.

The Mauritian private sector lacks key attributes needed for global competitiveness: i.e. it thinks too small for the global stage, it lacks the requisite knowledge, ambition, capital, vision, initiative, strategic thinking about the future and world-class managerial competence. This is partly because it has, since independence, survived on colluding with government to protect domestic business space and, like the population at large, it has developed a **dependency culture**. It is preoccupied with keeping its share of the Mauritian 'pie', rather than focusing on carving out for itself a piece of the regional or global 'pie', except when it has been forced to – in industries such as sugar and tourism, where core competencies have been developed and are now surplus to domestic needs.

For that reason, in all four areas, the growth of services exports will depend on whether foreign investors can be attracted to bring in the necessary technical operating know-how, market knowledge and linkages, managerial capacity and financial investment. Mauritius has since 2005 opened its economy and FDI regime dramatically. The Board of Investment (BoI) will now need to carry out targeted marketing to attract pre-identified foreign investors, who have the attributes needed to ramp up service exports in all four areas relatively quickly.

The Government of Mauritius has, since independence, driven development by playing a pro-active role in launching key initiatives. However, it has stayed too long in areas it should have exited after an initial push. Besides, the island's government has now become too large: there are too many ministries, commissions and quangos, which have been created to accommodate political patronage interests.

In the HLSS and HRD sectors, regulatory architecture for governance is fragmented, complex and unco-ordinated, especially for an economy the size of Mauritius. These bodies are not run along efficient lines (as they are in Singapore or Dubai, for instance). Instead they are handed out as prizes within the political community, and run on the basis of a deep-rooted culture of chronic and endemic patronage, resulting in even more deep-rooted vested political and ethnic interests. Thus a client state has been created, with high overhead costs (more than 5 per cent of GDP) that a globally competitive economy cannot afford. It has too many public employees and their dependents, forming too large a proportion of the voting population. Such structural **clientelism** inhibits significant change in the extant paradigm through the normal democratic process, because it introduces a major perverse bias in that process.

To export services on a globally competitive basis, this type of governance and economic structure (created in an era of externally subsidised protectionism of commodities and manufactures, which is not sustainable) is counterproductive because it inhibits competition and innovation. Therefore it needs to be changed and restructured dramatically – not over a prolonged period (because that is not an affordable luxury), but as soon as possible.

The respective roles of government and the private sector need to change in Mauritius with: (i) the government/state role being shrunk to a more realistic, affordable size; (ii) private choice and internal markets being introduced in universalised public services; (iii) public resources being targeted to assist the poor rather than subsidising middle-class consumption; and (iv) the private sector being significantly enlarged and enlivened by foreign inputs (in terms of know-how, HR and financial resources) from global firms (from Asia and the EU) that are well-established in global service export industries.

In addition, public investment needs to be accompanied by large private investment inputs into infrastructure and key public services via enhanced PPPs. In particular, education and health policies need to be revised substantially with an opening of these sectors to private investment in order to create both export- and domestic-market service capabilities.

Such profound, fundamental changes in the island's economic and governance paradigms have far-reaching implications for the role/size of government, for governance and for macro-, meso- and micro-policies in a number of areas (fiscal, monetary, industry, education, health etc.), all of which need to be more clearly understood.

A start has been made with the four symposia held to carve out niches in new service export industries, which have the potential of contributing between 10–15 per cent of GDP and a higher proportion of total exports. Each substantive chapter is sufficiently detailed to provide a clear roadmap of what needs to be done in each of these fours sectors, by whom, how and by when.

Nonetheless, follow-up action will require continual pushing by dedicated task forces in each area to actually make things happen: to follow up with investors who have expressed a clear interest; to follow up with ministries and regulatory bodies that are still blocking progress and get them to act as facilitators rather than gate-keepers; to raise to cabinet and Prime Minister's Office level issues on which there is inter-ministerial disagreement; and to follow up on essential infrastructure initiatives, without which export potential will be constrained.

References and bibliography

Böhm, Anthony (2003) *Global Student Mobility 2025: Analysis of Global Competition and Market Share*. IDP Education Pty Ltd.

Bank of Mauritius Annual Reports. See: http://bom.intnet.mu [accessed 5 January 2008].

Commonwealth Secretariat (2007) *Barbados: Frequently Asked Questions on Trade in Services*. London: Commonwealth Secretariat.

Daniel, John (1989) Distance Education for HRD in Mauritius. Official report prepared for the Ministry of Education and Human Resources, Government of Mauritius.

Eisenberg, DM et al (1997) Trends in alternative medicine use in the United States, 1990–1997: results of a follow-up national survey. Boston, Mass: Center for Alternative Medicine Research and Education, Department of Medicine.

Financial Action Task Force (FATF) (2000) *Reports on Non-Cooperative Countries and Territories*. Paris, France: FATF.

Franks, Julian, Colin Mayer and Luis Correia da Silva (2003) *Asset management and investor protection: an international analysis*. Oxford and New York: Oxford University Press.

Gerschenkron, Alexander (1968) *Continuity in history, and other essays*. Cambridge, Massachusetts: Belknap Press of Harvard University Press.

Global Insight (2006) Report on Outsourcing. Waltham and Lexington, Massachusetts: Global Insight. Available at: http://www.globalinsight.com/ [accessed 5 January 2009]

Joint Commission International *Hospital Standards* (third edition). Comprehensive Accreditation Manual for Hospitals (CAMH). See:

http://www.jointcommission.org/AccreditationPrograms/Hospitals/Standards/09_FAQs [accessed 6 January 2009]

International Monetary Fund (1993) *Balance of Payments Manual* (BPM5). Washington, DC: IMF.

IMF (2004) The Impact of Preference Erosion on Middle-Income Developing Countries. Working Paper. Washington, DC: IMF.

Mattoo, Aaditya, Robert M Stern and Gianni Zanini (eds) (2008) *A Handbook of International Trade in Services*. Oxford: Oxford University Press.

Meade, James E (1968) *The Economic and Social Structure of Mauritius*. Routledge.

Mistry, Percy (1999) 'Mauritius: Quo Vadis?' *African Affairs 98:551–569.*

National Productivity and Competitiveness Council (2005) *Competitiveness Foresight: what orientations for Mauritius?* Mauritius: NPCC.

Nicoletti, Giuseppe (2001) Regulation In Services: OECD Patterns And Economic Implications. OECD Economics Department Working Paper No. 287. Paris: Organisation for Economic Co-operation and Development (OECD).

Organisation for Economic Co-operation and Development (1998) *Harmful Tax Competition: An Emerging Global Issue*. Paris, France: OECD.

Financial Stability Forum (2000) Report of the Working Group on Offshore Financial Centres. Available at http://www.fsforum.org/publications/r_0004b.htm

Sharman, J and Mistry, P (2008) *Considering the Consequences*. London: Commonwealth Secretariat. See http://publications.thecommonwealth.org/considering-the-consequences-556-p.aspx

UN Conference on Trade and Development (2008) *Handbook of Statistics*. Geneva: UNCTAD.

UN Education, Science and Cultural Organization (2006, 2007) Global Education Digest, 2006, 2007. Paris, France: UNESCO.

World Bank (1998, 1999) Global Development Finance Reports. Washington, DC: World Bank.

World Bank (2006) Trade Research Papers. Washington, DC: World Bank.

World Bank (1998, 1999) World Development Indicators. Washington, DC: World Bank.

World Bank (1993) *The East Asian Miracle*. Washington, DC: World Bank.

Young, Michael *(1989) Open Learning & its Potential in Mauritius.* Official report prepared for the Ministry of Education and Human Resources, Government of Mauritius.